TISHA

The Story of
a Young Teacher
in the Alaska Wilderness

as told to
Robert Specht

ST. MARTIN'S PRESS   NEW YORK

For
Judith, Raphael, and Allegra

Library of Congress Cataloging in Publication Data

Hobbs, Anne.
Tisha: the story of a young teacher
in the Alaska wilderness.

1. Hobbs, Anne. 2. Education—Alaska. I. Specht,
Robert. 1928-   joint author. II. Title.
LA2317.H59A37   371.1'0092'4   75-40789

I'VE LIVED in the Forty Mile country of Alaska for a long time, but even now, every so often when I'm out rock-hunting or looking for fossils, I get lost. Sometimes I'll have to wander around for a while before I get my bearings. That's what happened to me when I first started to think about telling this story. I wasn't sure which direction to take, until I finally realized that the only way to tell it was the way I might have told it when I first came to Alaska.

That was back in 1927, when I was a prim and proper young lady of nineteen. From the time I'd been a girl I'd been thrilled with the idea of living on a frontier, so when I was offered the job of teaching school in a gold-mining settlement called Chicken I accepted right away.

The first time I heard the name Chicken I laughed. I didn't believe there could really be such a place. Sure enough, though, when I looked at a map of Alaska there it was (and still is), right up near the Yukon Territory.

Green as goose grass and full of lofty ideals, off I went, thinking of myself as a lamp unto the wilderness. The last thing I expected was that the residents of Chicken weren't going to think of me in that way at all. Far from it: before my first year of teaching was over half the population wanted to blue-ticket me out of the place.

All that was forty-eight years ago, yet I can still remember how excited I was on the day I set off for Chicken by pack train. For me it was the final leg of a long journey, and the pack train left from a village called Eagle . . .

September 4, 1927

I

Even though it was barely eight o'clock and the sun had just come up, practically the whole town of Eagle had turned out to see the pack train off. Counting the Indians, who'd come down from their fish camp for the dance the previous night, there must have been close to a hundred people gathered around—miners in hip-length boots, old sourdoughs in battered Stetsons, even women and children. In a few minutes I'd be leaving, going off into the wilderness, and I was kind of excited. I was scared too, and I must have showed it, because Mrs. Rooney asked me if I was feeling well.

"Yes, ma'am," I said. "I feel just fine."

"You look a little pale. You're not afraid of the trip, I hope."

"No. I guess I just didn't expect there'd be all these people," I said.

Mrs. Rooney dismissed them with a wave of her hand. "One thing you'll learn is that it doesn't take much to collect a crowd in Alaska. As for the trip, you don't have a thing to worry about. It's only ninety miles and you'll be perfectly safe. Mr. Strong will take good care of you."

But it really wasn't the crowd that was bothering me. Hardly anybody was paying any attention to me. To the people here this was just a little event, nothing like the riverboat coming in, which was really exciting to them. And I wasn't afraid of the trip, either. It was the horse I'd be riding for the next four days that was scaring me. I'd have felt silly admitting it, but he was making me so nervous I could hardly concentrate on what Mrs. Rooney was saying. It wasn't as if I'd never been on a horse before. Eight years ago, when I was living with my grandmother on her farm, I used to ride around on old Tom bareback. I was only eleven then, and Tom was a pretty big horse, but he always moved so slow and he was so gentle that you could almost curl up on his broad back and go to sleep and you wouldn't fall off. This one was mean.

He was called Blossom, but where he got that name I would never know. Maybe he looked like a blossom when he was a colt, but it was the last thing he looked like now. He was so huge that even if I stood on my toes I wouldn't have been able to see over the saddle, and he was scarred and wild-looking. From the minute Mr. Strong handed his reins over to me I'd been afraid of him. And Blossom knew it. He started rolling his eyes at me right away and tried to nip me a couple of times. After he caught the sleeve of my jacket once I made sure to hold the reins close to the bit and keep him at arm's length. But everytime I thought he'd settled down, he'd jerk his head up and nearly pull my arm out of its socket.

From the corner of my eye I could see Mr. Strong moving toward me down the line of horses and mules that were tethered together.

I wished I wasn't the only passenger. In another minute I'd have to mount up, and as scared of Blossom as I was, I was sure I'd make a spectacle of myself. We weren't getting along too well just standing side by side, so I couldn't foresee our relations improving when I was up on top of him.

The other animals in the train were loaded down with just about everything in creation: washboards, sacks of dried beans, bolts of canvas, even windowpanes. One mule started bucking, trying to shake off his burden of shovels and stovepipes and whatnot. The load shifted and it looked as if it was going off until somebody grabbed it at the last minute. The rest of the animals stood patiently while Mr. Strong adjusted a rope here and there or tightened a cinch.

4

". . . And if you have any problems at all," Mrs. Rooney was saying, "write to me and I'll be glad to give you any advice I can." She fingered the cameo brooch on the front of her dress. "And remember what I said—spare the rod and spoil the child. Show those kids right off that you're the teacher and you won't have a bit of trouble."

"I will."

"If you have to smack a couple of them do it."

Somebody went over to Mr. Strong's stable and started to close the doors. I caught a glimpse of the big sled that was in there. It was the size of a hay wagon, and I wondered how many horses it took to pull it. In a couple of months from now, after the first heavy snowfall, Mr. Strong would be bringing my trunk out on it.

The doors slammed shut and the odor of hay and manure drifted over. And then Mr. Strong was beside us, clearing his throat. Even though it was sunny and comfortable, he was wearing a mackinaw. It was open, and I could see the top button of his long underwear under his flannel shirt.

He was a tall, stoop-shouldered man, and he had such a courtly way about him that if he wore a beard he'd have made me think of Don Quixote. When I'd first met him yesterday his manners had seemed so out of place in this rough country that I thought he was joking and almost laughed. I was glad I didn't, though, because he acted that way with almost everyone. I'd been waiting over two days for his pack train to come in, but when I'd asked him if he could take me to Chicken all he'd said was, "Yes, madam, I can."

"Will you be going soon?" I'd asked him.

"Yes, madam. My pack train leaves for Chicken on the fourth, the fourteenth and the twenty-fourth of each month. I shall, therefore, be leaving tomorrow. Eight a.m. sharp."

"I'd like to go," I'd told him.

"The rent for your horse will be ten dollars per day. That will include your meals along the way and your lodgings. The journey will take four days. I hope that will be satisfactory."

I'd told him it would be fine and that was that.

"If you are ready, madam," he said to me now, "I shall assist you to mount."

Mrs. Rooney smiled up at him. "You will take good care of her, won't you, Mr. Strong?"

"I shall do my best." Compared to him, President Coolidge was a nonstop talker.

Mrs. Rooney looked at him coquettishly and brushed at the front of her dress. It had a lot of shiny spots where her corset poked against it. She'd been a widow for ten years, she'd told me, and I had a feeling she would have liked to marry him, but he wasn't interested.

He took the reins from me and dropped them over Blossom's head, then he bent forward with his hands locked together. I grabbed the saddle horn and he boosted me up. Once I was in the saddle the ground looked pretty far down. Blossom started to dance around and a few people laughed. I thought they were laughing at the trouble I was having trying to get him to stand still, but as soon as he settled down I saw they were laughing at my legs. The saddle was so big and wide that they stuck out like wings.

"Better do somethin' about them pins a hers, Walter," somebody called out, "or she'll be knockin' down every tree in the Forty Mile."

Mr. Strong shortened the stirrups until I could get my feet into them, but I was still spread out pretty wide. Some good-natured suggestions were offered by people close by, such as tying rocks to my feet, but Mr. Strong didn't see anything funny about them.

"When we stop over at my camp in Liberty tonight," he said to me, "I will have a smaller saddle for you." He looked at my clothes skeptically. "Are you sure, madam, you will not reconsider my offer of the coat?" A little earlier, when he saw how I was dressed, he had offered to lend me a coat, saying that the weather was very changeable. But I'd told him I didn't think I'd need it.

"I'm really very comfortable," I said now. "I mean it's such a lovely day."

6

If I was back in the States I'd have felt ridiculous, but here in Alaska nobody cared how you dressed. I was wearing the jacket of my pink Easter suit, a pair of boy's corduroy knickers I'd bought for the ride, cotton stockings and some old sport brogues. I knew that the flowered hat I'd bought in Portland the past summer would end up crushed if it was put on the pack animals with my other things, so I wore that too. My ensemble was completed by a nickel-plated revolver that a fellow had given me at the dance last night.

Mr. Strong was still skeptical. "Should you change your mind, let me know."

"Now, Walter," an old-timer called out, "why you want to go and hide all that nice young beauty under that old army coat?"

Mr. Strong started for the front of the pack train and I looked around, able to see the whole crowd for the first time. A few old men were sitting on the rail of the schoolhouse porch, giving encouragement to a couple of little boys on a small dog-sled. The sled was outfitted with some old baby-carriage wheels and the boys were trying to teach the malamute puppy that was pulling how to gee and haw.

Aside from Mr. Strong's stable and the stables of a couple of other freighters, the schoolhouse was the only other building here at the edge of town. Mrs. Rooney had showed me the inside of it and I was looking forward to teaching in it when I took over from her next year. Made of squared-off logs, it was good and sturdy. I only hoped the schoolhouse I was heading for now would be as nice.

Farther up the line of pack animals a few men were rechecking some of the loads, making sure that whatever they were sending out to mining partners or friends wouldn't fall off. But most people were just gathered around talking.

The Indians stood apart from the whites, and I wondered where they'd spent the night. There were about twenty-five of them, mostly men. Compared to the whites, who were laughing and joking about how much they'd drunk and danced, the Indian men were quiet, just watching what was going on

7

or making an occasional comment to each other. They looked so serious, all of them, that if I hadn't seen them having such a good time last night, I'd have thought they were angry or resentful. That was what I'd thought about them when I'd first seen them standing around in White Horse and Dawson. But now I knew better. They'd laughed more and danced better than almost all the whites in Eagle. And probably had more fun too. They were just different from the whites. When they didn't have anything to say they didn't say anything.

I felt kind of sorry for the Indian women, especially the girls. Most of them had changed to moccasins, but a few still had on high heels and bright shawls. In the crisp morning air they looked out of place, their silk stockings full of runs and their makeup all smeared. For all the attention the white men paid them now they might just as well have not existed. It hadn't been that way at the dance. The white men had been pretty free with them then—a little too free. The Indian women hadn't minded it, or the Indian men either, but the white women hadn't liked it at all. Only one or two of the white women had even danced with the Indian men. The rest looked down their nose at them or, like Mrs. Rooney, disliked them outright. "Dark faces all packed full of bones," she complained to me, "you never know what they're thinking." She hated the Indian women, saying that the way they carried on with white men it was no wonder the women like herself who were matrimonially inclined couldn't find a husband.

"How's the weather up there, Teacher?"

"Cabaret" Jackson's hatchet face grinned up at me, his Adam's apple looking as though it was going to pop through his skin. One of his eyes was closed and there was some dried blood in his nostrils, but he'd cleaned himself up pretty well and he didn't look too bad.

I wished I could give him a clever answer, but I never could think of the right thing when it came right down to it. "The same weather you have down there," I told him.

"Hate to see you leavin' here," he said. "Don't suppose you'd change your mind about what I asked you last night?"

8

"Thanks, Cab, but I don't think so."

He was the one who'd given me the revolver, telling me that I shouldn't be going into the wilds without a little protection. Last night, before he got too drunk and had a fight, he'd proposed to me, promising he'd give me everything under the sun. He'd been a real gentleman, but as soon as he got drunk he turned mean. In the fight he'd had, he'd beaten the other man bloody and got so wild he tried to bite the man's ear off. The whole thing had made me sick to my stomach. He probably wasn't a bad fellow at heart, but he wasn't the type I'd want to keep company with.

"Well," he said, "I'll be mushin' out there to Chicken some time after the freeze-up, and I'll just try you again when I do." He grinned. "Take care, Teacher."

"Teacher?" A girl with kinky hair and close-set eyes had come up near me along with her husband. I couldn't remember her name, but there was something so nice about her, a kind of a sweet smile she had, that I'd liked her right away. She was going to have a baby and she was a little embarrassed about her big stomach, so she kept kind of stooping over all the time. "Teacher, do me a favor, will you?"

"Sure." I liked that—the way everybody called me Teacher.

"My ma runs the roadhouse out to Chicken—Maggie Carew. Tell her I'm comin' along real good an' that I'm expectin' middle of December."

"And tell her it'll be a boy," her husband said. He was about as young as she was, a big stringbean. Last night he'd had to practically drag her out on the floor to fox-trot with him, but she'd been so embarrassed by her stomach she didn't even finish.

"You tell her it's gonna be a girl. I know it. My name's Jeannette," she said to me. "Jeannette Terwilliger. And this here's Elmer."

"Maggie Carew," I said. "Middle of December. I'll tell her."

At the front of the line Mr. Strong had mounted up. Holding a coiled bullwhip, he wheeled his horse and slapped a few of the animals on the rump. To the accompaniment of whoops

9

and hollers from the crowd, the pack train slowly moved out.

"Don't you fall in love with any a them gum-boot miners out there, Teacher," I heard Cab yell to me, "they'd marry ya just for a grubstake."

"Make sure you come on back after break-up," someone else called, "and don't ride ol' Blossom too hard."

There was no chance of that, for after all his fussing and dancing around, Blossom wasn't moving. I kept trying to kick him in the ribs, but my feet were out too far, and he hardly felt it. So all I could do was jiggle the reins and tell him to giddap.

Then someone behind me whacked Blossom across the rump and I grabbed for the saddle horn as he plunged forward. Cries of encouragement went up from the crowd and I held onto Blossom for dear life as he caught up with the pack train and kept going. I felt my hat slowly lifting from my head, and then it was gone. But I didn't care. All I wanted to do was stay on. By the time we passed Mr. Strong I was sliding off and I braced myself for a fall. And then miraculously Blossom slowed down and stopped just short of a corridor of birches that led into the forest.

Shaking, I watched Mr. Strong ride back and pick up my flowered hat. I knew I was as white as flour when he rode up and presented it to me, and I was ready to burst into tears. But he was a gentleman, not even giving the slightest sign that he noticed it. "Madam," he said graciously, "since you're not familiar with the trail, I think it better if you allow me to lead."

As he went past I looked back at Eagle. There were a few people waving good-bye, including Mrs. Rooney, and I felt sad. For the past two weeks I'd done more traveling and met more friendly people than ever before in my life. Up to now the longest trip I'd ever made had been from Colorado, where I was born, to Oregon, where I'd been teaching. But in the past couple of weeks I'd traveled to Seattle, taken a boat up the Inside Passage to Juneau, then come North through places I'd only read of but never thought I'd see—Skagway, the Chilkoot Pass, White Horse, Dawson, the Yukon Territory, and finally here.

Along the way I had so much attention paid to me by men that sometimes I didn't think I was me. Even though I'd heard that there weren't too many women in the North, I hadn't expected to be treated like a raving beauty wherever I went. But I was. In White Horse and Dawson, when I checked into a hotel overnight, the clerk told me there'd be a dance given in my honor. And during the week that I'd spent on the riverboat, sailing north down the Yukon, I'd been invited to sit at the captain's table every night. A couple of times, in my cabin, I'd look at myself in the mirror thinking that maybe I'd changed in some way, that maybe I was really much prettier than I'd always thought I was. But after a good examination I knew I was just the same plain Anne Hobbs—same gray eyes, not a bad nose, good white teeth. One of the front ones was a little crooked, so about the best I could say was that if I didn't open my mouth and if my hair were still long I might have a faint resemblance to Mary Pickford. But even here in Eagle, where the riverboat had left me off, there'd been a dance given for me.

The last of the pack animals passed me and I took one more look at the town. People were moving off now, and beyond them the log cabins and white frame houses looked snug and comfortable. It was a beautiful place and I was sorry to leave. I couldn't see the wharf from here, but I could see the green waters of the Yukon River snaking for miles in each direction.

Blossom started to move, following the pack animals along a rutted wagon road that disappeared into the corridor of birches. The birches were beautiful, flaming with the colors of autumn, and they grew so thick on each side that I couldn't see the mountains beyond them. Wanting to ride alongside Mr. Strong, I gave Blossom a little kick, but he didn't pay any attention. I tried giving him a few more, then I gave up.

It was easy going for the first couple of miles, the wagon road gently curving through the forest, the only sounds the clatter of the pack animals' cowbells and the clop of their hooves. After a while my backside began to ache a little and I felt some stiffness in my shoulders, but I didn't mind. Blossom wasn't giving me any trouble and it was warm enough so I could open my jacket. It was hard for me to believe this was Alaska. Even though it was only the beginning of September, somehow I'd expected to find snow on the ground and cold weather. So far, except for a few nippy days and some nights when it came near to freezing, it hadn't been much colder than it would be back in Forest Grove, Oregon.

The wagon road ended suddenly and turned into a trail that was barely wide enough for one horse to pass through at a time. Trees and buckbrush pressed in on each side. Branches and bushes tore at my jacket and pulled the threads out. Now I realized why Mr. Strong had offered me the coat. If I could have I'd have ridden forward and asked him for it before my jacket was ruined, but even if I could get Blossom to move faster, the trail was too narrow for me to pass the animals ahead. Most of the time I couldn't see more than half a dozen of them because the trail twisted and turned so sharply. Twice when I caught sight of Mr. Strong through the trees I yelled to him, but the growth was so thick and the cowbells made so much noise that he couldn't hear me. Once I thought he saw me and I waved to him frantically, but he just gave me a pleasant wave back and went on.

The farther we went the more uneven the trail became and I kept slipping and sliding all over the saddle. The muscles in my legs were aching from trying to hold on. After a while I tried to stop Blossom so that I could get off, but no matter how hard I pulled on the reins he kept going. When I kept it up, he turned and tried to bite my foot.

An hour later when we were climbing up the side of a steep hill, I knew I wouldn't be able to hold on much longer. We'd been climbing for about fifteen minutes, and I was hoping that when we reached the top I might be able to jump off. But as soon as we did the land dipped suddenly and Blossom started down a canyon side that was so steep I was afraid I was going to go tumbling over his head.

By the time we were halfway down my hands were hurting

so badly I could barely hold onto the saddle horn. My jacket was just about ruined and all I wanted to do was whimper. Then things became worse. Without warning the sun disappeared and everything was gray and chill. A few minutes later big feathery snowflakes were drifting down and it was like being in the middle of winter. When I finally reached the bottom of the canyon, my teeth were chattering. My hands were so numb I couldn't move my fingers.

The pack train had stopped and so did Blossom. Mr. Strong came riding back, the olive-drab coat over his arm. He shook his head when he saw how I looked, but he didn't say anything. If he'd asked me how I was I would have started crying. Leaning over, he helped me on with the coat. "I believe you'll be more comfortable now," he said. "There are mittens in the pockets."

"Could we stop here for a while?"

"I'm afraid not, madam, I have U.S. mail to deliver and we have twenty-five miles to cover before nightfall. I must stay on schedule. We'll have a rest stop at Gravel Gulch."

"How far is that?"

"Seven or eight miles."

I knew I wasn't going to make it without a rest and maybe he suspected it, because whenever he could he rode back to see how I was. Snow kept drifting down, melting as fast as it hit the ground. Finally it stopped. Once when he rode back he complimented me on how much better I was sitting. "You're not sliding all over the place now."

"Thanks," I told him, "but it's not me. The snow melted on the saddle and my pants are stuck."

He smiled for the first time since I met him. "Are you hurting badly?"

"Kind of."

I wasn't a crybaby, but for the third time in as many hours I was ready to burst into tears.

He thought for a moment, then he said, "We'll stop at the next creek for about twenty minutes and you can stretch your legs."

13

The twenty minutes went like twenty seconds. Then I was back in the saddle again. I tried as hard as I could not to cause Mr. Strong any bother or hold up the pack train, but I just didn't have the strength in my legs to keep holding on without a rest once in a while. Besides that, the saddle was rubbing me raw in a couple of places. We finally figured out the best thing to do. Every time we came to the top of a hill or canyon Mr. Strong took Blossom's reins and led him while I walked or slid down by myself. It worked out fine because I could make it down five times faster than the pack animals. By the time I got to the bottom my shoes were full of dirt and stones and I had to spend some time getting stickers and foxtails out of my stockings, but it gave me a rest.

When we'd started out from Eagle I'd been looking forward to what I'd see along the way, but long before we reached Gravel Gulch I was aching so badly that I didn't care about anything except getting there. I had leaves and all kinds of twigs down my back and I'd been slapped by branches and brush so many times my face was raw. On top of that I was getting so hungry my head was aching. So when Gravel Gulch came into view I hardly minded when Blossom speeded up, even though it hurt.

It was only a few cabins nestled in a gulch, the slopes around them thick with willow and tamarack, but it looked beautiful. Before we came to them we crossed a few acres of ugly ground that was dotted with excavated mounds of yellow-looking dirt. They were tailing piles, I found out later, the gravel that was left over after gold had been taken from the ground. But then I didn't care what they were, all I wanted to do was get off Blossom before I fainted or died.

Four men and a woman were waiting for us. The sod roof of the cabin they were standing in front of must have been over a foot thick. There were still some vegetables left in the garden that had been growing on it, and I thought to myself that my Grandmother Hobbs would sure like to have seen a garden growing up in the air like that.

The men were glad to see us, but they seemed a little shy

14

when they saw me and went right to the pack animals instead of saying hello. The woman wasn't shy at all. Her name was Mrs. Ross. Short and fat, with jolly red cheeks, she was stuffed into a lumberjack shirt and a pair of Levis rolled up at the bottoms. She came right up to me, took in my flowered hat and the apparition underneath it and said, "Gracious, what'na heck happened to you?"

She wasn't expecting an answer and I didn't give her any. "One of you galoots get this poor thing down from there," she said. A man came over to me and lifted me out of the saddle as if I was a toy. When he set me down my knees gave way, and the next thing I knew the woman was practically carrying me into the cabin.

She sat me down beside a cookstove that had all kinds of things warming on it, took off my coat and jacket and told me not to move. I didn't have to be told. If she'd have wanted to kill me I wouldn't have raised a finger to stop her. She was swabbing my arms and hands with a washcloth when somebody started to come in. Whoever it was shut the door right away when she told him and everybody else to stay out until I came back to life.

I told her my name while I dried myself off with a towel she gave me, and she asked me where I was headed.

"Chicken," I said. "I'm the new teacher."

"Chicken! Honey, from the looks of you, you ain't even gonna make it to Liberty."

She was so hearty and outgoing that she made me feel better right away. If she'd been wearing a shirtwaist and long skirt she'd have reminded me of Miss Ivy, a teacher who'd taken me in when I was still in high school.

She didn't let the men in until she was sure I wasn't going to faint or cry, then she served up a delicious lunch of hot bear soup, hot sourdough bread and moose pot roast.

The men at the table didn't have too much to say, talking a little with Mr. Strong about their "clean-up"—the gold they'd taken from the ground—and speculating about the kind of winter they thought they were in for. I could tell they'd have liked to talk to me, but they were being polite and letting me eat. I was starved and ate so much finally that I could hardly move when I was done.

Mrs. Ross shooed them outside as soon as they finished so that I could lie down for a while. A half hour later when it was time for me to get up, I was glad the men weren't around. The insides of my thighs were so chafed I waddled around like a duck for a few minutes.

Before I got on Blossom again Mrs. Ross gave me an old stained pillow to put under me. It made it a little harder for me to balance myself, but it helped.

Once we were out of Gravel Gulch the going was easier. The country smoothed out into a series of gently sweeping hills, and I wished I weren't so saddle sore, so that I could really appreciate it. Sometimes, when we'd be riding across the crest of a hill I could see for hundreds of miles in every direction and I'd feel expectant and afraid at the same time. It was all so big that it made me feel as if something exciting was going to happen, yet so quiet and lonely I felt lost in it. But as big as it was, when we'd stop to water the horses at a creek and have a drink ourselves, there'd always be an old tin cup sitting between some rocks or hanging from a nail driven into a tree.

Darkness came slowly after a long twilight, but once the sun was down it became cold fast. It was past eight o'clock when we reached Liberty, and I was so bone-weary I hardly paid any attention to what was going on. Even if I had there would have been nothing to see but an old sagging cabin and a smelly stable nearby.

All I wanted to do was get into a bed and never wake up, so when Mr. Strong told me that after the horses were unloaded and stabled we'd have something to eat, I asked him just to show me where I was going to sleep. An old man who tended the stable for him hobbled ahead of me to a one-room cabin that smelled stale with sweat. He took three bedrolls down from a shelf and laid them out, then put some horse blankets on them. Before he left he told me that I'd be most comfortable

16

nearest the stove. There was a kerosene lamp hanging over a homemade table, and some water warming on the small stove, but I didn't even bother to turn the lamp down or think about washing or brushing my teeth. I just lay down on the bedroll, pulled a couple of blankets over me and tried to sleep.

From the start I kept drifting in and out, too exhausted to wake up and too sore to fall into a deep sleep. I felt the floor-boards move under me when Mr. Strong and the old man came in and lay down, and during the night I heard one of them snoring.

I kept dreaming that I was still on Blossom and that he was walking all the way back to Eagle with me. No matter what I did I couldn't stop him. When we arrived I felt terrible. I'd been riding for two days and I was back where I started.

II

It was dark and cold the next morning when Mr. Strong shook me. "There's hot water on the stove, madam," he said. "You will have twenty minutes to wash up and prepare yourself. Then we shall have breakfast and be on our way."

Ordinarily I loved getting up early and starting a new day, but after he went out I had to force myself to move. It took me five minutes before I could even stand. I had charley horses in both my legs and I didn't know which part of me hurt most. On top of the potbellied stove there was a kettle of water. I limped with it over to a wooden counter, poured some hot water into a basin, then got some cold water from a big barrel. The water didn't look that clean so I decided I'd skip brushing my teeth.

It was just starting to get light when we finished breakfast and were ready to go. But this time when Mr. Strong cupped his hands to boost me into the saddle I was too stiff to raise my foot. He and the old man had to get together and lift me.

Our next stopover for the night, Mr. Strong told me, would be Steel Creek, twenty-four miles away. "We'll stop at Dome Creek for lunch," he added.

"Everybody here in Alaska seems to live either on a creek or a river," I said.

He didn't think too much of my observation. "It's natural enough, madam. If they didn't they wouldn't have any water."

18

I was tempted to say they could always dig a well, but I didn't.

He'd found a smaller saddle for me as he'd promised, and it helped a lot at first by not rubbing me where I was raw, but after a while it started new raw places.

I'd thought Blossom had been mean the day before, but today he was even worse. Now that I had a smaller saddle I thought I'd be able to make him mind me. Instead he showed me right from the start who was boss. He'd stop whenever he felt like cropping some late grass or a few leaves that were still green, then to make up for lost time he'd jog along till he caught up with the pack train, punishing every bone in my body. I told Mr. Strong about it and he gave me a small box of chocolate creams. "Feed one to him every so often. It will keep him in a good mood."

They kept him in a mood, but it wasn't good. He was as smart as he was mean. After I gave him the first chocolate he kept turning his head every few minutes for another, whinnying and making terrible throaty sounds until I gave in. Twenty minutes later I gave him the last chocolate, showed him the empty box and tossed it away so he knew there was no more. After that he was worse than ever. I couldn't do anything to make him obey, until finally I just stopped caring. I rode hunched over, only seeing the creeks we crossed as Blossom splashed through them, and once I watched his legs turn blue as we sloshed through a patch of late blueberries. Sometimes I fell as much as a quarter of a mile behind the pack train.

It was about an hour after we left Gravel Gulch that I looked up to see the pack train halted and Mr. Strong waiting for me. Up ahead was what looked like a field of cotton. A light wind rippled its surface, and it was so beautiful that it made me forget how bad I was feeling.

"What's that?" I asked Mr. Strong.

"Tundra."

"I mean the white stuff." I didn't think it could be cotton, but it was.

" 'Alaska cotton,' " Mr. Strong said. "From this point on,

madam, you'll have to look where you're going. We're going to cross all that."

"I don't mind at all," I said.

He stared at me owlishly. "Have you ever crossed a nigger-head flat?"

"No . . ."

He wheeled his horse and the pack train started forward. I soon found out what he meant. At first I enjoyed myself. We rode through acres and acres of silvery bolls, their long silky fibers waving like pom-poms atop a slender stem. Then we hit swamp. Out of it grew great big hummocks of matted grass that looked like giant mops. They grew so thick that I thought of getting off Blossom and walking on them. Like the other animals, he wasn't having easy going. The mud sucked at his hoofs, and he kept slipping all over the place and stumbling over submerged roots. We slowed way down and soon fell behind the rest of the pack train.

I was so busy holding on that I didn't see the herd of caribou until we were almost on top of them. I heard them first, making peculiar coughing sounds. Then, as though they'd come out of nowhere, there they were a few hundred yards ahead on solid ground. They were grazing, eating some kind of white moss, a forest of antlers over their heads and a shawl of white around their shoulders. The closest of them lifted their heads, big eyes staring curiously. Then they went back to grazing as if they hadn't seen a thing.

What happened next went so fast that it was over before I knew it. We were about forty feet away from a caribou mother and a calf that were separated from the rest of the herd. All I saw at first was something moving fast—a humpbacked shape that was charging down on the calf in one moment and in the next was launching itself through the air.

It was a huge grizzly, and it landed on top of the calf with a terrible bone-crushing sound. The calf tried to get out from under but it didn't have a chance. I watched, horrified as the grizzly, snarling and raging, held the struggling calf down with one paw. Then, like a wrestler, it wrenched the calf's neck back, snapping it.

Blossom reared and I went tumbling into the mud, praying he wouldn't fall on me. Scrambling and stumbling, he managed to stay on his feet, then ran off. The whole herd started to move at the same time, antlers clacking, all of them pushing and shoving at each other in a panic to get away. A few stumbled and fell, but were back on their feet in a moment. Then the whole herd was bounding off.

Only the mother stayed, watching as the grizzly tore a great chunk of flesh from the twitching body. I started to back off, but I must have moved too fast. The grizzly dropped what he was eating and snarled at me, flashing bloody fangs.

I was too scared to move until I was sure he was more interested in his meal than in me. Then I started to back off slowly, the mud sucking at my shoes. Finally I turned and stumbled away.

After I felt I'd gone a safe distance, I turned around. My heart almost stopped as I stared into a pair of eyes.

The caribou mother had followed me. Only ten feet away, she looked enormous now that I was on foot. She let out a mournful wail that scared me even more and I screamed at her hysterically. "Go away! You hear me? Go away!" I started to cry.

At that she wheeled and loped off. I saw why a few seconds later: Mr. Strong was riding toward me, leading Blossom. Covered with mud from head to toe, aching all over, I couldn't stop crying. There was even mud up my sleeves. Mr. Strong got down from his horse and came over to me and I threw my arms around him. He stood straight as a statue, giving me a soft pat on the shoulder once or twice. "Now, madam," he said after a couple of minutes, "you mustn't take on so. Whatever happened you seem to have weathered it."

Finally I was able to blubber out the whole story.

"It is something you must get used to in this country," he said. "We will find some dry ground and after you change clothes you will feel better. Can you ride now?"

"I guess so."

"Madam, where is your hat?"

"Back there somewhere. I don't care about it anymore."

He rode back a ways before he found it. When he returned with it and I saw the shape it was in I told him to throw it away. He said he'd prefer not to.

"It is very becoming on you. Perhaps we can wash the mud off at the next creek."

The revolver lay heavy against my thigh. I hadn't even thought to use it, I realized. I mentioned it to Mr. Strong.

"It was fortunate you didn't. That grizzly would have torn you to pieces."

As soon as we reached some dry ground he unpacked the horse that had my things on it, then turned around so I could change. Luckily, I'd bought an extra pair of knickers back in Eagle, but having to put on a pair of practically new pumps, I wished now that I'd bought some boots. Mr. Strong had advised me to, but I wanted to save the money.

"After this," he said before we mounted up again, "I want you to keep up with the pack train."

"I'd like to, but I just can't get Blossom to mind me."

That made him mad. Without saying a word he walked over to a tree and broke a branch from it. He swished it around a couple of times, then grabbed Blossom's rein. First he jerked Blossom's head from side to side, punishing his mouth with the bit, then pushed him backwards until he almost fell. Blossom was scared and so was I. He tried to rear, but Mr. Strong held onto the rein. Then he lashed out at Blossom's neck with the switch while he held the rein tight. Blossom snorted and whinnied in panic, but Mr. Strong wouldn't stop. Dirt and stones were flying all over the place. How he held onto that big animal I didn't know, but he must have hit Blossom on the neck and face about twenty times. When he was done Blossom was quivering so badly I felt sorry for him. Mr. Strong's hat had fallen off. I gave it to him when he handed me the switch. He was sweating, and with his hat off, the top of his head bald, he didn't look so forbidding.

"If he gives you any trouble after this, whack him on the neck. He'll mind."

I didn't have to. All I had to do from then on was tap him and he did what he was supposed to do.

After that Mr. Strong became more friendly. Up to then I didn't think he liked me, but after a while he even asked me where I'd come from and how I happened to come to Alaska.

I told him about how I'd been teaching in Forest Grove Elementary in Oregon when the territorial commissioner of education visited there last year. "He gave a lecture in the auditorium about teaching here, and he made it sound so exciting and adventurous that I made out an application. And here I am."

"Where were you brought up?"

"In Colorado. My father was in the mining business," I said. Somehow it sounded better than saying he'd just been a coal miner.

"You seem a little young to be out on your own."

"I'm almost twenty," I said.

"You don't look it."

I knew he was going to say that. Just before I'd left Forest Grove I'd gone into a barbershop and had my hair bobbed. I'd figured that since I was going to be teaching somewhere in the wilds, it would be easier to take care of if it was short. Up to then people always took me for being older than I was, but from then on they kept telling me I looked like a kid.

"I meant no offense by that, madam," he said. "I was twelve when I left home myself and the experience hasn't hurt me yet."

"I was an old woman compared to you. I was sixteen when I left Colorado and started teaching in Forest Grove."

As we rode he told me a little about himself, of an unhappy childhood in North Carolina, then running away to go to California. He was in his late twenties when he came to Alaska to look for gold, and he'd been in the Forty Mile country for twenty-one years now. He was on the town council and was a member of the school board in Eagle.

The two of us having left home early gave us something in common. He didn't stop calling me madam, but I could tell he felt kind of fatherly towards me. All the rest of that day, seeing how badly off I was, he helped me down and let me walk a little even when we weren't going down a steep hill. It meant

23

that the whole pack train had to slow up and I really appreciated it.

It was getting towards dark and I was thinking that we were never going to reach Steel Creek, when we came to the foot of the steepest trail we'd come across so far. The brush around it was so thick and high that it formed a tunnel. Even without packs it would have been a tough trail for the animals to climb. Now, since it was the end of the day and they were tired, they balked at it and I didn't blame them.

They weren't the best animals to begin with—I'd seen finer horses pulling vegetable wagons—and they were overloaded. Besides that, most of the loads weren't packed on them right and half of them had sores full of pus and blood where the loads were rubbing against them. One of the mules whose back was the worst of all kept trying to knock his pack off against every tree he passed. I mentioned it to Mr. Strong, but he said they'd be all right.

Now he kept smacking the lead animals on the rump with his coiled whip and yelling at them, but it didn't do any good. They were played out. I'd thought he was mad when he'd whipped Blossom earlier in the morning, but this time he went into a rage.

Dismounting, he searched around in the brush until he came up with a length of dead limb as thick as a two-by-four. Then swearing to beat the band, he clubbed the first few animals all over their bodies. I thought he'd gone crazy and was going to kill them, but they moved. One after the other they disappeared up into the tunnel of brush, dirt and rocks coming down behind them. When Mr. Strong reached me, he threw the limb aside and took Blossom's reins.

Leading Blossom to his own horse, he mounted up. "This will be a tough climb, madam. You're going to have to hold on."

Before I could say anything, he'd spurred his horse forward, jerking Blossom's reins, and the next thing I knew I was charging up through the tunnel after him. It was so steep I couldn't see how we were going to make it to the top. I could barely

24

see ahead with all the dust that had been raised, and a couple of times I was almost blinded by branches. It was a full five minutes before we broke out of it. When we did the horses and mules were dripping sweat onto the ground and breathing so hard they sounded like bellows. My backside was raw and I was all for just dropping off Blossom and giving up then and there, but when I asked Mr. Strong if I could get off, he shook his head, too winded to talk. It took him a minute before he could say, "Walk your horse over there." He pointed to a spot about a hundred yards away and I nudged Blossom over to it.

I didn't know what to expect, but what I saw made me forget every ache and pain I had. The sun was below the distant mountains, and the land in between was covered with a strange veil of gray. Pine and spruce loomed up from the slopes below me, and beyond there was so much land, all of it bursting with spruce and tamarack, that I felt like a speck of dust that could be swept away in a second. Winding through it for as far as I could see were the waters of the Forty Mile River. And directly below, on the other side of the river, looking almost unreal, were twenty acres of tilled farm land. A big red barn was set to one side of them, and near that was a log building with bright patches of flowers all around it. Another half acre, directly behind the building, was lined with the orderly green rows of a vegetable garden.

"Steel Creek," Mr. Strong said, riding up beside me. "That's the creek, branching into the river down there. And that's the Prentiss roadhouse."

There was no problem getting the pack animals down to the river. Once they saw what was below they came to life, knowing that feed and a warm stall were waiting. They were so anxious that Mr. Strong had to keep holding the lead horse back, afraid that once the animals started to move fast there'd be no stopping them. If one of them was to fall he was liable to drag all the rest down. I knew how they felt. I couldn't wait to get there myself. Mr. Strong had told me I'd be able to take a hot bath when we reached Steel Creek.

As we kept going down and drawing near the river, I won-

dered how we were going to cross. The river wasn't high, but
it was flowing pretty fast. When we reached the bank I was
glad to see a thick cable stretched across the water. It was
anchored to the cliff face on this side and to a big iron tripod
on the other. There was a raft pulled up on the opposite shore
that had a line attached to the cable.

No sooner did we arrive at the river than about a half a
dozen people appeared on the other bank. Except for a girl in
bib overalls, they were all men. One of them hallooed and
yelled a question, but what with the rushing water and the
animals milling around, I couldn't hear. Mr. Strong understood.
He shook his head violently from side to side and waved a hand
to make sure they understood he was saying no.

Almost as soon as we were at the bank, Blossom began to give
me trouble for the first time all day. He kept heading for the
water, and each time I turned him away from it he'd try again.
He'd been so good that I'd dropped the switch a long way
back. Now I wished I had it.

Mr. Strong dismounted, and I thought he was going to grab
Blossom and help me down. Instead, he started untethering
the pack animals. As each one was untied it splashed into the
waist-deep water. After the third one went in Blossom was so
mad at my holding him back that he started trying to bite my
foot again, his teeth clicking evilly.

"Mr. Strong, can you help me? I can't hold Blossom!"

"Give him his head, madam. He knows what to do."

"You mean let him go in the river?"

"That is correct."

"Can't we use that raft?"

"We don't need it. Rest assured, madam, it's not necessary.
I've been doing this for years."

You may have, I thought, but I haven't, and I wished I had
the courage to tell him that. The lead animals had reached
the middle. Almost up to their haunches, they had to fight to
keep their feet in the powerful current. I couldn't swim, but
even if I could cross the Channel like the champion Gertrude
Ederle I still wouldn't be too anxious to do it with Blossom.

But I took a deep breath, eased my hold on the reins and let Blossom go. Hungry and bad-tempered, he plunged right in.

To my surprise, it was easy. Once I stopped caring about getting splashed, I began to enjoy it. I'd seen cowboys cross rivers in picture shows and they'd done it in deeper water than this. I was feeling so good that I even waved once to everyone on the opposite bank.

Then Blossom slipped.

He went down on his hind legs and I almost slid off. While he was down the water hit us in the side with so much force that we almost went over. Blossom held his feet, but he started losing ground. The current was pushing us into deeper water. As hard as he tried, Blossom couldn't hold out against it. He slipped again, and I felt the shock of cold water up to my waist. I began to panic. With Blossom not able to get any purchase on the slippery bottom, it was only a matter of time before we'd be swept away.

He knew we were in trouble and fought harder than ever to make it to the opposite bank. If I wasn't so busy just holding on, I'd have had the sense to point him downriver and ease him over to the bank gradually, but I was too scared to think. Suddenly he stumbled. His forelegs went down and I was pitched forward at the same time that his head snapped back and it cracked against my forehead. Dazed, I hardly knew what was happening after that. All I knew was that I couldn't faint and I had to hold on.

I grabbed a handful of mane and had a quick flash of the people on the opposite bank whirling away from us. Then they were gone. A big blood-red blotch kept coming between me and everything else. I heard Blossom blowing and snorting, and once I felt the two of us being pulled down, only to be pushed right back up again.

I couldn't tell how long it was before I realized that Blossom had calmed down. The red blotch in front of my eyes had disappeared and left me with a headache, but somehow I was still in the saddle. Blossom was swimming. Moving along smoothly, he was heading for the bank. I felt him touch bottom, and a few seconds later he heaved himself up out of the water. Once we were on dry land he shook himself so hard that even if I'd wanted to I couldn't have stayed on him. I slid to the ground and landed hard.

It took me a minute before I started telling myself that I'd better get up. I was shivering with cold, but didn't have the strength to move.

I'd finally managed to sit up when I heard someone coming. It was a girl. Breathing hard from running, she leaned down, one of her braids dangling in front of me.

"You all right, ma'am?"

I managed a nod.

"Can you walk if I help you?"

She got me to my feet and we were making our way along the bank when Mr. Strong came riding up. He wanted to put me up on his horse, but I wouldn't let him. I didn't want to look at another horse right then. Between the two of them they brought me to the Prentiss roadhouse.

Inside, a stocky woman with gray hair and a bossy manner took me in charge right away. Holding me away from her so she wouldn't get wet, she told the girl to unfold the canvas tub, and then ushered me into a room. There she told me to take off my wet clothes, and dry myself off. She came back with an old flannel bathrobe a few minutes later, steered me into a bathing room and eased me into a portable tub that was full of steaming water. It burned me where I was raw, but it felt wonderful everyplace else. She was furious at Mr. Strong. "That old tight-fisted sonofagun," she said, when I leaned back against the wooden frame of the tub, "—it was his fault you went in. If he'd of let us send the raft over it wouldn't of happened. But he wanted to save the money."

The girl came in then carrying a big copper kettle. "This is my daughter Nancy," the woman said. "I'm Mrs. Prentiss. This isn't the first time this kind of thing's happened." She turned to her daughter, "You remember when he lost those two mules loaded down with parcel post?"

"Yes'm." The girl let the hot water into the tub slowly.

28

"You stay here with her. I got supper to make and I don't want her falling asleep in there. Be a heck of a thing if she ended up drowning in *here* after all that."

She left. Nancy finished pouring the water and sat down in a homemade chair. I slid further down along the smooth rubber lining and let my head rest against the frame. I'd rather have been left alone, but Mrs. Prentiss wasn't the kind of person you argued with. Nancy was uncomfortable. Her green eyes kept looking everyplace but at me.

"Thanks for helping me," I said.

She made a little motion with her head to say it was nothing, then looked down at her fingers. She had on an old middy blouse under her overalls and her fingernails were bitten down to the quick. She could have been pretty if she didn't keep her mouth pursed so tight.

"We didn't think you were gonna make it."

"Neither did I."

"Everybody figured Chicken was gonna have to do without a teacher for another year."

When she saw me smile she grinned, trying to hide the cavities in her front teeth. I told her she didn't have to stay. "I won't fall asleep."

"You sure?"

"Positive. It feels too good."

I stayed in the tub for another hour, until Mrs. Prentiss came for me and brought me back into the room. She'd already laid out bandages on the top tier of a bunk bed and made me lie down on my stomach on the bottom tier. Then, even though I told her I could do it myself, she insisted on bandaging all the places where I was raw. "I've raised eight kids," she said. "You don't have anything they don't. In some places they got more, so settle down. You got two more days before you reach Chicken. You won't make it with a raw behind."

She was none too gentle, but she was thorough. After she finished, she handed me a suit of boy's Stanfield underwear. "It's scratchy," she said, "but it's warm."

29

She ordered me to stay awake until she brought me some dinner. I found out later that the meat was bear cub, but it tasted like pork and it was delicious. No sooner had I finished it than I fell asleep.

Breakfast the next morning was solemn. The big main room of the roadhouse was cheerful and clean, the board floors almost bleached white. There were flower boxes on the windowsill. The whole place was so spick-and-span it made me uncomfortable, but not half as uncomfortable as the Prentisses did. All ten of them, including Nancy, sat at the long table sullenly, as though someone had cheated them and they were angry about it. I wished Mr. Strong was here, but he'd eaten already and was out getting the animals loaded up. After Mrs. Prentiss introduced everyone in the family to me they didn't say a word. She seemed to dominate them like a circus lion tamer with a cage full of cats. After a couple of minutes of silence, she looked at them with cold green eyes. "Ever see a finer lookin' bunch?" she said contemptuously. "Talk your ear off, don't they? My nine mules—happy as sunshine, the whole lot of 'em."

"How long you been teaching?" she asked me a minute later.

"Two years."

"You must have started when you were in diapers."

"I'm older than I look," I said.

"What do you think of somebody who's had plenty of schooling and still can't read?"

"I don't know," I said. "There could be a lot of reasons."

As soon as Mr. Prentiss finished his breakfast and got up, the rest did also. I thought at first that maybe none of them wanted to be left alone with her. But as soon as they were gone I realized they knew she wanted to talk to me alone.

"I got a favor to ask you," she said. "I want my Nancy to stay with you at Chicken."

I was too surprised to answer.

"I'm willing to pay, mind you," she went on, as if that meant I didn't have any excuse for refusing. "I'm not asking nothing for nothing."

"But Nancy and I don't even know each other, Mrs. Prentiss."

She brushed that aside. "That doesn't matter. You're a teacher. My Nancy can't read too good and I think you could help her."

"But I don't even know if I'll have room for her. I've never been to Chicken."

"There'll be room. And if there isn't she'll sleep on the floor." When I didn't say anything, she found another argument. "Look, Teacher, you're a cheechako. You don't know the first thing about this country. Nancy could be a big help to you."

"Let me think about it," I said, wanting to get away.

Mrs. Prentiss' tone changed. She stopped pushing. "I'll give it to you straight, Teacher. I don't know you, it's true. I don't know anything about you, but I think you'd be good for Nancy. I'm talking to you because she asked me to. I could send her to school in Eagle, but she doesn't like that Mrs. Rooney, says she's more interested in men than in teaching. Besides, the kids there call her bonehead because she can't read."

The door to the kitchen was ajar and I had the feeling Nancy was behind it, listening. I got up. "Let me think about it," I said again.

The stable next to the roadhouse was almost as neat as the roadhouse itself, with plenty of fresh hay all around, and a clean stall for a cow. Mr. Strong was almost ready to lead the animals out. When I told him the story, he didn't seem surprised at all. "It's a good idea," he said.

"But we're complete strangers."

"That has nothing to do with it, madam," he said. "If I were you I would take her."

"Why?"

"You're new to this country. You're going to be all alone. Living in the bush isn't easy for anyone, much less for someone like you. Nancy can teach you a great deal."

"Suppose we don't get along?"

"You can always send her home."

31

I stayed in the stable, trying to decide what to do. I thought about Miss Ivy. If she was in this situation, I knew, she wouldn't have thought twice about taking Nancy. She'd been my teacher in high school, and if it hadn't been for her I'd probably never have become a teacher myself. When my family had broken up and my mother couldn't support me anymore she'd taken me in and treated me as if I were her own daughter. She hadn't made any bones about it either, just took me in and kept me with her until I graduated, as if she wasn't doing anything but what was simply right and proper.

When I thought about it that way it seemed to me that taking Nancy to live with me wasn't a big thing at all—especially since what Mr. Strong had said was true. I *didn't* know anything about living in the wilds. Having someone like Nancy to show me the ropes would make things a lot easier. I could help her and she could help me.

Before the pack train left I told Mrs. Prentiss that it was all right, and she said she'd send Nancy out with Mr. Strong some time in the next few weeks.

I hadn't seen Nancy around at all, but as we were moving out she appeared around the corner of the roadhouse. "Bye, Teacher," she called.

"Bye, see you soon." I smiled.

She didn't smile back.

III

From Steel Creek on the going was easier. Right from the start I felt better. The air was nippy, but I was well bundled up. Besides the suit of long underwear I was wearing, Mrs. Prentiss had given me a pair of bib overalls one of her boys had outgrown, a pair of his boots and a flannel shirt. With Mr. Strong's coat on top of it all, I didn't have to worry about being cold.

My flowered hat was in such bad shape that I gave it to Blossom. With a couple of holes cut in it to let his ears through, it really looked almost rakish on him. I settled for an old wool pom-pom hat that I could pull down over my ears. I was feeling so good I started paying attention to the country.

All during the trip down the Yukon I'd kept wondering what it was that made this country so different from what I'd known so far. I'd thought it was the bigness, but it wasn't only that. It was the rawness. Back in Oregon the trees billowed out fat and heavy even at this time of year. Here they were tattered, leaner and tougher—the tall spruce looking like huge giants ready for a scrap. Everything was that way, like the thick groves of willow that some animal had chewed half up, stripping the bark from them. They just kept on growing anyway, unkillable. Even the clouds overhead seemed to move faster. The air was all charged up, as if something was going to happen.

I'd have thought that with all the noise the cowbells were making, we wouldn't see hide nor hair of any wild animals, but it was just the opposite. The noise made them curious, and every so often I'd look off and see something watching us. Once it was a whole bunch of foxes. They were frisking on a shelf when we came on them, two blues, a couple of blacks and one cross fox. They stopped fooling around and just stared at us as nervy as you please, then went right back to what they were doing.

I'd always thought wolves traveled in packs until I saw one all by himself maybe a hundred yards off the trail. I'd never seen one before, but I knew right away it had to be a wolf. It looked bigger and meaner than I'd imagined, long snout, heavy ruff around the neck and eyes as calculating as the Devil's. He paced us for almost a mile, sometimes showing up ahead of us, and I'd have sworn he was thinking as clearly as I was. "You can bet on that," Mr. Strong said. "He smells the horses—hopes maybe one of them will drop dead."

He gave up hoping finally and disappeared.

We were a few hours out of Steel Creek when a settlement appeared in the distance—a line of about fifteen cabins set back from the banks of the Forty Mile River. A few small boats were pulled up on the bank and there were some food caches standing on poles in back of the cabins.

"An Indian village," Mr. Strong said. "We'll stop there."

I'd seen a couple of Indian villages from the riverboat coming down the Yukon, but never close up. Before that I hadn't even known there'd be Indians in Alaska. I thought there'd be Eskimos. This village looked so picturesque I couldn't wait to get there.

But when we drew near I was shocked. It was a shanty-town, worse than any of the worst sections I'd seen in all the coal towns I'd lived in. There might have been three or four decent-looking places, but the rest were hovels, sway-backed cabins and sagging shacks that were patched with everything the owners could get their hands on—tarpaper, rotting planks, scraps of galvanized iron, even old animal hides. The whole place looked as if all the garbage and slop from Eagle had been dumped here. Rusting tin cans, rags, paper, shreds of hide, bottles and fishbones littered the ground. There was no breeze blowing and the stench that hung over everything was nauseating. I was glad it was chilly. If it had been hot it would have been unbearable.

As we rode in people stared at us from doorways. I'd thought that the Indians I'd seen at Eagle were poor, but these people had nothing. They made me think of pictures I'd seen in a stereoscope once of starving Negro sharecroppers, except that these faces looked Oriental. The clothes were the same, though: worn dresses that hung like sacks on the women, patched and baggy overalls on the men. On one man we passed I recognized the frayed jacket of a riverboat captain.

Mangy dogs, half starved and chained to stakes, snarled and leaped at us as we went by. They were jerked back and landed in their own dung. A few children kept pace with us, giving the horses plenty of room. Barefoot and in rags, noses running, they were having a good time. One little boy, with open running sores all over his head, tripped over one of the dogs and barely avoided being bitten. Another boy had the same kind of sores all over his neck. They were from tuberculosis, I found out later.

We stopped in front of a frame house that had paint peeling all over it. I thought that maybe it was where the chief of the village lived because a lot of the Indians were gathered in front of it. Mr. Strong seemed to know everybody, greeting a few people by their first name.

"Betty, how's little Charles Lindbergh?" he asked a mahogany-colored woman who was holding a tiny baby. The dogs all over the village were making such a racket he almost had to yell.

"He fine," she yelled back, lifting the baby a little to show him off. "Strong like bear."

"*Skooltrai* here?" Mr. Strong said.

The woman nodded and at almost the same time the door to the house opened. An Indian and a white girl came out, and no two people could have looked more different than they did. Maybe it was because the girl was so beautiful, but I thought the Indian was one of the ugliest men I'd ever seen. He was tall and thin, the skin over his cheekbones drawn so tight that it glistened, and his eyes were small and set wide apart. His shirt was open at the throat and his neck looked as though somebody had once wound barbed wire around it, it was so covered with scars.

They were followed by a little boy. He must have been about eight years old and you could see he was part white. Like the other kids, he was as skinny as a rail.

"Good day, Miss Winters," Mr. Strong called to the girl. Up to then he'd been smiling and friendly with everybody, the way you'd be with children. But he didn't look friendly now. "This young lady is bound for Chicken," he went on, "and she needs a short rest. I would appreciate it if you would accommodate her."

The girl didn't act any friendlier to him than he did to her, but she came right over to me.

"I'll give you a hand," she said, reaching up.

She was really lovely, with bright blue eyes and long black hair tied back with a red bandanna. She was wearing moccasins, but even then she was taller than I was.

"I'm Cathy Winters," she said, after I was able to stand by myself.

"Thanks," I said. "I'm Anne Hobbs."

She indicated the tall Indian beside her. "This is Titus Paul."

I told him I was glad to meet him, but he didn't return the compliment.

She asked the little boy to get her mail, then brought me into the house. Her place was less than half the size I'd thought it was from the outside, one dingy room with a cracked brown linoleum on the floor and a tiny bedroom. She helped me off with my coat and I plopped down on a battered couch.

"I hope I'm not putting you out."

There was a small table in the center of the room with the remains of a meal on it and I smelled the delicious odor of fried fish.

36

"Not at all. Titus and I just finished eating some grayling he caught this morning. Plenty left over if you're hungry."

"Thanks. This is all I need."

"Want to wash up?"

"I sure do."

She set about getting a basin and a washcloth and I just sat back and watched her move around. She had on a dress that was as beautiful as her figure, some kind of homespun embroidered with Indian designs around the hem and the half-length sleeves. It was tied with a leather thong at the waist. She looked so smart and neat that even if I hadn't been so sweated up and grimy I'd have been jealous of her.

The little boy came in then and put her mail on the counter.

"This is Chuck," Cathy said, taking a pitcher and dipping it in a barrel of water. "He'll be keeping you company the rest of the way. Chuck, I'd like you to meet Miss Hobbs."

He was too shy to look at me.

Cathy tipped the pitcher over the hand basin and poured the water in. "Oh come on," she said to him. "Is that the way I taught you to say hello? Go on," Cathy encouraged him. "She won't bite you. She's a teacher just like me."

"Please . . . to . . . meet you," he said gravely.

"I'm pleased to meet you too," I said.

She told him to run along and he went out, grateful to get away.

After I washed up I felt a little better, and over a cup of coffee I found out why her place was so small. She was the schoolteacher here and these were her living quarters. The rest of the house was the schoolroom. I admired her. She didn't have much of a place, but she'd certainly made it comfortable. There were books all over and all kinds of Indian articles on the walls—a quiver full of arrows, bows, a couple of wooden ceremonial masks and dozens of other things. A colored framed print of Jesus that hung on one wall looked out of place.

"Are you here all alone?" I asked her.

"Sure." She must have realized what I was thinking because

37

she said, "I know how you feel. I felt the same way when I first came. But there's nothing to be afraid of here. If you like, I'll show you around. You should walk a little anyway—get the kinks out."

Outside, Mr. Strong had untied a badly sagging load on one of the animals and laid the contents out on the ground. He and the Indians who'd ordered stuff were stooped around it. They had their money ready as he handed them their goods: a frying pan for one, kerosene lantern for another, canned milk, a teapot. The others just looked on.

The onlookers made way for Cathy and me when we came out, and Cathy introduced me to them in their own language. I caught the words *"skooltrai"* and "Chicken" as she explained who I was. Then she reeled off their names to me, almost all of them Biblical: David Solomon, Paul Joe, Ruth James, Isaiah John. The older people nodded pleasantly. The younger ones, especially the girls, were kind of shy. They giggled when they were introduced. The ones with babies carried them on their back in a blanket. The older women, like most of the men, looked listless and tired, half of them with cheeks that had a hectic flush and eyes that glistened. I didn't know until Cathy told me a little later that they were the symptoms of TB. Half the village had it. The sores on some of the children were from glandular TB, Cathy said.

"You got chewing gum?" a squat, flat-featured woman asked me after Cathy introduced her as Mary Magdalene.

"Mary, where are your manners?" Cathy said.

"Hunh," Mary said. "I not need manners. Need chewing gum."

Cathy took me from one end of the village to the other. There wasn't much to see, but the more she showed me of it the worse I felt. I'd always thought of Indians who lived in the wilds as being strong, proud people able to live off the land, but here there were up to seven and eight people huddled in small one-room cabins. Through a couple of open doors I could see that except for some crude bunk beds, a stove and a few chairs and boxes, most of them were bare. The caches that squatted on poles in back of many of them should have been packed with dried meat and fish. Most of them held pitifully little, Cathy told me.

"They won't be empty in the winter, though," Cathy said bitterly. "We'll be using them for the dead, keep them there until we can bury them in the spring." She saw the look on my face. "Sorry," she said. "It doesn't take much to get me started. You've got your own troubles."

I couldn't understand it. "Why do they live this way?"

"It's not an easy question to answer. Anyway it's too long to go into now. The main thing is not to judge what you see here by white standards. Most of these people didn't meet whites until about thirty or forty years ago. Up to then they were living in the Stone Age."

"What kind of Indians are they?" I asked her.

"Athapascans. That's the general designation for all the Indians up here. Then that's broken down into tribes. These people are Kutchins—Takhud Kutchins."

On the way back we passed a huge caldron boiling over an open fire. The odor from whatever was bubbling around in it was awful. An old crone, her spindly legs bowed so badly they looked like they were going to snap, was trying to get something out with a wooden spoon. But she was too short and couldn't reach over without almost falling in. Cathy said something to her in Indian, took the spoon and tin enamel plate from her and scooped out some pieces of salmon. When she handed it back the old woman took it gratefully. She had only a couple of teeth in her mouth and two lines of tobacco juice ran down each side of her chin.

"What's that cooking in there?" I said.

"Fish heads, animal guts, rice. It's the dog pot. For them." She waved a hand toward one of the dogs. The old woman sat down on the ground and began eating. "That's Lame Sarah. That little boy who's going along with you—Chuck—he's been living with her. As you can see, he hasn't been eating steak and

39

potatoes. She can barely take care of herself. Thank God he's getting out of here."

When we were ready to leave, the old woman and Chuck were standing by one of the mules, which had an old beat-up saddle on it. She was buttoning up Chuck's mackinaw. When she finished, she hugged him to her, murmuring endearments. He was only half listening, though. His eyes were on the mule and he looked worried. It towered over him the way Blossom did over me, and I knew exactly what was on his mind. The old woman let him go.

"Up we go, Chuck," Cathy said to him. She tried to lift him into the saddle, but he pulled away from her. "No!" he yelled. He was scared and I didn't blame him. A few of the kids were looking on, kind of anxious and envious at the same time. Cathy kneeled down in front of him. "Chuck, if you want to see your mother you're going to have to ride that mule."

Mr. Strong came over and asked what the matter was.

"He's a little afraid to get on," I said.

"Is that right," he said. Without another word he grabbed the back of Chuck's mackinaw, lifted him bodily and plunked him down on the mule's back. "You stay put," he warned him, "savvy?"

Terrorized, Chuck didn't answer, but he looked as though he were about to cry.

"You didn't have to do that," Cathy said. I didn't say anything, but I agreed with her. Mr. Strong acted as if he hadn't heard her.

"We are about ready to go, madam," he said to me. He glanced down at Cathy's feet. "Are you too destitute to buy shoes, Miss Winters?"

Before we left her house she'd slipped on a pair of black rubbers over her moccasins. I noticed that a few of the Indians were wearing the same thing.

"What makes you ask?" Her voice was cold as ice.

"I know the Indians are accustomed to wearing such foot-gear, but I've never seen respectable white women do so. They

40

prefer shoes. From the rear I might have taken you for a squaw."

"Nobody asked you to look at my rear."

He got red, and I almost blushed myself. I would never have been able to say anything like that to an older person. Not that Cathy was being fresh or disrespectful. She was just giving tit for tat, but if it had been me I would have just shut up.

"Are you ready, madam?" he asked me.

After he boosted me up, he went down the line once more for a last check of everything.

"Do me a favor, Anne," Cathy said. She tossed her head in Mr. Strong's direction. "For all he cares, Chuck is just another piece of baggage—maybe less. Look after him, will you? He's hardly ever gone further than a few miles out of this village and he'll be scared to death."

"I'll look after him."

Cathy spoke to him in Indian, pointing to me a couple of times. "Remember," she said, "if you need anything you speak English. If you get scared, or you have to go to the toilet, you tell the teacher here, savvy?"

"*Aha*," he said.

"No more *aha*," Cathy said. "From now on it's yes, understand?"

He nodded.

"I say yiss and I tell Tisha."

She reached a hand up to me. "Good luck."

"Good luck to you, Cathy. I wish we'd had more of a chance to talk."

"Drop me a line when you get to Chicken if you feel like it."

I told her I would.

The pack train moved out then. We followed the curve of the river, and the last I saw of the Indian village before it disappeared behind us was the white wooden cross that stood on top of the church. Then that disappeared over the tops of the trees. I was glad when it was gone. The whole place was awful,

41

and I just couldn't see any reason why they couldn't clean it up. I didn't want to say it to Cathy, but I wouldn't have stayed there for five minutes.

Mr. Strong slowed down and let the pack train move ahead. "I trust you're feeling much better, madam," he said when Chuck and I reached him.

"Much."

"Good. I would like to make up for some of the time we have lost."

"It's all right with me, but I don't know about Chuck."

He was still scared stiff, just barely managing to hang on.

"Don't worry about him," Mr. Strong said. "These Indians can take anything. . . What did you think of that young lady back there?"

"I liked her."

He was still angry, and I thought he was going to say something about her, but he changed the subject. "We will stop for lunch in a couple of hours, then push on until nightfall. We will spend the night at the O'Shaughnessy roadhouse. I trust you will bear up until then."

I would, but I didn't know about Chuck. Indian or whatever, he was only a little boy and he was going to need rest along the way.

He made out all right as long as we stuck to the river bank, but once we veered off and started going through rough country he looked as though he was going to be sick.

"Do you want to stop, Chuck?" I asked him. Pale and sweating, he was too miserable to answer.

A few seconds later the mule jumped over a dead tree and he went tumbling off. He landed on his hands and knees and didn't get up. Instead he started to retch. By the time I was able to get Blossom to stand still long enough to get off, Chuck had thrown up and was crying.

I led him over to the tree, sat down with him and put an arm around him.

Mr. Strong made his way back to us a few minutes later leading both Blossom and the mule.

"He fell off," I said.

Mr. Strong wasn't too happy. "Is he hurt?"

"No, but he's pretty badly upset."

Mr. Strong waited until he was able to stop crying, then he said, "Chuck, I think maybe you go back home, huh? I give you your stuff, you go home."

Chuck looked stricken. "You no want me?"

"You fall off mule. No can ride. We ride far, sleep tonight long distance from here, ride more tomorrow. Too tough for you."

"I ride," Chuck promised. "You take me I no fall down no more."

Mr. Strong raised a finger. "You fall once more you go home, savvy?"

He tried as hard as he could and my heart went out to him for it, but it was a losing battle. He managed to stay on for another mile before he fell off again. It made me wince, but he scrambled right to his feet and ran after the mule, trying to get it to stop. It wouldn't though, and he stood in the trail, tears of anger streaming down his face. "Stink'n mool!" he called after it. "Dirty black stink'n white mool!"

I stopped Blossom. In a couple of minutes Mr. Strong would be coming back. "Chuck, do you know your way back to the village from here?"

"Yiss," he said.

"Maybe you can try again when Mr. Strong comes through next time."

He wrung his hands. "Tisha," he said earnestly, "you talk Mista St'ong me? You talk him? Say one more time Mista St'ong he let me come I stay on stink'n mool. I stay on, Tisha, I stay on."

"I'll talk to him, but I don't think he'll listen to me."

He wrung his hands again, glancing up the trail, then dropped his hands in defeat. I felt terrible for him.

There was a big boulder a short distance away. I headed Blossom over to it and stopped him beside it.

"See if you can climb up and get on with me."

He clambered up and somehow we got him on in back of me. Then we rode on, his arms tight around my waist. Up ahead, Mr. Strong came in sight. He looked at me questioningly.

"He asked me if he could ride with me for a while," I said. "I'm getting pretty good now. I don't mind."

Whether he believed me or not, he wheeled his horse without saying anything. Chuck's head leaned against my back.

"Tisha?"

"Yes?"

"You one darn good white woman," he said, tightening his arms around my waist. It made me feel good when he did it.

Somehow we made it to the next rest stop. How I didn't know, but we did. This time it was a sagging old cabin that had sunk into the ground about a foot. I had to stoop down when I went through the door. Inside it was dark and dingy, half of it floored with planks and the other half dirt. A man and his wife owned it and from the way they acted you'd have thought they'd taken vows of silence. After the man asked Mr. Strong how the trip had been they hardly said anything. The man gave Mr. Strong and me a basin of water to wash with while the woman began ladling out some stew she had on the stove. When Mr. Strong finished washing, the man threw the water outside. He didn't fill the basin for Chuck. I said that Chuck would probably want to wash up too, but he didn't pay any attention to me. Mr. Strong sat down at the table and indicated the other place that had been set. "Sit down, madam."

"Isn't Chuck going to eat?" He'd sat down on the floor beside the stove and was leaning against the wall.

"You hungry, Chuck?" I asked him. He nodded up and down a few times.

Mr. Strong said, "I am not being paid for his transportation, madam. I'm doing it out of charity. Rest assured, he can take care of himself."

"I'll be glad to pay for his meal," I said. "Is that all right?" I asked the woman. She looked at Mr. Strong and he nodded, so she got a bowl for Chuck, cut a slice of bread and handed them to him where he sat. He finished off every bit of it.

We had a half hour before we were to leave and I spent part of it showing Chuck how to ride the mule. "You say whoa when you want him to stop, say giddap and give him a little kick when you want him to go." It took a little while for him to get it, but once he saw he could control the animal, he stopped being afraid. By the time we were ready to go, he was having fun. "Giddap, mool," he said, and we were off.

The longer we rode together, the more I liked him. If he was sore—and he had to be—he didn't complain about it. Instead he'd jump down every so often and lead the mule along. Walking didn't seem to bother him at all. Sometimes, when the horses had tough going, he even drew way ahead of us. When we caught up with him, he'd lead the mule over to a rock or a log and clamber back into the saddle without any help.

"I told you, madam," Mr. Strong said to me the first time he did it. "These Indian kids are hardy."

Our next overnight stop was the O'Shaughnessy roadhouse. It was run by a pleasant Irishman with a thick accent. Since I was a woman he gave up his bedroom, and I shared his bed with his wife, a plump Indian woman who saw to it that Chuck was well fed and bedded down in a warm sleeping bag in our room. I tucked him in and was going out when he called to me. "Tisha . . . You talk me?"

He wanted company. He was scared being in a strange place. I sat down on the sleeping bag. "I bet you'll be glad to see your mother," I said.

"Oh yiss," he said.

"She must be very nice."

"She beyoodeeful, Tisha—like you."

"I'll bet. Is your father in Chicken too?"

"Yiss."

"What kind of a man is he?"

"Big man," he said. "Got plenty guns, lotsa things. Got big glass eyes see far." He curled both his fists in front of his eyes to make binoculars. "I no like him," he added.

"Why not?"

"He no like me and Et'el."

45

"Is Ethel your sister?"

"Mmm . . . You got nice school?" he asked drowsily.

"I don't know. I haven't seen it yet."

"You let me come?"

"Sure. Do you like school?"

"Like too much," he said enthusiastically. "School plenty warm. Big. Miss Wintuhs make good grub for kids. You make good grub you school?"

"I never have, but I probably could. What do you like to eat?"

He didn't answer. He'd fallen asleep.

IV

We were up at five the next morning and on our way an hour after a hearty breakfast.

Right from the start Chuck was lively as a squirrel, riding that mule as though he'd done it all his life. In fact a couple of times he gave me a turn, slapping the mule to make him jog and pretty near falling off in the process.

He was comfortable around me, but not around Mr. Strong. For the whole trip I never heard him say a word when Mr. Strong was in earshot. Not that he talked much when we were alone either. Aside from the talk we had before he went to sleep the previous night, the only real conversation we had was about George Washington.

"You know Geo'ge Wash'ton?" he asked me.

"I've heard of him," I said.

He started giggling. "He chop down cherry tree."

"What are you laughing at?" I asked him.

"Cherry *tree*. Fun-ne-e-e." He kept giggling.

"Why is it funny?"

"Cherry grow on *tree*. I no believe."

"They do, though."

"You see?"

"Oh, yes."

"See *apple tree*?"

"Loads of 'em."

That really made him laugh. "How apple get on *tree*?"

47

"They just grow there. Oranges, pears—they all grow on trees."

He shook his head. It was hard for him to accept. "Potato?" he said mischievously.

"No, not potatoes."

"Leddus?"

"No, lettuce grows right out of the ground. You know that."

He laughed so much he had *me* giggling about it. When you saw it from his point of view, big pieces of fruit hanging from a spruce tree, or a birch, it did seem kind of funny.

Around noon, Mr. Strong stopped the pack train as we were making our way through a dense growth of cottonwood. The cowbells that had been clanking all the way down the line were quiet all of a sudden, and all I could hear were the merry waters of the meandering creek we'd been crossing and recrossing for a while.

"There it is, madam," Mr. Strong said. "That is Chicken."

I could barely make it out through the trees—a settlement about a mile away and a little below us. It was too far to really see what it was like.

"If you don't mind, Mr. Strong, I'd like to change my clothes."

"What is the matter with what you have on?"

Miss Ivy had always told me that first impressions were important. "Always look your very best," she said to me once, "No matter where you are you must try to be a lady."

"I'd feel more comfortable if I were more properly dressed."

Mr. Strong dismounted. "Will you want to wash up too?"

"I'd like to."

He was nice about it, unpacked the suitcase I asked for and brought it to the edge of the creek.

"We camp here?" Chuck asked.

"No," I said, "I'm going to change and wash up." I took off the army coat, Chuck watching me, interested. I asked him to turn around before I took off my shirt and knickers. "And don't look until I tell you to."

"Why I do this, Tisha? he asked with his back to me.

"It's not important," I said. "Just stay that way until I tell you it's all right." It would have been too much trouble to explain. When it came to modesty he didn't have any.

After I finished I put the army coat back on and brought my suitcase back. I'd changed into a long black skirt, cotton stockings and white blouse. "You look quite nice, madam," Mr. Strong said gallantly.

He put my suitcase back, then started moving down the line, checking the loads for the final time. "When we break out of these trees," he said, "the animals are going to be in a hurry."

There weren't as many as we'd started out with, about ten left now. The rest had been left along the way.

I looked off at the settlement, my stomach doing flip-flops. This is it, I thought. I'm almost there. I'd come to a far place, just as my Grandmother Hobbs used to tell me I would. When I was a little girl back in Colorado I used to hate the places I lived in: Blazing Rag, Big Four, Laveta, Evansville. Mining towns full of company shacks, they were all ugly. I felt sure I'd be living in them forever, but Granny said no I wouldn't and she'd been right.

"You be a teacher, Annie," she used to tell me, "an' you can go anywhere in the world you want."

When I thought about her now I could see her as clearly as if she were right in front of me. As a little girl I used to wish that when I grew up I could be just like her. She wasn't like anybody else in our whole family. The rest of us were light skinned and had blue eyes—or gray eyes like mine—and we were all very serious most of the time. But not Granny. She was a full-blooded Kentuck Indian and her face had been brown and broad, with wonderful black eyes that usually sparkled and laughed. If it hadn't been for her I couldn't think of what might have happened to me. More than likely I'd be sitting around somewhere feeling sorry for myself—the one thing Granny wouldn't ever let me do.

My father had never cared anything about me, nor my mother either for that matter, but Granny had adored me.

49

Every time my father lost his job or left the house I was sent to live with her, and I couldn't wait to get there. I'd sit on the train coach overnight with my cardboard suitcase on the seat beside me and I could barely sleep for being so happy. She had a little farm in Deepwater, Missouri that had hardly any kind of a house on it at all, just a little ramshackle place in the backlands, but I thought it was wonderful. It made me smile just to think about it now. All the house had was one tiny bedroom that, even though it was three feet above the kitchen, had no stairs to it. Whenever Granny and I went to bed we had to shinny ourselves up. She must have been close to seventy the last time I was there, but she was able to scramble up almost as fast as I.

Living with her had been like living with another little girl who was just older and smarter than I was. There wasn't anything she couldn't do, except maybe handle a plow. At home my father had never let me help him because he said that I couldn't do anything right, but Granny had let me help with everything—milking the cow, tending the chickens, cooking and baking. She even let me help plant the vegetable garden, another thing my father wouldn't let me do. I couldn't keep the rows straight, he used to tell me. But Granny said she didn't give a hoot about straight rows. The potatoes I planted in her garden grew all over, sometimes crossing into the spinach, which curved around behind the tomatoes. It was less of a garden than a living salad, but when it all came out of the ground Granny couldn't get over how smart I was to have performed such a miracle, or so she told me.

I'd lived with her for a whole year that last time, and I'd never forget how terrible I'd felt when my mother finally wrote me to come home because my father was working again. Granny couldn't read, so I'd even thought of not telling her what was in the letter, but I couldn't lie to her. She felt as bad as I did, but there wasn't anything we could do.

That last night we'd spent together we tried to pretend that it was just like any other night. We went to bed right after supper the way we always did and I read to her from the Bible

50

for a while. I knew the Book of Psalms was her favorite, so I was reading from that. Granny had decided she couldn't abide beds after my grandfather died, so we were lying on thick patchwork quilts on the floor. It was warm enough so that we didn't need a blanket, and she was curled up beside me, her knees pulled up and poking at her cotton nightie, her hair done in a long braid down to her waist. Her eyes were closed, and after a while I thought she was asleep, so I put the Bible away.

Before I leaned over to turn down the oil lamp I looked at her face, seeing the deep lines in it. It was so dark and looked so Indian that I could almost imagine her living in a tepee, sewing hides and things like that. She wasn't asleep, though. Her eyes popped open and she smiled at me. She was a tiny little thing, thin in the shoulders and heavy in the waist. Even though I was only eleven I was bigger than she was.

"You fooled me," I said.

It was a game we played sometimes. If she fell asleep while I was reading I could go without washing my hands and face the next morning. But if she caught me I had to wash my neck and my ears.

"No, I jus' dozed off. I really did."

She took my hand and squeezed it. I could feel the calluses on hers. "I'm gonna miss you, Annie."

I'd tried hard not to whine or cry up to then, but I couldn't keep it up. I managed to blurt out, "Granny, I don't want to go home ever again. I just don't want to. Please let me stay." Then I started to bawl so hard I didn't think I'd ever be able to stop. Granny got up and held onto me the whole time. She didn't say a word until she knew I was done.

"Annie . . ."

"Uh-huh."

"You know I don't want you to go home . . ."

"Yes."

"An' you know I never told you a lie."

"I know."

"Then you know if I tell you you're a lucky girl, that's the truth."

51

"How can I be lucky?"

" 'Cause a lot of people when they unhappy, they can't do nothin' about it. But you can, 'cause you're smart. You got brains. An' when a person's got brains they got a ticket to any place they want to go—a ticket to the whole world."

"What kind of a ticket?"

She tapped her head. "Right up here. Didn't you tell me that if you was to work hard an' really study you could be teachin' school by the time you're sixteen?"

"That's what my teacher said."

"Then that's what you got to think about, about bein' a teacher an' gettin' outta them dirty minin' places."

"I'll never be able to do it, Granny, never." I was ready to start crying all over again, but Granny told me to stop right away. "An' listen to me, 'cause I ain't gonna say this twice."

She told me to sit up. "You're gonna do big things some day, Annie—real big things. But you can't do them big things if you're gonna go round feelin' sorry for yourself." She stopped for a second and she looked a little sad. "Your pa's my son, child. He ain't an easy man, but he ain't a bad man neither. Whatever you think about 'im you just remember he always stood on his own two feet an' he learned you the same. An' he always paid his own way. That's what the Hobbses is like—all of 'em. Maybe him and your ma ain't been too understandin' of you, but they fed you good an' give you a roof. That's more than many's got . . ."

"But they don't really want me, Granny."

"Yes they do. They jus' don't know how to show it. But never mind that. If you got just *one* person in the whole world who loves you an' believes in you, why that's wonderful, don't ya see. An' you got one—me. *I* love you, an' I believe in you. So anytime you get to thinkin' you ain't gonna make it, or that you can't do somethin' for your own self's sake, you do it for my sake. Will you?"

"Yes."

"Promise?"

"I promise."

"That's what I want to hear. You'll see, Annie. Some day you're gonna go off to a new land just like a pioneer—just like your grampa an' me did. 'Cause you're that kind—a big person. An' that's the kind that goes to a new land."

"But there's no new lands, Granny. They're all gone."

"Shoot, child, there always be new lands."

"Where?"

"California maybe, I don't know. Or Alaska . . . Now there's a new land, Alaska."

I asked her what she knew about it, but she'd begun to get sleepy and so had I. A few minutes later we were asleep.

"Madam?" Mr. Strong had finished checking the animals over and had mounted up again. "I asked you if you are ready."

"Yes," I said, "I am."

As we moved forward I thought of that last morning I'd spent with Granny. When it was close to train time a neighboring woman had ridden into the yard with a buckboard. Granny had gone as far as the main road with us, then we hugged each other good-bye. She'd felt like a strong little bird.

As the buckboard drove off and I turned around to see her waving to me I had to fight to hold in the tears. "Don't worry," the driver said, "you'll be back some day."

I hadn't answered her, not knowing how to explain that I wasn't crying because I was going away, but because my grandmother had looked so small and alone as she stood in the middle of the road gently waving good-bye.

I'd never seen her again after that. She'd died during the first year I'd been teaching. I hadn't found out about it until three weeks after it happened. She had died in her sleep, my mother wrote me, and she had left me a legacy.

She sure had, but it wasn't the legacy my mother had written me about. It was one she'd given me a long time ago when I needed it most. And for that I'd never forget her.

"You'd best keep a tight rein on him, madam," Mr. Strong

was saying. As soon as we'd broken into the open, just as he'd predicted, the pack train speeded up and so did Blossom. I pulled back on the reins.

We'd descended into a small level valley. About a quarter of a mile ahead were maybe twenty-five or thirty buildings strung along the same side of the creek we were on.

"Is that all of it?"

"Just about."

I'd imagined it would be something like Eagle—a town— but from this distance it looked more like the Indian village we'd gone through. It couldn't have been built in a better place, though, set down snug on the valley floor. Low hills ringed the valley, rolling away from it into a blue haze of high mountain peaks. The creek was deep and narrow here, spilling down from the slope behind us. It got wider as it went, and right smack in the middle of the settlement a wooden bridge arched across it.

Blossom was just aching to break into a gallop and I had all I could do to hold him to a walk. It must have rained here recently, because halfway there we started winding around craters filled with muddy water.

"Keep away from those holes, madam," Mr. Strong cautioned me sharply when Blossom came close to one. "Some of them are deep. Fall in and you're liable not to come out."

I told Chuck to be careful too, then I asked Mr. Strong what they were.

"Prospect holes. Some of them go down forty feet. These miners don't bother to fill them up after they've dug them."

The ground was pock-marked with them all the way into the settlement and the ground got muddier as we went.

"Looks like everybody's waiting for us," I said. There was a whole crowd of people, maybe twenty or thirty, gathered in front of a tiny cabin. It wasn't much bigger than a hut, but with the American flag fluttering over it I figured it for the post office.

"They don't have much else to do but wait. It's a big day

for them. The women curl their hair, everyone spruces up. Some of them even take a bath."

Whether he was being sarcastic or not, I started grinning. The sweet fragrance of wood smoke wafted over and I felt proud enough to burst. I'd really done it, I thought, I was really a caution. I'd traveled through the wilderness just the way Granny Hobbs had done. Now here I was riding toward a frontier settlement as though it was the most natural thing in the world. Mr. Strong saw the look on my face and he smiled.

"What do you think of it?"

"It looks wonderful," I said.

It wasn't anything like the Indian village at all. The street between the creek and settlement was wide, with patches of late grass here and there, no tin cans, no trash. Even from here I could see vegetable gardens in a few backyards, along with dog kennels and stacks of corded wood. As soon as we neared the edge of the place the crowd started calling and waving. Between their hollering and sled dogs doing the same thing in their own way you'd have thought it was the Fourth of July.

The whole place was about three city blocks long, the post office right in the middle, opposite the wooden bridge. The first couple of cabins were a letdown. They were in bad shape, one just a rotted skeleton, roof gone and weeds spilling out the door, the other all boarded up. As far as I could make out, a few others down the line weren't lived in either. The ones that were lived in, though, were solid and sturdy, with traps, harness, washtubs and all kinds of stuff hanging from posts and railings. One of them even had a dogsled leaning against the side of it.

No sooner did we pass the first few cabins than Blossom broke into a jog and I couldn't hold him back. We jittered past a cabin that had a young birch tree growing from the sod roof, then almost ran into half a caribou carcass that was hanging from a tripod. Blossom was heading right for the stable, which was on the creek side of the road a little beyond

55

the crowd. Somebody was way ahead of him, though. A man in knee-length boots ran out to cut him off, yelling and waving a beat-up fedora. Blossom gave up. It was too muddy for him to risk trying to dodge, so he just slowed down and ambled up to the crowd as though that's where he was headed all along.

A little old man appeared under him and grabbed his rein. "Steady as she goes." He smiled up at me from under the brim of a yachtsman's cap, a shrunken pug-nose face and teeth stained from chewing tobacco. "There y'are," he said, "safe in port. Hop right on down, little lady."

"What a fool," another old man said to him. "Can't ya see she can't make it by herself? Wait'll I get a box."

Everybody who hadn't moved out to stop the pack animals and help Mr. Strong unload them stood around and stared up at me. If I hadn't been in Alaska for a couple of weeks I wouldn't have realized that most people were wearing their dress-up clothes. But now I was used to how drab everybody looked and how old-fashioned their clothes were, so I knew that even though the men's shirts were wrinkled and you could hardly tell what the original color was, the fact that they had a tie on meant they were dressed up.

Chuck had found his mother, I saw—a slight dark Indian woman who had a little girl by the hand. From the quick glimpse I caught of her as she kneeled down to hug him she looked like a beauty.

I kept smiling and getting smiles in return. A heavy-set Indian woman wearing a shawl gave me a big grin and waved. She had a little girl with her—half-white, I could see. I waved back to her. There were a few other children around, and one little boy in a gray cap and knickers looked away when I smiled at him.

I tried to figure out which building was the schoolhouse, finally realizing that it had to be a big frame house with a homemade flagpole in front of it. It was opposite the stable a little further up. Mr. Strong had described it to me and I knew that my living quarters were in it too, so I was glad to see that it was larger than Cathy's place.

The second old man came back with a box and set it down. "Here you be, missis." He was almost hunchbacked, he was so stooped over, with a beard that hung from him like weeping willow.

What with everything else that had gone wrong on this famous trip, I should have known I wasn't going to make a dignified entrance. I let one foot down while the bearded man tried to steady me. As soon as I put my weight on the box it collapsed right under me and the next thing I knew I was sitting in the mud and everybody was staring down at me. I could hear a couple of the kids laughing and I was so embarrassed I wanted to disappear right then and there.

The old men helped me up and fussed around trying to get some of the mud off me until they were pushed aside by a big burly woman.

"Awright, awright, awright. Leave 'er alone before you wind up killin' 'er. I'm Angela Barrett," she announced. "You're the new schoolmom, I take it. What's yer moniker?"

I told her, and she led me over to another woman who was wearing a long navy blue coat buttoned up to the neck. She had a broken nose. "She's the new schoolmom, awright," Angela said to the woman.

"I'm Maggie Carew," the woman said. "What's your name, honey?"

"Anne Hobbs." My skirt was clinging in back of me and I could feel water trickling down my legs. I just hoped it didn't make me look ridiculous.

"Let's get you over to the schoolhouse."

I'd been right about which building it was. When we stepped up onto the porch, Angela Barrett moved to the closer of two doors. It was studded with mean-looking nails that stuck out about three inches. "This here's the schoolroom," she said, opening it. "The other door there's to your quarters. Watch out for them nails."

As I followed her in my heart sank. The room was big, but it wasn't like any schoolroom I ever saw, and it was in a shambles. A few assorted tables and chairs were piled in one corner, and some boxes in yet another corner held old books and papers. Piles of dust and dirt were everywhere, and a few yellowed papers littered the floor, mice droppings all over them. The plank flooring was buckled and warped, higher in the center than it was at the walls. The tables and chairs all sat at an angle and I felt seasick just looking at them. Light came in through windows fogged with smoke and grime.

"Needs a little cleaning up," Maggie admitted, "but I'll give you a hand with it." Her broken nose made her look tough, but I had a feeling she was pretty decent. I guessed she was about forty.

The other room was neater, the same size as the schoolroom, but except for a brass bed that had no mattress, two chairs, and a big potbellied stove, it was empty.

"How do you like 'er?" Angela Barrett asked. She must have weighed two hundred pounds and she towered over me. Her voice was rasping, and there was a red rash on her nose and all around it. I tried to think of something nice to say.

"It's a good big room."

"Glad you feel that way," Angela said. "You're the one's gonna be livin' in it."

"Do you think it will take much time to get it ready?"

"What do you mean ready?" Angela asked. "It's ready now."

Both women were staring at me as if there was something wrong with me. I was almost afraid to ask the next question. "Don't I have to have a mattress?" I said. "Or blankets, or a table?"

It took a moment before they seemed to realize that I had a point.

"Where'na blazes'd it all go?" Angela said, as if she'd turned her back for a minute and somebody had snatched everything away. "It's your fault, Maggie, you're the school janitor. It's your responsibility."

"When there's no school there's no janitor," Maggie said tartly, "and there ain't been a school here in well over a year."

"What are we gonna do?" Angela said.

58

Maggie thought for a minute. "Come on," she said finally.

Angela and I followed her outside. At the post office, almost all the pack animals had been unloaded. The stuff everyone had ordered was lying on the ground: boxes of candles and flashlight batteries, sacks of flour, crated gasoline cans and cans of kerosene, tied-up bundles of dried fish and a whole bunch of packages of parcel post.

"How about my cornflakes?" the bearded old man who'd tried to help me was saying to Mr. Strong. He could just straighten up enough to look Mr. Strong in the eye. "I had a dozen boxes of cornflakes on order an' you didn't bring 'em."

"They'll arrive in due time, Mr. Spratt."

"That's what you told me the last three times. I ordered them cornflakes by parcel post four months ago an' they should be here. You got 'em stuck there in the warehouse at Eagle, now don't ya?"

A lot of people were beginning to mutter that the old man was right, and Mr. Strong was getting mad. "You heard what I said, Mr. Spratt."

"I heard you. An' I know you ain't brought'm 'cause it don't pay you to bring'm out with the rest of the parcel post right now—take up too much space on them precious horses a yours. Well you darn well better bring'm out next time, or I'm writing to Washington D.C. You got a mail contract says you bring out *all* the mail—not what personally suits ya."

"Uncle Arthur, hold on a minute if you can," Maggie broke in. "We got a problem that needs everybody's attention . . . This is Anne Hobbs, our new teacher," she said to the crowd.

"I don't doubt she's a teacher," a quiet voice said from somewhere, "but she sure don't look new."

There was some laughing, but Maggie cut it short.

"Miss Hobbs here needs some help," she went on. "Some of you mutts have borrowed everything there is in the teacher's quarters. There's nothin' left in there and I mean nothin'. I ain't sayin' who took what, but it's got to be packed back here pronto. The poor girl's got an empty cabin."

59

"What do you need, Miss?" a tall good-looking man asked. He was trying on a heavy fleece-lined jacket he must have ordered.

"Just about everything."

"I've got a couple of good Hudson Bay blankets I can spare."

Angela Barrett snorted. "Leave it to Joe. Gives you a couple of blankets one day, tryin' to climb under 'em the next."

"How about the rest of you?" Maggie said.

"We got a good set of tin dishes she can borrow," a girl of about ten said. She was with two older girls who looked like twins, both of them rawboned and husky. "Can she, Pa?" she asked. A red-haired man beside her nodded.

After that the offers came thick and fast—a broom and pan, a rocking chair, a wash boiler and a dozen other items. One man said he'd taken the chifforobe and would return it. Everybody got into the spirit of the thing, telling me not to worry, they'd take care of me. It made me feel so good that when Maggie Carew asked me if I wanted to say a few words, I was just about able to say thanks and that I was glad to be here.

The men were as good as their word. While I kept busy cleaning and scrubbing up the place the rest of the day, everybody kept trooping in carrying things. Within a few hours I not only had a firm straw mattress for the bed, but also a blanket, a pillow, a table and some chairs. Someone even thought to bring a water barrel. My prize possession was a wood-burning cookstove. It took four men to carry it in, and it was a beauty. Black wrought iron with shining nickel-plated fittings, it had hardly been used. All I needed was a stovepipe and I could start cooking.

The two old men who'd helped me down from Blossom brought me presents. "Uncle Arthur" Spratt, the little bent-over man who'd been angry about his corn flakes, came by with a few jars of wild cranberry jam he'd preserved himself. The man in the yachtsman's cap gave me a can of bear lard. "It's kinda sweeter'n the lard you're used to," he said, "but you just add a little salt to it and it's just as good."

60

Granny sure knew what she was talking about, I thought. People who go to a new land *are* big people, kind and generous.

I didn't even have to clean the place alone. Five of my pupils showed up to help. The three Vaughn girls were first—Elvira, the girl who'd asked her father for the tin dishes, and her older twin sisters, Evelyn and Eleanor. Then Maggie Carew's two children came over. They all went to work with a will, so that by late afternoon the windows were sparkling and the whole place looked and smelled clean. While we were working the man who'd promised me the blankets rode up. "I'm Joe Temple," he said when he came in. The two blankets he'd brought were almost new. I offered to pay him for them, but he said forget it. "Use them for as long as you like."

He was good-looking and he knew it. He was too old for me—I figured he was about thirty-two or thirty-three—but I could have thought of half a dozen teachers in Forest Grove that would have taken to him right away. "You've got your work cut out for you," he said, looking around the room. He was still holding onto his riding crop and he slapped it against his boot a couple of times. I'd unpacked all my dresses and hung them wherever I could find a nail. "I haven't been Outside in a couple of years," he said, looking at them, "but I thought they were wearing dresses shorter than that."

"They are. I guess I'm pretty conservative."

"Not all the time, I hope." I didn't know how to take that so I didn't say anything. "You'll have to let me take you out to dinner," he said.

"I didn't see any restaurant signs coming in."

"Right down the street—Maggie's roadhouse. She's the best cook in town."

"Maybe after I get settled."

"Settled or not you're going to have to eat dinner. How about tomorrow night? I won't bite you."

"All right, you're on."

He whacked his crop against his boot again. "See you around six," he said, going out. "I'll go over and tell Maggie now."

61

Wow, I thought, things really happen fast around here. I haven't been in Chicken more than a few hours and already I have a date.

Maggie Carew came by a little before dark and sent the children home. "Place looks a lot better," she said.

"Thanks to you. I appreciate your helping me."

"Don't mention it. Joe Temple tells me you're comin' over the roadhouse with him tomorrow night. Fast worker, that one," she said admiringly.

"What does he do?"

"Mines, like everyone else. Darn good miner too. Got a college education to boot. Do 'im good to go out with a white woman for a change. You hungry?"

"Starved."

"Come on over the roadhouse when you're ready and I'll fix you some supper. On the house."

"Thanks, but Mr. Strong said he'll be coming back with some food and I was to wait for him."

She went to the back of the room and opened the door that led into a small storage room—the cache. Her high-buttoned shoes made a lot of noise on the plank floors. "You'll have plenty of room for your outfit," she said.

"Outfit?"

"Your grub for the winter, flour, sugar, all a that."

"I don't have any."

"Didn't they tell you to have an outfit shipped in when you were hired?"

"No."

Now that she'd mentioned it, I realized I didn't have even a bit of food.

"That makes sense. Well, don't worry, you won't starve. When the freeze-up comes Walter Strong'll bring one in for you. It'll cost you a little more, but not that much. We'll help you out in the meantime. Well, I got supper to make. Drop by the roadhouse later if you like."

Just then I remembered her daughter. Her face lit up when I told her what Jeannette had said. "Thinks she's gonna have a

62

girl, eh? Well, I hope so. If she's anything like Jennie that'll be two good things I got outta this life."

As she went out I asked her what all the nails in the doors were for.

"Bear," she answered. "Last teacher here threw a fit when one came sniffin' at the door one day. I'd have'm hammered down if I was you. Kids might hurt themselves."

Alone, I sat down on the bed and looked the room over. It needed a lot of work. The floor was as bad in here as it was in the schoolroom. In some places it had dropped below the walls and I could see the ground outside. The walls were in bad shape, too. They were just rough planks with canvas stretched over them like wallpaper, and the canvas was peeling in places. But I didn't care. This was the first place I'd ever had to myself. Right now, with everything piled all over, it looked like a secondhand store, but when I fixed it up it would look nice, nicer even than Cathy Winters' place.

It was getting chilly, drafts coming in from the spaces around the molding. I went over to check the potbellied stove. Maggie Carew's son Jimmy had built a fire in it to get the dampness out, but I'd forgotten to keep it up. Opening the door, I saw that the wood he'd put in was just embers now. I tried to start it up again, but I didn't have any kindling. There was no water left either, so I took a pail and went outside.

In the Vaughn cabin, next door, pots and dishes were rattling as the girls prepared supper. A couple of them were talking, but I couldn't make out what they were saying. Standing there outside, the darkness falling fast, I felt lonely all of a sudden. Except for the sounds from a few cabins, everything was quiet. There weren't as many people here as I thought there'd be. Out of all the buildings on each side of me there were maybe only six that had people living in them—the Vaughns' next door, the Carews' roadhouse, Angela Barrett's cabin and a couple of cabins way down at the far end.

The only other cabin that was occupied was on the other side of the creek. The unoccupied ones were shells, most of them—the windows taken out, the doors gone. The rest were outbuildings, privies, stables, tool sheds and the like. Most of the people who'd been waiting at the post office lived on the outlying creeks.

It was a little like being in a ghost town. Twenty and thirty years ago this had been a thriving settlement, men had streamed in here looking for gold, built these cabins and dreamed about making a big strike. Most of them were gone now. Almost everyone here now had come after the rush was over, like me.

The sun was gone, a faint orange glow in the purple sky.

I filled the pail with water and started lugging it back, stopping halfway to rest. I couldn't even see inside my quarters it was so dark. I felt a little scared. Maybe it was because everything looked so rough and bare, I didn't know. Suddenly it didn't seem so friendly. Back in Oregon, where I'd taught up until last June, the nights were made for a nice walk or a soda at the drugstore. Here it was all wilderness. At night everything went into hiding. I picked up the pail and hurried back into my quarters.

Inside, it was almost too dark to see. I thought about going next door to the Vaughns and asking if I could wait there for Mr. Strong, but I didn't want to bother them. Besides, if I was going to get used to being on my own I might as well start now.

I thought I remembered seeing a couple of stubs of candles somewhere. I was lucky. I found them right away, along with a box of matches, in one of the fruit boxes nailed above the counter. Lighting the candles, I put one on the counter and the other on my table. Then I sat down to wait.

The candles didn't give too much light and they made shadows go jumping all over.

After a while I began to get cold, so I got up and walked around, stopping to listen for the sound of Mr. Strong returning. But it stayed quiet outside. Too quiet, I thought. I couldn't hear a sound.

A slight wind shook the door and for some reason I thought right away of the grizzly that had pounced on the caribou

64

calf. I caught myself listening for the soft pad of an animal outside.

The door to the schoolroom was open and it looked like a big dark hole, so I closed it. My footsteps sounded hollow on the plank floors and I realized suddenly that I had no protection here at all. All I had between me and the wilderness outside was a few walls. I didn't even have locks on the doors. Anyone who wanted to could walk right in through the schoolroom or my front door. They could even come in through the cache, since it had a door that led outside. I tried lodging a chair in front of the doors, but the knobs were too high.

My nickel-plated revolver, still holstered, lay in a box beside the bed. Tying it around my waist, I felt a little better.

A half hour later Mr. Strong still hadn't come back. One of the candle stubs was flickering out and the other had only two inches to go. Once it was gone I'd be left in complete darkness. There was a gas lantern hanging from the ceiling, but there was no gasoline for it. Even if there had been, I wouldn't have known how to work it.

Then I heard footsteps outside.

I knew they didn't belong to Mr. Strong. He'd gone to make some deliveries on some outlying creeks and I'd have heard his horses. The footsteps couldn't belong to a neighbor either, because they were coming from the brush back near the outhouse. They padded closer, moving around the side of the house. I waited, hoping they'd pass by, and yet something told me that whoever they belonged to was coming after me.

I was right. They stopped in front of the porch. I got to my feet, wondering if maybe I ought to slip out through the cache and run next door. Before I could make up my mind the footsteps came up on the porch and I was too scared to move. A second later I almost jumped as the ghostly outline of a face appeared at the window, then ducked away. Then there was a soft knock at the door.

Taking the revolver out, I stayed still as a rabbit, hoping whoever it was would go away. When the knock came a second time, I decided that whoever was out there could get in just by turning the doorknob anyway. He'd be less antagonized if I invited him in than if I didn't. The revolver was too heavy for me to hold in one hand, so using both I pointed it at the door. "Come in," I said, "but be careful."

The chair I'd left in front of the door slid forward and I could just make out a dark man with thick black hair staring at me from the porch. As soon as he saw the gun he raised his hands. He was nervous, but he smiled. He was darker than a Spaniard, and his teeth looked deadly white.

"You better be careful," I said. "I shot a bear with this once." I was so scared I didn't know what I was saying.

He stopped smiling. "I can believe that," he answered.

"Did you come to see me?" I asked him.

I was hoping he'd say he got the wrong cabin by mistake, but he didn't. He said, "Yes."

"Well, you can come in if you want, but I'd much rather you didn't." That sounded silly, I realized.

He stayed at the threshold and kept his hands up. "I just came to talk to you," he said.

"What about?"

"My mother sent me over to see if you'd like to have supper with us."

As soon as he said that I realized how silly I was being. He wasn't even much older than I was, I could see now, and he was embarrassed. So was I. "Oh."

"Can I put my hands down?"

I nodded yes.

"I won't come in," he said, "so could you point that gun away?"

"Sure," I said. "I'm sorry. You can come in if you want." I meant it this time.

"That's all right. I'm sorry I scared you. My father said you came in with the pack train today, and my mother thought this being your first night, you wouldn't be set up to cook. She thought maybe you'd like to eat with us."

"Oh," I said again. "That's awfully nice of her, but I better not. Mr. Strong is coming back soon and he'll be bringing dinner with him."

He looked uncomfortable. "Well, my mother said to tell you that if you need any help at all you just let us know."

He looked the room over, not able to think of anything else to say.

"Do you live here in the settlement?" I asked him finally.

"No, a little further up Chicken Creek," he said.

I tried to think of something else to say, but for the life of me I couldn't.

"I guess I better be going," he said.

I was disappointed. Now that I wasn't afraid of him I wished he could keep me company until Mr. Strong came back. But he said good-bye and closed the door before I could even think to ask him his name.

"That was young Fred Purdy," Mr. Strong said when he finally came back. He seemed pleased that I hadn't accepted the invitation. Later, as we were finishing the cold chicken he had brought, he smiled when I mentioned how I'd held the gun on Fred.

"You'd have been more than safe with him. Fred undoubtedly will never amount to anything, but he is a fine young fellow . . ."

"Why won't he ever amount to anything?"

Mr. Strong nibbled the last piece of meat from the chicken bone he was chewing and laid it on the plate, satisfied.

"Couldn't you see? He's a half-breed," he said, wiping his hands. "Mother's Eskimo, father's white."

"He seemed very nice."

"He is. Smart too. Smarter than most breeds. The whole family is as good as they come."

"Then why won't he ever amount to anything?"

He got up and began to collect the plates. "I told you," he said patiently, "he's a breed—a product of race mixture. That's what happens when you mix the races. I've seen it all my life— seen it in the South, see it here. It's always the same—the off-spring have to suffer."

He made it sound as if anybody who wasn't all white had some kind of a disease. It kind of disappointed me in him a little. I wondered what he'd think of me if he knew my grandmother had been Indian.

"What is Chuck's father like?" I asked him, changing the subject.

"Joe? Good miner, good trapper. You can bet your bottom dollar he regrets ever having involved himself with a native woman."

"Joe Temple is Chuck's father?"

"Why do you look surprised?"

"He's supposed to take me to dinner tomorrow night."

"Well, it's nothing for you to be concerned about. Mr. Temple is a gentleman and he will treat you like a lady."

"But he's married."

"No, he is not and I'm sure he thanks God for it."

Married or not, I still felt funny about going out with him.

Before Mr. Strong left I knew just about everything there was to know about everyone here. As far as the Purdys were concerned, he respected Mr. Purdy even though he felt he'd lowered himself by marrying an Eskimo woman. He advised me to act towards them the way he did himself—"the way you'd act towards anybody who abides by the law no matter what their color is . . . You know what I mean, just about the same way you'd act towards niggers."

V

After Mr. Strong left I was so tired I could hardly keep my eyes open. Leaving the gas lantern on, I lay down on the bare mattress with my clothes on, and pulled a couple of blankets over me. But I couldn't sleep. It was so quiet outside that the creek sounded as though it was right in the room. The slightest draft made the doors rattle. It was cold out too. I could feel it slipping in through the cracks in the floor and walls. Then a small animal began moving around the side of the house, and every time I closed my eyes I imagined that something was going to charge into the room and pounce on me.

Finally I got up, pumped up the light in the lantern and got my Bible. But I couldn't concentrate on it. My ears perked up every time one of the horses snuffled in the stable across the way or kicked the side of the stall. I wished I was in Blossom's place. At least he had a bar across his door and plenty of company.

I started to think about the next few days. Besides having to get these quarters into shape, I had a lot of work to do in the schoolroom before school started. There were hardly any supplies, no blackboard, no paper that I could find, and not many books. When I had mentioned the shortages to Maggie Carew, she didn't seem to think anything of it. "You'll make out," she said.

It was almost the same thing Lester Henderson had told me

when he interviewed me in Juneau. He was the commissioner of education for the whole Territory and when I told him I was worried because I'd never taught in a one-room schoolhouse, he'd told me not to be.

"Forget it," he'd said. "You're going to do fine." He was a big, broad-shouldered man, as easygoing as a Saint Bernard.

I could remember looking out the window of his office and seeing all the ships moored in Gastineau Channel far below. The *Dorothy Alexander* had been among them, the boat that would take me to Skagway.

"It'll be much easier than you think," he'd gone on. "I doubt that you'll have many more than ten pupils, and I know you'll be able to handle them. What does concern me a little is your age. May I be frank with you?"

"Of course."

"You're just about one of the youngest teachers I've ever sent into the bush. Ordinarily I'd place you here in Juneau first, or some other more well-populated place. The only reason I haven't is that it's not easy to find qualified people who will go into the bush. Does that surprise you?"

"Yes." I really was surprised. "When you lectured at my school I figured you'd be swamped with applications."

"Well I'm not. I hope that doesn't make you less enthusiastic."

"Not at all."

"Good. You see, I fought hard to get these Territorial schools established. It wasn't easy, but I did it because I believed that where there is even one child who needs schooling—not ten as the law says there must be—there should be a school for him. What I'm trying to say, Miss Hobbs, is that education is so important to me that despite my misgivings about sending a nineteen-year-old cheechako into the bush country, I'm going to send you anyway."

"A cheechako is a greenhorn, isn't it?"

"The greenest. You've done some reading about Alaska, I see . . ." He paused, then went on. "Before you leave this office I'd like to give you a bit of advice. I have the feeling

70

that you are a pretty tolerant young lady—young enough to be open to new ideas. Where you're going you'll find that most people are not. They have their own code and they don't take to anybody who tries to go against that code or change it. In short, I hope you're not going into this job with, well . . . shall I say missionary zeal?"

"I don't think so," I said, but I'd gotten all red. More than once I'd thought of myself as being like a young Florence Nightingale. I had even imagined the smiles on the faces of hardy backwoods parents as their children came home from my log-cabin school brimming over with the learning I'd given them. "I've tried to keep my mind open," I added maturely.

We talked a while longer and he shook my hand warmly before I left. "I want to hear from you," he said, "and I don't mean that I want to hear from you only in your regular monthly report. Write to me anytime you need help or advice. Alaska's a big place, but it's just like the small town you've been teaching in. We all know each other, and we're concerned about each other. If there's anything I can do for you, let me know immediately."

He'd meant it, I knew, and it made me feel good even now. I'd write to him tomorrow about the books and supplies before Mr. Strong left. But now that I was here I was more worried than ever about being able to handle the job. Teaching in Forest Grove, I'd had everything mapped out for me. There was a system, a time for study, for recess, for lunch, for auditorium, for everything. There was order and routine. Here I didn't even have a register, I realized, or report cards. I wondered what I would do if I couldn't control the class. What if they didn't like me or didn't want to listen to me?

The more I thought about it the worse I felt. All I had was a high-school education. I knew my subject matter pretty well, but suppose a couple of the children were smarter in some subjects than I was? I didn't even have a library I could go to for more advanced materials. Suddenly the whole idea of coming here seemed like a big mistake. I was going to fall on my face, I was sure of it . . .

The sun was streaming through the window when I woke up, but the room was so chilly and damp that my breath steamed. There was still some water left, and Mr. Strong had brought coffee, so I set about making a fire. Five minutes later the room was so full of smoke I had to go out on the porch.

Outside, the sun shone down on hills covered with frost. As though there had been a shower of diamonds the night before, the whole valley sparkled and glittered with the reflected colors of autumn.

Across the road Mr. Strong's stable was open and I heard him murmuring to the horses and moving around. A few moments later he came out leading four of them, but stopped when he saw the smoke billowing out of my doorway.

"It's only the stove," I told him. He nodded and continued to lead his horses to one of the big prospect holes filled with rainwater. Breaking the light crust of ice in a few places, he left them to drink, then made his way past me. In a few moments he had cleared the smoke from the house.

After he started a fire in the stove, he took me over to his store, a small log building about five cabins away.

The inside of the store was so crowded with things that except for a narrow path to the counter and some sitting space around an oil-drum heater there was hardly room to walk. Canvas parkas, snow shoes, animal traps and just about everything else hung from the ceiling. Odors were all over the place —of wool and cotton from a counter loaded with pants, overalls and long underwear, of furs and hanging slabs of bacon. In front of the heater a deep pan of yellow water gave off the rank smell of cigarette butts and tobacco juice.

Looking the shelves over, I felt a lot better. There was everything here, even tins of butter. Inside of a few minutes, Mr. Strong and I had loaded up two sacks with canned goods, cereal, flour, sugar and other staples. A little while later, after I'd rustled up some bacon, eggs and hot coffee for us on top of the pot-bellied stove, he paid me my first compliment. "It is heartening to know, madam, that there are still girls around who can make a proper breakfast." He gave me the key to the store,

72

something he said he'd never done with anyone else. I was to take what I wanted as I needed it, and we'd settle up once a month. In return I agreed that if anyone wanted anything while he was away I would give it out and keep a record of what was bought.

By mid-morning I had the furniture in my quarters arranged fairly nice. I was working in the schoolroom when I heard footsteps on the porch. It was Fred Purdy and what I thought at first were two younger sisters with him. Only one of them was his sister, though. The other was his mother. I doubted she weighed more than ninety pounds. She was even smaller than Granny Hobbs, and cute. She was Eskimo for sure—round dark face, wide mouth and strong uneven teeth. She just seemed to light up when she saw me and I liked her right off.

"Ah, the teasher," she said. "I am so happy to meet you. I am Mrs. Purdy, and this is my daughter, Isabelle."

She put a hand out and it felt small and capable. "My son Frayd have tell me how pretty you are," she said after I introduced myself. "Before he say only lynx is pretty. Now I see for myself. Indeed, you are very lovely."

She was like a little queen, and she wasn't putting it on. She was dressed beautifully too—in a cloth parka that looked like a Fifth Avenue design, and a soft fur hat.

When I invited them in she complimented me on how much I'd done with the cabin. We all sat down and had a cup of tea and talked for a while. Before I knew it I was telling them about the trip out on Blossom, but instead of it coming out the way it really was, it sounded funny, especially the part about my landing on my behind in the mud outside the post office. I never heard anybody laugh the way Fred did when I told the story—with so much fun and enjoyment that it made me laugh myself. By the time I told how I'd walked in here to find hardly a stick of furniture we were all doubled over.

"Indeed, Ahnne," Mrs. Purdy said, wiping away tears, "there is mush work to do in this place." She grew serious. "You cannot live here in sush . . . sush . . ."

Fred supplied the word. "Conditions."

73

"Conditions, yes. Thank you, Frayd."

"Do you really think it's so bad?"

"It is not terreebul, yet it is not good. There are many things to do here." She sent Isabelle out to play, then went around the room, shaking her head. "If you are to live here, you must have home that is comfortable, warm." She pointed to the baseboard where light was coming in. "This must be fixed or in winter you will freeze to the death. No, this will not do." She reeled off all the other things that had to be fixed—sagging shelves, loose floorboards, crippled tables in the schoolroom.

"You will work here," she said to Fred, "and Father will do your chores at home."

Fred grinned. "Yes, boss."

"How mush work, you think?"

"Oh . . . Couple months maybe."

She smiled. "You wish to open school when, Ahnne?"

"In a few days if I can."

"You will do it in a few days, Frayd, no?"

"I will do it, boss, yes."

Before they left Mrs. Purdy asked me if I'd like to come to supper that night. I couldn't because Joe Temple was taking me over to the roadhouse, so we made it for the next night.

A couple of hours later Fred came back driving a wagon that looked like a long thin buckboard. It had a load of rough boards on it and a big tool box.

We were a little shy with each other at first, but after we worked together for a while we were gabbing about everything under the sun, from the Marines in Nicaragua to Lindbergh's trip across the Atlantic. I told him I was surprised he knew as much about what was going on in the world as I did.

"One thing everybody does plenty of around here is read," he said. "There's not much else to do at night."

By noontime he'd connected a stovepipe to the cookstove and run it up through the roof. After we had a fire going in it I made lunch for the two of us—canned ham and sweet potatoes. "There has to be something else people do here at night besides read," I said while we were eating.

74

"Every other Friday night there's a dance. We've been having them at the roadhouse, but as soon as the schoolroom's in shape we'll have them there."

"When will the first one be?"

"You call it. You're the teacher."

We decided on a week from the following Friday.

While we worked people kept dropping by to lend me more things they thought I might need, a kettle, some spoons and knives, even an old encyclopedia. I told Fred that I knew people in Alaska were hospitable, but I hadn't expected it to be like this.

"Everybody wants to do what they can to make you stay," he said.

"Why should they think I won't?"

"For the same reason the teacher who was here last didn't. This is tough country, especially for a cheechako."

"When do I stop being a cheechako and become an Alaskan?"

"Maybe by the time the river goes out in the spring."

"What do you mean—maybe?"

He looked at me almost the way Mr. Strong did that day when he'd ridden back to give me his army coat—as if I was a foreigner. Only Fred's look was a little different. The only thing I could liken it to was the way one forest animal might look at another to see if it was its own kind. If it wasn't there was no offense taken. The animal just loped off. It gave me a funny feeling.

"Well," he said, "some people never really become Alaskans. They never get to like it the way it is. They just tolerate it."

"I don't know what you mean."

"It's hard to explain, maybe because it's something you have to feel inside. All these old sourdoughs around here—they're real Alaskans. They came here way back before I was born, when there was nothing out here but raw land. They fought the cold and the rivers, built cabins and barely stayed alive. They were lonely and went hungry, froze their feet and their hands and hardly ever took enough gold out of the ground to keep themselves in grub, but they made it."

"You think I'll make it?"

"No reason why you shouldn't. Just make sure you've got good footgear and plenty of warm clothes—and take people's advice."

"When they give it to you, you mean. Up to now I keep finding things out hit and miss." I told him about Mr. Strong offering me his old army coat back in Eagle. "When I turned it down he didn't try to convince me I was wrong."

"That's the way it is. If somebody tells you something you have to listen the first time. They won't tell you twice. They'll let you find out for yourself."

"What do you think of Mr. Strong? You think he's an Alaskan?"

"He sure is. He cuts it a little thin sometimes and he's tough on horses, but he's skookum—he's got guts. The people around here don't appreciate him much because once in a while he'll lose some mail or other stuff in the river."

"Stuff like me you mean."

That made him laugh. "I heard about that," he said. Then he went on as though it wasn't anything out of the ordinary. "What most people don't realize is that he's been mushing that trail for over twenty years and no matter what it's like— blown in, flooded or frozen—he shows up here on time if he possibly can. Twenty-four days out of every month he's on trail all alone and he's usually here like clockwork on the eighth, the eighteenth and the twenty-eighth. But if he shows up a day late once in a while, or he won't pack parcel post out here in summer, people get all riled up at him and start sending letters to Washington D.C. saying the mail contract ought to be taken away from him. Well, he's still got it—because there's nobody else can do the job better. You'll see what I mean after the freeze-up."

I wondered if he knew what Mr. Strong thought of him and his family, and I had a feeling he did.

We kept working all day and he didn't go home until a little before Joe showed up.

Joe came in wearing the fleece-lined jacket I'd seen him trying on when I arrived, and he had a tie on. He was surprised I was ready. "I was ready an hour ago," I said.

"You're still operating on Lower 48 time," he said, helping me on with my coat. "You're going to have to get used to Alaska time."

"What's Alaska time?"

"An hour or two early or an hour or two late. Maybe more depending on the weather. If somebody doesn't come at all you know something held them up and they'll be along the next day, or the next."

"I hope the school won't work that way."

The roadhouse was about five cabins down from me. Inside it reminded me of a frontier stagecoach stop I'd seen once—rough plank floors, ceiling black with woodsmoke, a couple of long tables covered with oilcloth and a bunk room and stable in the rear. I wished I had the old upright piano in the corner, though. I could have used it in the schoolhouse for music appreciation and singing. I made a mental note to ask Maggie if she'd let me bring the class in occasionally.

There wasn't anybody else in the place, so except for Maggie and her family, Joe and I had the place to ourselves. Maggie gave us a small table against the rear wall. The stable was on the other side of it and it took me a little while to get used to the horses that kept snuffling and sniffing the whole time we ate.

The boiled moose tongue she made was delicious, and while we ate I found out that Joe had gone to Washington State University. He'd come to Alaska in 1920, right after he got out of the Army. After we finished eating, Maggie and her husband sat down with us while her two little boys sat at one of the big tables listening.

"Heard you dropped in for a visit with Cathy Winters," Maggie said. "Did you see that Indian guy she's living with?"

77

"I was in her place. It didn't look to me as if anybody was living there but her."

"I don't mean *living* with," Maggie said impatiently. "I mean doing things she shouldn't with." Her two little boys, Jimmy and Willard, were all ears. "He's a tall lean thing, ugly as sin and scars all over his neck. What's his name?" she asked her husband, raising her voice a little because he was hard of hearing.

"Titus Paul." He was a small intense man. His false teeth were uncomfortable and he kept clicking and grinding them.

"I just saw him for a second," I said. "I wasn't there for very long."

"Well I'll bet a Stetson to an old spud she's living with 'im," Mr. Carew said. "She don't act like any white girl *I* ever saw. Spoils them Indians rotten."

"She's one a them communists," Maggie said, "—believes in free love an' all that. She won't be around much longer. Comes spring they'll send her Outside on the first water—kick 'er right up the Yukon. How's the Purdy kid comin' along fixin' your place up?"

"Fine. It won't look like the same place when he's done."

"He's a good kid for a half-breed," she said.

"Mr. Strong didn't seem to think too much of him, or his family for that matter."

"Mr. Strong's a little old-fashioned," Joe said to me. "You know, white man's burden and that sort of nonsense. The last I heard he was trying to get the town council in Eagle to pass a law saying the Indians had to be out of there by sundown."

"Who says that's a bad idea?" Mr. Carew asked. "I'm no crazier about siwashes than he is. Half-breeds either for that matter."

While we were talking Mr. Vaughn came in. Living right next door to me, he'd dropped in a couple of times while Fred and I had been working. He'd stayed about an hour each time, offering advice and telling Fred how things should be done, but he hadn't lifted a finger to help out. A widower, he told

78

me he'd raised his three girls practically by himself. I'd heard him yelling at them once or twice, and just before Joe had come over earlier I'd heard him slap one of the twins when she dropped something and it broke.

After Mrs. Carew poured him a cup of coffee he just sat and listened for a while. Finally he asked me what kind of teaching I was going to do. "Are you going to get fancy and teach a lot of tripe, or are you going to teach the three R's?" Somehow, the way he said it put me on the defensive.

"I'll teach the best way I know how, I guess. Arithmetic and reading are important, but there are other things too."

"Such as?" Mr. Vaughn asked. He had a goiter as big as an orange on one side of his neck and I kept trying not to stare at it.

"Literature and poetry. Civics, music."

"Sounds pretty fancy, all right," Mr. Carew put in.

"Sounds that way to me too," Mr. Vaughn said.

"Hey, give her a chance, will you?" Joe said. "She hasn't even started yet."

"What's wrong with us being interested?" Mr. Vaughn said. "That's why we have a school board."

"I'm glad you are," I said. "Does the school board meet very often?"

"When we think it's necessary," Mr. Vaughn answered. "We'll let you know when we think we should have a meeting."

A little while later Joe walked me back to my place. It was clear out when we'd gone into the roadhouse. Now it was so misty you could hardly see three cabins ahead.

"What's a sy-wash?" I asked him.

"Siwash? An Indian."

"That's what I thought. Is it an Indian word?"

"French. *Sauvage*. Savage. The old-timers weren't too finicky about their accent."

He came in with me and built up the fire in the stove. I thanked him for the supper.

"My pleasure," he said. "We'll have to get together again soon."

"Maybe after I get settled."

"I have plenty of time till trapping starts. You name it."

"I'll tell you the truth, Joe. I feel a little funny about going out with you."

"Why?" He saw I was embarrassed. "I see . . . Mary Angus?"

"I guess so."

"Don't let that worry you. We went separate ways a while back."

We dropped the subject and after a couple of minutes he left.

The next day while Fred and I were working I asked him about Joe and Mary.

"It's pretty much of an old story," he said. "Mary lived in the Indian village and Joe was doing some mining near by. They fell in love and took up housekeeping. They were like man and wife for a long time until they finally broke up about a year ago. Then a few months ago Mary came out to be with him. I don't think he really wanted her to, but she's still in love with him, so she did."

"Where does she live?"

"About a half-mile from here, on the way to my house."

Later on we stopped off at her cabin when Fred took me over to his house. It was a lovely walk, the sun settling down behind the mountains in a sea of liquid gold. The woods were silent except for here and there a few camp robbers hopping around in the trees, having some last minute arguments. We followed a wide trail alongside Chicken Creek, then turned north after a quarter of a mile.

Mary Angus' place was stuck back off the trail. There was so much buckbrush and willow growing up around the back of it that I didn't see it until Fred pointed it out. He'd said it was just an old line shack, a place put up by a trapper to stay in overnight as he moved along his trapline, so I hadn't expected it to be much. But it was awful—an old weathered shack that looked as if one good wind would blow it right over. A stovepipe leaned out of the roof and a couple of broken window panes had rags stuffed in them. It made me think of the greasy little shed the Rag Man used to live in when I was a little girl back in Evansville. None of us kids even knew the Rag Man's name, but every so often we'd go over to the junkyard where his shed was and throw stones at it until he came hobbling out on a heavy old cane. Then we'd run away screaming. We were so afraid of him that whenever I did something bad my father used to threaten to give me to him.

Mary Angus was out in front sawing some wood, and when she turned around it was hard for me to believe she was the same woman I'd glimpsed a few days ago. I'd had the impression then that she was beautiful. And at one time she must have been, with a lovely long face and dark eyes that were slanted a little. Now, although she was probably in her mid-twenties, she was old and tired. Her face was pock-marked and there were dark circles under her eyes. She was flushed and perspiring from the work she'd been doing. When Fred introduced us she smiled and I felt worse than ever. Most of her back teeth were gone. "I . . . am . . . happy . . . to . . . see . . . you," she said in this tiny little voice. It was like a little girl reciting. Fred had told me she didn't speak English too well, so I spoke slowly.

"I'm glad to meet you too," I said. "Is Chuck around?"

"In cabin. He sick."

"Can I say hello to him?"

She gave Fred a quick questioning look and he nodded slightly. When I asked Fred about it later he told me that white people didn't usually go into Indians' cabins, at least not white women.

Inside, the odor was so bad I almost gagged. It was like being in a tiny foul pit. The floor was dirt, and Chuck was lying on some kind of fur robe, a couple of dirty blankets pulled over him. The small Yukon stove was going full blast and there was some gray stew bubbling in a coffee can on top of it. An oil lamp on a shelf gave off a faint yellow light. It was a nightmare, the smell from a slop jar so foul I had to breathe through my mouth. Chuck had a cold. I stooped down alongside him.

"How are you feeling?" I asked him.

"Bad sick," he murmured.

He looked it too. If I could have I'd have taken him home with me right then and there. He needed a clean bed, some good nourishing food and a place where he could breathe.

I heard a little sigh. It was from his sister. She was lying fully clothed on some kind of small wooden frame lashed together with leather strips. She was asleep.

"You take care of yourself," I said. "I'll see you in school when you're better."

He didn't answer. He wasn't in any shape to be interested in me, school, or anything else. I went outside so furious at Joe Temple I wanted to scream.

"How can he let them live like that?" I asked Fred when we went on. "Can't he help them out at all?"

"He probably would if Mary would go back to the Indian village," Fred said.

"Couldn't he at least move her into one of those empty cabins in the settlement? A couple of them are ten times better than that shack."

"The people there don't want her."

"Fred, that's inhuman. Joe lived with that woman. Those are his children. It's all wrong."

"There's nothing anybody can do about it."

"There has to be."

"What Joe does is his business—his and Mary's. That's the way it is."

He didn't seem to want to talk about it, so I didn't say anything more, but I was a little disappointed in him for saying something like that.

His own house was beautiful, a big log cabin that was built on a knoll. A few outbuildings were around it, and telescoping out from the rear of it were a couple of smaller cabins.

I'd seen other cabins built the same way, added on to like that. I asked him why people did it.

"The only time you can build is during the season—that's about four months. So you build your main cabin, then keep adding on every year."

As soon as I walked in I realized why his mother had thought my place looked so terrible. She had a lovely home. The whole place sparkled with friendliness and good cheer. Potted plants and growing herbs lined the windowsills and three braided rugs lay on the highly polished floor. I couldn't get over it, especially since the Purdys had made just about everything that was in it themselves, from the glass-fronted cupboards in the kitchen area to the bright curtains on the window sewn from flour sacks.

It was a nice evening, with everybody talkative and good-humored—and a delicious dinner to boot. The only one who didn't have much to say was Fred's father. After I was introduced to him, he disappeared into one of the back rooms, and during supper I almost had the feeling that if he could have he'd have eaten by himself. The only time he really said anything was when I asked him where he was from. "New England," he said. Then, as if he didn't want me to ask any more questions, he asked me where I was from. I told him, and that ended the conversation between us. Right after dinner he excused himself and went into the next room. For the rest of the evening I could see him through the curtained doorway, working on a crystal radio he was making.

Before I left Fred asked me if I'd ever seen gold in the raw. I told him no, so he took a preserve jar down from a shelf. He handed it to me and everybody laughed when I nearly dropped it. It was about ten times heavier than I'd thought and it was filled with dull yellow flecks mixed with black powder. "That's flour gold," Fred said. He brought over another jar that was filled with nuggets ranging in size from pinheads to little pebbles. The two jars had their whole season's cleanup in them—maybe two thousand dollars worth of gold. It wasn't very much for a family to live on, but Fred said they expected to do better next year. They were going to prospect some ground during the winter that they thought would have some real good pay in it.

The next afternoon I got to see some gold mining done. Fred took me over to Lost Chicken Hill, where Uncle Arthur and Mert Atwood were going to be sluicing for the last time. "They don't have much of a setup," he told me on the way, "but you'll be able to see what it's all about."

"How come they're the only ones still mining?"

"They have a little water left. Nobody else has. No water, no mining."

"What do you mean 'no water no mining'?"

"Well," he said, "you've got to wash tons of dirt to get a few ounces of gold. You can have the richest ground in the world, but if you can't pipe water to it it's not worth a cent. The run-off's all gone now. The rivers, the creeks—they're all low. There won't be enough water for mining again until after the winter's over and the snow starts to melt."

"How about for bathing? I notice the creek in front of the schoolhouse is low too. Suppose it dries up?"

"It'll freeze before that happens."

"Then what do we do?"

"Chop ice or go bathless."

"I'll let you know what I decide."

"Oh I'll know, don't you worry." He laughed. "Everybody'll know."

It took us a half hour to get there, through a couple of canyons and over a stretch of tundra, then across a hillside that blossomed red with waist-high fireweed.

The two men were waiting for us, their sluice box set up on a slope. About ten feet long and open at both ends, it looked like a small gangway. Alongside of it was a big heap of pay dirt they'd excavated with pick and shovel. There must have been a couple of tons of it.

I was afraid I'd be in the way, but they went out of their way to make me feel welcome. I liked Mert the best. He was

84

the one who'd brought me the bear lard. A barrel-chested little man, he was so shy that the first few times I asked him something he took off his yachtsman's cap each time he answered. They'd dammed up a stream farther on up the slope, he explained to me, then they'd dug a trench from it all the way down to one end of the box. As soon as I was ready, he said, he'd go up and let the water go.

"You worm-eaten dub," Uncle Arthur bawled, "why you think she came over—ta spend the day with ya?"

Mert started up the slope apologetically. "Somethin' wrong with his cerebral machinery," Uncle Arthur complained. "Been goin' around with 'is hat off too long. Froze 'is brain box." He rested a hand on the sluice box. It was like a claw. The two last fingers were gone and the rest looked as though they'd been badly burned. Fred told me later that they'd been frozen.

Mert didn't come back for ten minutes. A few minutes after he did the water began to seep down the trench. Before long it was gushing down and running through the box pretty fast, gradually building up force. As soon as it had a "good head," as Uncle Arthur called it, the two men started shoveling in the paydirt. The water swept it right through the box. Even rocks as big as a fist clattered along easily. And that was all there was to it, Fred said, whatever gold was mixed in the dirt would drop to the bottom of the box where it was caught in the "riffles," wood slats. The dirt and rocks were washed through, running down to the bottom of the slope, where they added to the other tailing piles already built up by earlier sluicings during the season. Now I understood what Fred had meant. Pay dirt without water was just ordinary dirt.

It was over in about twenty minutes, when the water ran out, and Uncle Arthur and Mert leaned against the box, sweat staining the back of their shirts. They were both staring down at the muck in the bottom of it. Their final cleanup was down there. Four months' work with pick and shovel was ended.

I thanked them for letting me come over, then we left. On the way back I asked Fred if he knew how they'd done.

"Not too good," he said. "They never do."

"Never?"

He shook his head.

"Then why do they do it?"

"It's better than working for wages."

When you looked at it that way, maybe he was right. My father had worked down in the mines all his life, six days a week, and he had nothing to show for it. However little Uncle Arthur and Mert had, at least they were their own men.

"Now that everybody's done mining, what do they do?"

"Get ready for winter. Trapping'll start around the beginning of November."

"Why wait so long?"

That made him laugh.

"What are you laughing for? Is that a dumb question?"

He said, "No," but he was as amused as Chuck had been at the idea of fruit growing on trees. "You see, when you go out trapping," he explained, "you've got traps to tote, food and supplies, and sometimes you go pretty far. Then you've got to tote the furs back. You need a sled for all that."

"And for a sled you need snow."

It was a dumb question, all right. We both tried to keep a straight face, but it was no use. One look at each other and we were laughing.

Later on I asked him why the place was called Lost Chicken.

"Somebody found it once, then lost it. By the time they found it again they'd named Chicken Chicken."

"They must have lost a lot of places, those old prospectors." Besides Lost Chicken I'd heard of Lost Delta and Lost Fork.

We worked for another two days before my quarters and the schoolroom were finally finished. When they were done you could see the difference right away. Fred had glued the canvas back on the walls where it had been peeling and patched the bad spots, the tables and chairs in the schoolroom were sturdy, and I even had a "blackboard"—a couple of dark green window shades tacked to beaver board. He'd also made me a couch for my quarters by nailing three boxes together. Maggie Carew gave me a mattress for padding, and covered with a blanket and pillows it looked fine. He stayed for supper, and before he left we had a cup of cocoa and some cookies to celebrate.

"I'm really grateful to you," I told him. "I don't know what I'd have done if you hadn't helped me so much." I meant it too. A lot of people had loaned me things and even lent a hand once in a while, but he'd done just about all the work.

"Forget it," he said. "I was glad to help out. Maybe I'll drop by after school tomorrow and you can tell me how you did."

"Will you?" I'd told him how scared I was.

"Sure."

We sat talking for a while longer. He didn't want to go and I didn't want him to either, which really surprised me. Usually I never knew what to say to boys when I was alone with them. But with him it was just the opposite. Here we'd been together for practically three whole days and I felt I could have gone on talking to him the whole night. I'd never met any boy like him. He said he'd only gone as far as the sixth grade in school, but he read everything he could get his hands on and he was interested in everything—history, current events, motors, even metallurgy. He'd taken me for a walk to show me around and pointed out all kinds of rocks and minerals, white quartz with glints of pyrite in it, lodestone, feldspar. I'd never heard of most of them. He said he had a book about them and when I asked him if he'd lend it to me so the class could start a rock collection he said he'd be glad to.

He was just getting ready to leave when there was a knock at the door. It was Mr. Vaughn. "I brought you over the flag," he said.

It was for the pole outside. He'd had one of his daughters wash it for me.

"Thanks," I told him. "You didn't have to bring it over special, though. The girls could have brought it with them in the morning."

"No trouble," he said.

He kept standing in the doorway. "Schoolroom all done?"

"Ready and waiting. Did you want to see it?" I asked him.

"Wouldn't mind at all."

He came in and nodded to Fred. Fred said hello, then he said he'd better be going.

"Not before we show off your handiwork," I said.

I brought the oil lamp and the three of us went inside. I showed him the blackboard Fred had made, the shelves. He'd even made a couple of shelves low down for the two little kids I'd have. Mr. Vaughn just glanced around. He didn't seem too interested. "It'll do," he said.

I was a little disappointed. The least he could have done was tell Fred he'd done a good job, but all he said to him was, "Well, you'll be able to get back to your own work now."

Then I realized he'd come over just to see what we were doing. It embarrassed me and it made Fred feel uncomfortable too. He walked out right after Mr. Vaughn did. "I'll see you tomorrow," I called after him.

Before I went to sleep I went into the schoolroom again. I stood behind my table and imagined the kids sitting in front of me. It felt exciting. The room looked wonderful. I'd scrubbed the Yukon stove so it looked almost new and it was all ready with kindling and logs. On one of the shelves there was a whole row of books—a few readers, a dictionary I'd brought with me, and the old encyclopedia someone had contributed. I'd kept a few of the rocks Fred had pointed out to me when we took a walk, and they were sitting on another shelf. It was just a big bare room now, I thought, but in a few weeks, after the children began to draw and make things, it would look more like a schoolroom. Looking at the empty tables and chairs, I thought of so many things I wanted to say to the class that I went back inside my quarters and started jotting them down. They were things like our being as much a part of America up here as the people in any of the forty-eight states, and how important it was for all of us to be fine, well-educated citizens. When I went to bed I was so keyed up it was hard to fall asleep.

VI

School was supposed to start at nine, but by a quarter to they were all outside, so I went out and brought the folded flag with me.

With the oldest boy helping me, I ran it up to the top of the pole and then we all said the Pledge of Allegiance. Right then and there I knew I couldn't say one of the things I'd planned on. They all sounded too high-falutin' and phony. In fact, once we were in the schoolroom I couldn't say anything at all. I had stage fright. For a full minute the whole class stared at me silently and, completely tongue-tied, I stared back at them. The only sound was everybody's breathing and the squeak of the floorboards.

"How do you like the schoolroom?" I finally managed to croak.

"Real spiffy," Jimmy Carew said. He and his little brother and the Vaughn girls had seen it already, and so had Isabelle. Robert Merriweather and Joan Simpson hadn't. They all looked around, murmuring their approval. I was proud of it. Fred had done a wonderful job. All the tables were coverd with oilcloth and he'd painted the place with some pale green paint we'd found in Mr. Strong's store. The color was a little on the bilious side, but it brightened the room up and made it look larger.

"It smells good," Joan Simpson said. She was six years old, blue eyes, blond hair. I'd have to teach both her and Willard Carew to read.

After we found seats for everyone I wrote my name across one of the shades and said I was glad to be here. Then I shivered. "Before we go on," I said, "does anybody know how to build a fire in that stove?"

The schoolroom was so chilly that everybody sat with coats and parkas on. I'd tried to work the Yukon stove, a squat black metal affair a little bigger than an orange crate, but couldn't get a fire going in it. Out of the many hands that volunteered I picked Robert Merriweather. Twelve, he was the oldest of my three boys and big for his age.

He showed me right away what was wrong. I hadn't used enough kindling. "Also," he said, "you didn't open the damper enough. You need a good draft when the fire first starts." After he filled the stove with more kindling, he placed a couple of slender logs inside, then a couple of hefty three-foot logs on top of them. "You see," he said, "this kind of stove is made for long logs, so you don't have to keep feeding it so much."

"What do you know about that?" I said. "I thought all stoves were alike."

"Oh, no," a few children protested.

"Some you have to put small pieces in, like a cookstove, some large like this one," Elvira Vaughn said.

"That one's real ornery," Jimmy Carew said.

They loved the idea that here I was a teacher and I didn't know something. I'd intended to spend the morning getting acquainted and had rehearsed how I was going to start off asking them about themselves, but I didn't have to. Since they'd already taught *me* something, they didn't think twice about asking me questions.

"How come you don't know anything about stoves?" six-year-old Willard Carew asked. "*Every*body knows about *stoves*."

"Well, they don't use wood stoves very much where I come from."

"Then how do they cook?"

"Can anybody tell Willard?"

Robert Merriweather raised his hand. "I can. They use gas stoves. We had one before we came here to Alaska."

90

"What's a gas stove?" Willard asked.

Robert looked at me to see if I'd let him go ahead. He seemed to be the kind of a boy who'd always been kept in check, and he was self-conscious. I nodded to him.

"You turn on a switch and put a match to the burner and it lights right up. It's a million times better'n a wood stove."

From there we went on to talk about furnaces and steam heat and fireplaces.

"My father says a fireplace is the biggest waste of wood there is," Eleanor Vaughn said. She turned to her twin sister Evelyn, who was as husky as she was. "Isn't that right?"

"That's right."

"Ah, your father knows everything," Jimmy Carew said sarcastically.

After we decided which chairs and tables would be most comfortable for everybody and who would sit with whom, I asked them what they thought they were coming to school for.

" 'Cause we have to." Jimmy answered. That brought a laugh.

"All right, that's one reason. How many want to?"

Everyone's hand went up.

"Wonderful. Why?"

The hands went up again. I called on Jimmy's brother Willard. "There's nothin' else to do," he said with typical six-year-old honesty.

"Another reason. Next."

"To learn readin', writin' and 'rithmetic," Eleanor Vaughn said. She and her twin looked exactly like their father, the same big teeth and stern frown.

"Fine," I said. "What else?"

Silence.

"Nothing else? Anybody here know how to play the harmonica?"

"I do," Robert answered.

"Anybody want to learn?"

"Me," Jimmy said.

"All right, you'll learn."

"Here in school?"

91

"Certainly. That's what school's for—to learn what you want to learn."

"I'd like to learn sewing," Elvira Vaughn said.

"Me too," I said. "I'm terrible. Any good sewers here?"

Isabelle Purdy raised her hand.

"Think you can show Elvira how?"

"Sure," she said.

"That takes care of sewing. Anything else anybody wants to learn, they can learn it—as long as they keep up with their work. Maybe we can even learn a little bit about each other, like where we're all from."

The Purdys had come from Canada, we found out, the Carews from Pennsylvania. It gave me a chance to use one of the few teaching aids I had—a big map of the U.S. and Canada. It was my pride and joy and I wasn't about to pass the chance up.

"Where are you from, Teacher?" Elvira Vaughn asked me. Like her two sisters, her first name began with an E, but there the resemblance ended. She was slender and demure, not as sure about everything as they were, and more curious.

"I was brought up in Colorado."

"Where's that?"

"Who can show us on the map?"

Isabelle Purdy raised her hand, went to it and pointed to Colorado.

"Where would you say that is?" I asked her.

"Ma'am?"

"What part of the United States—North? South? West?"

While a couple of hands waved frantically, she stared at the map, then shrugged and gave me a smile.

"I know, Teacher, I know," Jimmy Carew shouted.

"Did you live in a big city?" Elvira Vaughn asked.

"No. My family always lived in coal-mining towns."

"Do they do that the same way as gold mining?"

"I don't think so," I said. "When you mine coal you have to tunnel deep down into the ground."

92

"They do that here too sometimes," Robert Merriweather said. "It's what they call drifting."

"Was the school you went to anything like this one?" Isabelle Purdy asked. She had the same kind of cheerfulness as Fred and her mother—always ready to break into an easy smile. And she was as immaculate as her mother, too. Her white middy blouse made her a standout. Most of the others had come to school in the same bib overalls and shirts they wore every day—even the girls. One of the Vaughn twins had a grimy shadow that came halfway up her neck. We'd have to start working on good health habits, I thought.

"Something like it," I said, "but we had different grades in each classroom."

"Can you drop your teeth out?" Jimmy's little brother Willard asked.

"No, I can't," I said. "Can you?"

"My father can," Willard said proudly. "He can hand 'em right out to you on his tongue." He illustrated for me.

"My father's got a goiter as big as a baseball," Eleanor Vaughn bragged, turning to her twin sister again.

"That's right," Evelyn said on cue. They were like two comics in a vaudeville show.

Before we broke for lunch I gave my six older children a diagnostic arithmetic test and while they were taking it I kept Willard and Joan busy making cut-outs and pasting.

After lunch we appointed monitors for taking care of the stove, cleaning the board erasers, sweeping the schoolroom and the outhouse and raising and lowering the flag.

Right in the middle of it we had an unexpected guest. Uncle Arthur walked in. Wearing a long gray coat that almost dragged the floor in front, he told us to just go ahead with what we were doing and pay him no mind. He stood by the door looking on, hands clasped in back of him while we went about our business.

"D'ya have an extra chair, missis?" he finally asked me.

The class seemed to take his being there for granted and I couldn't bring myself to ask him to leave, so I sent one of the kids into my quarters for one. He sat down, folded his arms under his beard and just looked on for a while.

He didn't say anything until after I'd tried a couple of the kids at oral reading, then he said, "When you gonna have penmanship drill, missis?"

"Maybe in a couple of days or so," I said.

"I could give ya plenty songs you could use for makin' circles 'n' straights if you like." He took a pad from his coat pocket. "Show ya right now if you want."

"Can he, Teacher?" Jimmy asked. "They're fun."

I'd never been much for penmanship, maybe because my own penmanship was so bad. If he had a way to make it fun I was all for it.

I told him to go ahead and he opened the pad. He wrote a capital N for us, chanting as he did it. "Ya make a loop and go down, climb a hill to the top, then go down to the bottom and there you stop." He recited a few more rhymes for other letters and the children were fascinated. "That teaches the kiddies how to write a good hand, ya see."

"We don't have time to do it right now," I said, "but I'd appreciate it if you'd teach me the rhymes."

He promised to write them all down for me, and then he left. I complimented the class on how well they'd behaved while he'd been there.

"Him and those other old-timers always drop by," Jimmy said. "They like to. *You* know—they're kinda lonely."

A little later I found out I was going to have to be careful how I explained things. Jimmy asked me why everybody had to come to school at the same time and eat lunch at the same time. "How come you can't do things when you feel like it?"

"If everybody did it would be like a three-ring circus," I said.

"What's a three-ring circus?" Elvira asked.

"Well," I said, 'it's like a chautauqua, only it's bigger. It has elephants and clowns and—"

"What's a shuh-tawk-wa?" Jimmy asked hesitantly.

I explained that a chautauqua was a fair, only to have Elvira ask what a fair was. By the time I was finished nobody really

94

had any idea of what a three-ring circus was like. They had never seen clowns, or jungle animals, or acrobats. They knew nothing about all the things that the children in Forest Grove knew about—radio programs and air shows, movies and automobiles. If I was going to cite examples I'd have to pick things they were familiar with—gold mining and trapping, dog teams and hunting. Talking about the future of air transportation or radio left them uninterested—until I told them that one day soon airplanes would probably be bringing the mail right here to Chicken, or that maybe in another year or two they'd be able to listen to all the radio shows that people Outside could tune in on.

One thing I could see was that I didn't have to worry about keeping their attention. Everything was new to them and they were hungry to learn.

Their big problem was reading. The only pupil who could read well was Isabelle Purdy. The rest of the class had trouble reading orally from a third-grade reader. The Vaughn twins were thirteen, but their sister Elvira, three years younger, could read better than they could. A few of the children could do fifth-grade and sixth-grade arithmetic—Robert Merriweather was good enough to do seventh-grade work—but their reading comprehension was terrible.

It had been almost a year and a half since there'd been a teacher here, and except for Isabelle and Robert, none of them knew anything about history or geography or social studies. I'd have to figure out some kind of a starting point—some way of getting them interested enough in history and geography so that they wouldn't be bored by them. Before I could do that, though, I'd have to get them to feel like a class, not like just a bunch of kids that happened to be in the same room. They weren't used to talking with each other much—at least not about anything that didn't have to do with mining or trapping or local gossip. They needed something that would bring them together and let them show off what they could do.

When 3:30 came nobody wanted to go home, which was fine with me. I invited them all into my quarters for cookies and hot cocoa. I still wasn't used to the cookstove. Trying to put just enough wood in to keep the oven at the right temperature was driving me crazy, but the cookies I'd made weren't too bad.

"Oh, looka that," Elvira said, admiring my coat. It was wool suede with a mouflon fur collar and cuffs. She ran her fingers along the sleeve. "Feels nice," she said.

Her sister Evelyn pinched the fabric expertly and shook her head. "You won't be able to wear that around here too long."

"Why not?" I asked. It had cost me $35 and it was my prize possession.

"Come winter it won't be warm enough."

"That's right," Eleanor agreed.

"So what?" Elvira said. "It's still nice to look at."

The cocoa was just about ready and I'd started to pour it when Jimmy Carew called to me. "Is this yours, Teacher?"

I nearly had heart failure. He'd found the nickel-plated revolver and was showing it to Robert and little Willard.

Taking it from him, I put it on the highest shelf in the cache, shoving it back out of sight.

School was over for the day.

Fred popped in a little while after they left and asked me how I thought I did. I told him I'd been scared at first, but now I felt pretty optimistic.

"The only thing I'm not sure of, though, is how to make one class out of them."

"What do you mean?"

"Give them the feeling that they're all learning together, find a project they could all work on. Back in the States it was easy. I could take them to a museum, or to the local dairy or cannery, then we would talk about it and write compositions about it. Besides that, everybody was in the same grade, so they had a lot in common to begin with. Here they're all in different grades. What I need is some kind of a project they can all work on, something local. I'm going to take them on field trips, but I need something else."

"You could take them to see some of the old sourdoughs."

"You think they'd like that?"

96

"The kids? They'd love it. So would the old men."

"That's not a bad idea. The only thing I'd have to do is make sure I don't wind up getting lost. I still don't know my way around here."

He laughed. "Make a map."

"Did you say a map?"

"Uh-huh."

I could have kissed him. "You just found my project for me."

I was just about to explain the idea to him when there was a knock at the door. It was Eleanor Vaughn. At least I thought it was. She and Evelyn looked so alike I couldn't tell them apart yet. "I'm sorry to bother you, Teacher," she said, "but I lost a mitten. I thought maybe I left it in the schoolroom."

We took a look around, but it wasn't there.

I didn't think anything about it until later, when I remembered how her father had dropped in the night before. Fred had been with me then too. It could have been a coincidence, but I had the uncomfortable feeling it wasn't. I tried to remember how the twins had been dressed when they came to school. They lived only right next door, and after I thought about it I realized that all they'd had on were sweaters. Neither of them had worn mittens.

VII

If there's one thing that fires up a class for the day's work, I'd found, it's some good rousing singing the first thing in the morning. And this class was no exception. Right after we went through *Yankee Doodle* and a few other songs, I started my two beginners out with some busywork, then gave reading-comprehension tests to a few of the older kids. While they were busy I worked with Isabelle and Elvira on long division.

In the middle of it Willard got bored with what he was doing and started scaring little Joan by telling her a bear was going to get her next time she went to the outhouse, so I had to separate them temporarily.

About mid-morning Merton Atwood showed up. He was even quieter than Uncle Arthur, glancing down shyly every time I happened to look his way. He watched Elvira do a long-division example at the board, then Isabelle, but when my oldest boy, Robert, did an example I saw him raise his hand.

"Mr. Atwood?"

"Mert." He shifted uncomfortably.

"Mert."

"How come that didn't come out even?" he asked me, pointing to the board.

"That's long division with a remainder," I said. "You come out with a fraction."

He stayed until lunchtime. The example was still on the

board and he went up and stared at it. "That easy to learn?" he asked me.

"Long division? Easy as pie."

"Alwuz been in'risted in learnin' that. Alwuz wan-ned to, but never did."

"Come by after school some time and I'll show you."

"I might do that," he said. "I just might."

"You could do me a favor too."

"What's that?"

"Could you draw me a simple map of Chicken here on the board with a dot to show where everybody in the class lives?"

He did it for me. He drew in Chicken Creek and then drew lines for the two other creeks that Joan Simpson and Robert Merriweather lived on. After lunch I told the class about the project I had in mind. "It's something we can all work on together," I said. "We're going to make a map of Chicken, something like this one, but bigger. We're going to use one whole wall for it. Everybody can draw a little picture of their own cabin and we'll put it up in the right place."

They liked that idea, of having the place they lived in and their name right up where everybody could see them. "But that's only part of the project," I said. "What we'll do is find out all about Chicken—its history and geography, what grows here, what's produced here, everything. After that we'll find out about other places."

"But there's nothing to know about this place," Jimmy said. "There's nothing here."

"Oh, I can think of a dozen things I'd like to know about it. Just one, for instance—does anybody know how Chicken got its name?"

Nobody did, so I asked Robert Merriweather if he'd ask around and write a report on it. He said he would. Then we decided that the next day we'd go on our first field trip to collect leaves and rocks and any other interesting things we could find.

After school, as the children went out the door, there was a roly-poly Indian woman waiting on the porch. She was bundled up in a light blue flannel coat that was made out of a blanket, and she had a little girl with her. "How you do, Tisha," she said. "My name Rebekah Harrin'ton. I come see you."

"I'm glad to meet you," I said. "Come on in."

"This my kid," she said when we were in my quarters. "Lily. Lily, you say how you do."

Lily peered up at me from under a peaked hat of wolf fur. I could barely see her eyes under it. "How you do," she said. She was charming.

Mrs. Harrington put a paper sack down on the table. She took out a few pounds of dried salmon. "F'you. Present."

"Thank you. I was just about to have some tea. Would you like some?"

"I like. Yes." I took her coat. She sat down and made herself comfortable, hitching her skirt up a little. She had on a couple of other skirts underneath it. "You got nice place," she said.

"Thanks to Fred Purdy."

"Ah, Fred he good boy, you make bet on that. Whole Purdy family got good people. Everybody like."

It took her a few minutes to get around to why she'd come, and it was just what I was hoping for. She wanted to enroll Lily in school. "You not got too much lotsa kids now?"

"Not at all. I don't have enough. How old is Lily?"

"Fo'. He be fi' soon—Janawary."

When she said "he" I looked at Lily again to make sure she was a little girl. She was. "She's a little young," I said, "but I think it'll be all right."

"Oh, he be one smart kid my Lily," she assured me. "learn like fire. Already he write A, B, F, P—many alphabets. My husbin Jake he teach." All of a sudden she became sad. "Only one bad thing, Tisha. Lily he scare come school all alone heself. Need Momma."

"You can sit with her till she gets used to it."

"You mean it?"

"Of course." With all the old-timers who'd been coming in I couldn't see any harm being done.

Her grin was as big as sunshine. "You one darn good joe, Tisha. I come with Lily tomorrow."

100

The next morning they were almost the first ones to arrive. After the Pledge of Allegiance I told the class that Lily was going to be their new classmate. "She's a little shy," I said, "so I'd like you to be especially nice to her."

"How about *her?*" Jimmy Carew said, pointing to Rebekah. "She comin' too?"

"Until Lily gets used to school and can come on her own." There were some snickers.

"Is anything wrong?" I asked. But nobody said anything.

I didn't think anything more about it, and once we got down to work the class didn't either, but the next day Evelyn Vaughn told me that her father said the school board wanted to have a meeting right after school.

The three of them came into my quarters looking solemn— Maggie Carew, Angela Barrett and Mr. Vaughn. I was surprised to see Angela on the board since she didn't have any children. I asked them if they'd like some coffee or tea, but they said no. The four of us sat around the table and Mr. Vaughn rapped his knuckles on it. "The meeting will come to order," he said.

They asked me a couple of questions about what I'd been doing, and I told them about the project. They didn't seem too impressed. Mr. Vaughn got right to it. "How come you're letting that Indian woman come to school?" he said.

"Mrs. Harrington? She's just sitting with Lily."

"Is that what she told you?"

"Yes. She said that Lily was a little scared to come by herself, so I said it would be all right if she sat with her until Lily was used to it."

"Well, we don't like it," Angela said.

"She's not bothering the class at all," I said. "She's quiet as a mouse."

"We want 'er kicked out," Angela said sharply.

"And the kid along with her," Mr. Vaughn added.

I was stunned. "Lily? But why?"

"She's under age. A kid has to be over five and under sixteen to go to this school. You know that."

"I know, but does it matter that much?"

"It matters to us," Mr. Vaughn said. "You have enough to do to teach our own kids properly without wasting time on some little siwash that doesn't belong here."

"I don't think it's doing any harm to let her come," I said to Maggie Carew. She hadn't said anything up to now and I had the feeling she'd be more receptive than the other two. "She's a bright little girl, and besides that we don't even have a full enrollment. We're supposed to have ten and all we have is eight."

"The law is that this school is for kids from five to sixteen," Mr. Vaughn said before Maggie could answer, "and the law's the law. Let's take a vote on it. I vote that Lily Harrington, being too young to attend this school, be expelled. How do you two vote?"

"I vote the same way," Angela said.

"Maggie?"

"You got a majority already," Maggie said. "You don't need mine."

"We'd like to make it unanimous."

"I'm all for throwin' Rebekah out," she said, "but I don't care about the kid one way or the other."

"You abstain?"

"Yeah." She didn't seem too happy about the whole thing.

"You've got your orders," Mr. Vaughn said to me. "See that you carry them out."

After they left I sat thinking about it. I couldn't believe it —that people could act that way. Just because someone was an Indian. I was ashamed of them. And I was ashamed of myself too. If I'd had any guts I'd have told them off, let them know what I thought of them. But I didn't. I'd let them buffalo me because I was new and I'd been scared of them. Now I had to tell Mrs. Harrington her little girl couldn't come to school.

I asked her to stay after school the next day, then I told her. The look on her face made me wish I was a thousand miles away. She knew as well as I did why the school board didn't

102

want Lily, but all she said was, "He sure like go school my Lily."

"I know. I'm going to write to the commissioner about it, Mrs. Harrington. I'm going to ask him if he can make an exception in Lily's case. I'm sure he will. In the meantime, if you want to, you could bring Lily over here after school a couple of times a week and I could tutor her."

"What tooda, Tisha?"

"Teach. I could teach her here in my quarters a couple of times every week."

"You do that?"

"I'll be glad to. Let's make it every Monday and Thursday right after school. You can learn at the same time."

She smiled. "Tisha, you make me too much happy. You bet we come!" She went out beaming.

That wasn't the end of it, though, because the next morning, right after we finished singing, Rebekah and Lily showed up again. With them was a big man, Rebekah's husband Jake, and all I needed was one look at him to know there was going to be a storm. He was as nice as could be to me, though. He took off his Stetson and said he was pleased to meet me. Then he asked me what swivel-eyed jackass said his little girl couldn't come to school.

I took him into my quarters and explained the whole thing to him.

"The school board, eh . . . Well, little lady, I gather *you* don't have any objections to my little girl gettin' educated."

"None at all."

"You sit tight then, while I have a little talk with the school board."

He slammed out of my quarters and went right next door to Mr. Vaughn. We could hear everything that happened from the schoolroom. He pounded on Mr. Vaughn's door and what followed after that was probably the finest and most eloquent cussing I'd heard since I was a little girl in Blazing Rag. It started off with him calling Mr. Vaughn a mangy, misbegotten,

103

worm-eaten egg-sucker and went on improving with every sentence. Not one of us in that classroom said a word the whole time. All we could do was marvel at it. There were a couple of silences in between the cussing, but it went on gathering steam for about five minutes without one word being repeated. "Now you potbellied, yelping, walleyed animal," Mr. Harrington finished off, "is my little girl goin' to school or ain't she?"

We couldn't hear what Mr. Vaughn said, but not ten seconds later Mr. Harrington strode back in as red as the smoked salmon Rebekah had brought me. "Little lady," he said, "Mr. Vaughn said that if it's all right with you, the school board would be pleased to have Lily attend your class." He even remembered to take off his hat.

"I'd be delighted, Mr. Harrington."

"How about you?" He asked Rebekah. "You want to give me a hand takin' out the sluice box or park here for a while?"

"I come help you, Jake," Rebekah said proudly.

"Well then let's go, woman. There's work to do."

I'd have kicked my heels together and jumped up and down if I'd been alone. The whole thing couldn't have worked out better if I'd planned it. Lily was in school, Mr. Vaughn got what was coming to him, and I was off the spot with the school board.

For the next few days everything went fine. The class really took to the idea of the map of Chicken. It started us talking about all the different kinds of maps there were, treasure maps and world maps, weather maps, and produce maps. We decided that since we had a whole wall to use we ought to show not only where everybody lived, but some of the things we'd found on our field trip. We'd come back loaded with treasures—birch and cottonwood leaves, samples of willow and alder, and rocks galore. Elvira Vaughn had even found a piece of black silicon with a shell fossil in it. After some discussion we decided to put some of them up on the map. The rest we'd make up books about—leaf books and fur-sample books, animal-picture books and food books. The project began to take on shape. When it was finished, we decided, we'd invite everybody in Chicken to come and see what we'd done. The class was so enthusiastic about it that I had trouble bringing them back to their regular lessons.

Robert Merriweather's report turned out to be excellent and I tacked it on the wall.

HOW CHICKEN GOT IT'S NAME

Chicken got it's name from the first prospectors who came here. There was a lot of Ptarmigans here and they thanked God for it because they were hungry. They were so grateful they wanted to name this place Ptarmigan, but they couldn't spell it. They named it good old American Chicken instead. This is what Uncle Arthur said.

Mert Atwood says this isn't true. Chicken got it's name because they found gold nuggets as big as chicken corn here.

No one can ever know the real truth, I guess.

Inside of a few days the schoolroom began to feel like one, with pictures and lesson papers all over the walls, our rock collection on one of the shelves, and a little herb garden sitting in tin cans on one of the window sills. Not that we didn't have our troubles. With everybody doing different things in one room there were bound to be arguments. When my three beginners were restless they'd get in everybody's hair. Willard would bother the older children or start scaring Joan and Lily by telling them about a wolf coming into their cabin some night to eat them up. They'd begin to cry, disturbing the others, so I'd have to find coloring work or something else for them all to do, or let Willard go home for a little while.

Aside from that the only other problem was interruptions. Everybody in and around the settlement seemed to feel the school was the one place open to the public any time. Mr. Strong had told everybody I had the key to his store, so every so often someone would come in wanting to buy something. A few times it was people like Angela, who lived in the settlement, and I was able to tell them to come back after school, but a couple of other times it was people who lived some distance away, like

Joe, and I had to leave the class. I finally posted a notice on the school door saying no goods could be purchased at the store during school hours.

On Friday still a third old-timer wandered in. His name was Ben Norvall, a wrinkled old basset hound of a man with drooping moustaches. He was just about the most well-spoken individual I'd met here so far. He could quote Shakespeare by the yard and he offered to lend us his whole set of Shakespeare's works if we promised to take care of it. He even told the class the story of Macbeth and they'd been spellbound by it. The only bad thing about him was that he looked and smelled something awful. I mentioned him to Maggie Carew and she told me not to let him in again.

"If you do," she said, "you're ruinin' it for the rest of us. No one's lettin' him in until he burns those clothes he's got on and takes a bath. As long as he's got a place to go he won't do it."

By the time the first week was over I felt pretty good. As far as I could tell the class was really interested in what they were doing and they liked coming to school. The only trouble I could see I might have was teaching Robert arithmetic. He was pretty good, and I'd have to do some studying to keep ahead of him. Aside from that I was pretty optimistic.

I shouldn't have been though, because on Monday I was in trouble with the school board again. This time it was over Chuck. He showed up Monday morning about fifteen minutes before school. Robert had already started the fire in the schoolroom stove, and I was inside my quarters making my bed. Outside, Jimmy Carew was tossing a ball against the porch base and talking with the Vaughn girls. All of a sudden he stopped and there was silence, until Jimmy said, "Where'd *you* come from?"

"From Louse Town," Evelyn Vaughn said.

"Who is he?" Jimmy asked her.

"Mary Angus' kid."

"You talk English?" Jimmy asked him.

"Yiss," Chuck said.

"Whattaya want here?"

"Come school."

"Like heck you are," Evelyn said. "This is a white school."

"I come here."

"Who says so?"

"Tisha, she say I come."

" 'Tisha'? Who the heck's Tisha?"

"He means Teacher."

"I know what he means."

I went outside. "Good morning, everybody," I said. "Hello, Chuck—nice to see you here finally. How are you feeling?"

He looked down at the ground and mumbled, "Good."

He looked anything but good, though. He was thinner than ever and his lips were all chapped. His clothes didn't help any. His mackinaw was so small his wrists stuck out and his pants were so big the bottoms were ragged from scraping the ground.

We had the Pledge of Allegiance inside because it was so cold out that ice bridges were forming all along the edges of the creek. After we sang I introduced Chuck, gave him a seat and started everybody working. When they were all busy I took him over in a corner and gave him a second-grade reader to read from for me. He didn't do well with it, but he did fine when I tried him with a first-grade reader. His arithmetic wasn't bad either.

The class was restless that morning, too many of them pre-occupied with giving each other looks about him. A couple of times he got hit by a spitball, but I couldn't see who did it.

During recess the older kids wanted to play dodge ball. After we showed Chuck how to play I took my three young ones on the side to play with them. After just a few minutes had gone by, the dodge ball game got out of hand. I didn't see it until it was too late. By the time I stepped in Chuck's nose was bleeding, and he was crying. They'd made him "it." I took him into my quarters, and after the bleeding stopped and he was cleaned up, I called everybody back inside. "Who started the rough stuff?" I asked Robert.

"Nobody," he said. "We all just did it."

"I'm surprised at you. You should have stopped it."

"It wasn't my fault. They don't want him."

"Who's 'they?' "

He didn't answer.

"Well let me tell you something—all of you. Whoever 'they' are, if 'they' do anything like this again, 'they' are going to be in trouble."

During vocabulary with the older children I gave Evelyn Vaughn the word "intelligent" to put into a sentence.

"Siwashes aren't very intelligent," she recited. A few of the older kids giggled.

"Can you tell me what the word siwash means?" I asked her.

"Sure. It's a dirty low-down black Injun."

More giggles. I felt like throttling her. "There are certain words," I said, "which I don't want to hear in this class room. One of them is siwash."

"What's wrong with it, Teacher?" Jimmy asked. "Everybody says it."

"It's a mean word—like hunkie or nigger or kike. Now," I asked Eleanor, "do you think you can find another sentence for me?"

"How about if I said *Indians* aren't very intelligent?"

"Do you really think that's true?"

"I sure do," she answered.

"All Indians?"

She nodded.

"How about people who are only part Indian?"

"You mean like half-breeds? I guess so," she said.

"I should tell you," I said, "that my own grandmother was an Indian. That makes me part Indian too. Do you think there's anything wrong with my intelligence?"

Eleanor shifted uncomfortably. "No."

"Is that really true, Teacher?" Jimmy said.

"Yes, it is."

"What kind of an Indian was she?" Elvira Vaughn said.

"Kentuck."

"I never heard of that kind."

108

"They're like any other kind—Comanche or Sioux, any kind of Indian."

"Oh, well," Jimmy said. "They're *American* Indians. They're different from the ones we got here."

"Why?"

"They just are."

"If they are it's not very much. Indians are Indians, and there are all kinds."

"Was your grandmother like these Indians?"

"I'll tell you the truth," I said. "If you saw her in the Indian village you'd think she was one of them."

"How come you don't look Indian then?"

"I guess I take after my grandfather. He was white."

"*That*'s why you're smart enough to be a teacher."

"Not necessarily. My grandmother was a pretty smart woman. A lot of people said she was smarter than my grandfather."

Robert Merriweather hadn't said anything up to then. He raised his hand. "If your grandmother was an Indian," he said logically, "then your father was a half-breed."

"I guess that's right. But you know something? Where I come from nobody cared about it. As a matter of fact whenever anybody found out I was part Indian they thought that was a pretty interesting thing to be. . . . Now we've got work to do, but just remember, what people are doesn't matter, whether they're Indian or Irish or Negro or anything else—they're just people."

When school was over for the day, Chuck hung around for a few minutes. "You tell truth, Tisha?" he asked me. "You Indian?"

"I'm part Indian, yes."

"You make moccasin?"

"No. I don't know how to do that."

"Cut fish?"

"Not too well."

"Trap?"

"I'm afraid not."

He thought it all over. "Funny Indian," he murmured.

Elvira Vaughn knocked at my door right after supper that night. She was all embarrassed. "My father said to tell you that me and my sisters won't be coming to school tomorrow," she said.

"How come?"

"My father said you'd know why."

I didn't sleep too well that night, and the next morning I was up at five. I did some washing just to keep busy, then I brought some wood in. By 8:30, when Robert arrived to start the fire, I was in the schoolroom putting some work on the board and listening for anybody who'd be coming. At a quarter to nine Isabelle Purdy and Joan Simpson arrived just as I went out to ring the hand bell for the first time. A few minutes later Rebekah brought Lily in, and right after that Chuck arrived. The Vaughn girls didn't show up at all. And neither did Willard and Jimmy. At nine I went out and rang the bell for late call, but there was nobody in sight. The settlement was quiet.

During recess I saw Willard and Jimmy playing up by the roadhouse. I decided to go over and talk to them, but as soon as I headed in their direction they ran indoors.

I tried to go on as if it was just a normal day, but every time I'd look at those five empty chairs I felt miserable. After school I must have sat for an hour drinking tea and trying to think what to do. Finally I threw on a sweater and went next door to the Vaughn cabin.

Mr. Vaughn opened the door.

"I wonder if I could talk with you for a few minutes?" I asked him.

"What about?"

"About the girls not being in school today."

"What about it?"

"Well, I know they're not sick. I wondered why they were absent."

"I kept them home."

"Will they be in school tomorrow?"

110

"We'll see," he said. Then he closed the door.

I stood there looking at the closed door, feeling like a little girl who'd done something awful. I started over to the roadhouse, then I changed my mind. I just didn't have the guts to stare into another face that might look at me as if I was a stone. So I went back to my quarters and stared at the walls for another hour.

I hadn't done anything wrong, but I still felt guilty. They were the ones who were wrong—Maggie and Angela and Mr. Vaughn. They were all wrong. They had no right to keep Chuck or Lily or any other little kid out of the school just because they thought they were dirt. There were plenty of people who'd thought I was dirt when I was a kid. I could even remember one teacher who used to favor the kids who came to school dressed in nice clothes. She was always calling on them and smiling at them, while she looked at the ones like me as if we were trash. She'd even made me wear a sign one day when she found lice in my head during health inspection. I'd gotten them from playing with two kids next door and I'd never had them before, but she made me sit in the corner all day wearing a cardboard sign with "Dirty" printed on it. As long as I lived I'd never forget that. Or her. I'd hated her from then on.

I tried to think what I'd do if I was Miss Ivy, but it didn't help at all. She just wasn't the kind of person you fooled around with. She'd have gone right up to Mr. Vaughn and Maggie Carew and told them she expected to see their children in school the next day and no nonsense about it, and that would have been that. By suppertime I couldn't even think about eating. I decided that I'd wait till after supper, then I'd go over and talk to Maggie. The idea of going through another day, and maybe more, with less than half a class was unbearable.

Maggie saved me the trouble, though. Just before six Jimmy knocked at the door. "My mother says is it all right if the school board comes over after supper?"

"Sure. You can tell her 7:30 would be fine."

Before 7:30 came I went through a half a dozen conversations with them, and if I was able to say half the things I'd thought of I'd get a speech prize. I gave them quotes from the Declaration of Independence, the Bill of Rights and the Ten Commandments and ended with some beautiful phrases about how education was the birthright of all Americans. As soon as they trooped in, right on the dot, though, I felt just as tongue-tied as I'd been on the first day of school. They were grim. They turned me down when I offered them tea.

I had the stove going really hot so they'd be comfortable. Angela Barrett took off her sweater right away and my eyes nearly popped out. Her arms had so many tattoos they looked like an art gallery.

"I prepared the minutes of the last meeting," Mr. Vaughn said, opening a composition book. "I'll read them."

"We can do without that," Maggie said.

"We're supposed to read the minutes," Mr. Vaughn said.

"What for?" Maggie said. "We know what we said."

"Are you making a motion that we waive them?"

"Wave 'em, fry 'em or boil 'em, I don't care. Let's get to what we come for."

Mr. Vaughn cleared his throat. "We'd like to know on what grounds you've taken Joe Temple's half-breed into the school."

"The same grounds on which I'd take any pupil in, Mr. Vaughn."

"He doesn't belong here. If you weren't a cheechako you'd know that. He belongs in the Indian village school."

"But he's not *in* the Indian village now."

"That has nothing to do with it. He shouldn't be in the same school with our children."

"I don't want to argue with you, but I don't see on what grounds you want to keep him out."

"According to the law," Mr. Vaughn said, "this school is open to, and I quote, 'white children and children of mixed blood who lead a civilized life.' You are aware of the law, I take it."

"Oh yes," I lied.

"Then there's your ground—'children of mixed blood *who*

112

lead a civilized life.' That kid isn't civilized. None of those Indians from that village are."

Now that it came right down to it, faced with the three of them I wasn't feeling as brave as I thought I would.

"Well?" Mr. Vaughn said.

"Isn't that your interpretation, Mr. Vaughn? Chuck can read, he can write, as far as I can see he's like any other little boy who—"

Maggie cut me off. "My kid says he can't even talk civilized." This time she was in agreement with them.

"Besides that he's illegitimate," Angela said.

"I hadn't even thought about that," Mr. Vaughn said.

"I don't see how I can do what you're asking," I said.

"Oh, you don't," Mr. Vaughn said.

"No. I just can't tell that little boy to get out of class for no good reason." And you wouldn't make me tell him either, I thought, if Chuck had a father who'd knock your block off.

"You've been given the reason. We're telling you the reason. We're not running a school for uncivilized siwashes and the law will back us up. Now are you going to tell him or do I have to do it myself?"

"I can't."

"Then I'll do it for you. We'd better take a vote on it to show we're doing it lawfully. I make a motion that the half-breed child known as Charles Temple be excluded from the school on the grounds that he does not lead a civilized life. How do you two vote?"

Maggie and Angela said aye.

"That settles it," Mr. Vaughn said.

Maybe it settled it for them, but it didn't for me. I was so mad I could have thrown the stove at them.

"We don't want you to have any hard feelin's, Annie," Maggie said. "We're just tryin'a show you what's best. You're still new here, ya know."

"I know."

"I'll take that tea if you're still offerin'."

I served her and Angela some. Mr.Vaughn didn't want any.

"Want you to know my kids think you're a good teacher, too." Maggie said, taking a sip.

"If there's no further business," Mr. Vaughn said, "we can close this meeting."

Not as far as I was concerned. Without my even having to think about it I heard myself say, "It's too bad I had to come all the way out here for nothing."

"How's that?" Mr. Vaughn said.

"I'm going to have to close the school."

About to take another sip, Maggie made a sound into her cup and put it down quickly. "You what?"

"I'll have to close the school," I repeated.

Mr. Vaughn's eyes narrowed. "What are you talking about?"

"I don't have enough of an enrollment," I said. I had to hold my hands tight in my lap, they were shaking so much.

"You got plenty enrollment," Maggie said.

"No I haven't," I said, trying to keep my voice even. It sounded to me as if I was squeaking. "Under the law there has to be ten pupils."

"You got my two boys, his three girls, the Merriweather kid, Simpson's little girl, and Isabelle and Lily."

"That only makes nine."

"I hear Nancy Prentiss is coming out. That'll make ten."

"*If* she comes out. Right now there's only nine."

"Well, so what?" Maggie said. "That's just a technicality. Plenty of schools don't make the enrollment." She snorted. "If you hadda rely on a full enrollment all the time there'd never be a school in the bush."

"I don't know anything about that," I said, "but this is my first teaching job in Alaska and I don't want to start out by breaking the law." My hands were sweating and my heart was pounding so loud I thought they could all hear it.

Maggie stared at me for a long moment as the point got home to her. Mad and disgusted, she pulled in one side of her mouth. "You telling us you'd pack up and git?"

"That's what I'd have to do, Mrs. Carew."

114

"You're bluffing," Mr. Vaughn said.

"No I'm not. You told me yourself—the law is the law."

He was so mad I was afraid he might smack me or something. "You dirty little snotnose," he snarled. "How dare you give us an ultimatum!"

"Simmer down, Arnold," Maggie said.

"Like heck I will." Even the veins on his goiter were standing out. "I never heard of anything like this in my life!"

"Will somebody please tell me what's going on?" Angela yelled.

"We're being blackmailed, that's what's going on," Mr. Vaughn said. "We've got a second Catherine Winters here— another Indian lover. I heard you're part siwash," he said to me, "now I believe it. For my part you can just pack up and get the heck out of here right now. As far as I'm concerned this meeting it adjourned." He walked out without saying another word.

Angela had her arms crossed in front of her. She didn't say anything, but her expression spoke worlds. It was pure hate.

"Angela, you go on back to the roadhouse," Maggie said. "I'll be there in a few minutes."

When she was gone Maggie said, "You're expectin' to teach in Eagle next year I take it."

"Yes."

"If I was you I wouldn't—not if you keep that little halfbreed in the class. They got a school board there too. If they don't want you they don't have to take you. They're not gonna like it when they hear about this."

"There's not much I can do about that."

She got up. "You got gall, I'll say that much for ya—more gall than a Government mule. You're a good kid and I like ya, but I'm gonna tell ya something and I'll tell ya right to your face—don't go too far or you won't be teachin' in Eagle or anywhere else in Alaska next year. People are goin' to be writin' to the Commissioner about this, more people than you think. You're a little too interested in siwashes for your own good."

115

"I don't want any trouble, Mrs. Carew, but that little boy is entitled to—"

"Never mind what he's entitled to. Maybe you don't want trouble, but you got a peck of it right now."

"I didn't ask for it."

She buttoned up her coat. "You got it nevertheless. I'd advise you to watch your step. I'm willin' to look the other way on this. Other folks won't. You'll find that out."

She walked out without saying good-bye.

VIII

The next morning I couldn't wait for the class to arrive, wondering if they were all going to show up. If they didn't I didn't know what I was going to do. By the time it was a quarter to nine I was a nervous wreck, and I swore to God that if the whole class came, from then on I'd cause the least trouble to Him of anyone who was ever born. They all showed up though, even the Vaughn girls, and when we sang that morning you could have heard my voice clear over to Steel Creek I was so glad.

But I found out right away what Maggie meant about people not looking the other way. There was a couple named Dowles who lived in two separate cabins down near the end of the settlement. Even though they were married they hadn't talked to each other in years. The wife was a little bird-like woman and she'd loaned me a wash boiler. She scuttled in during the morning and said she needed it. I had some clothes simmering in it and I told her I'd give it to her after school if that was all right. Then about 11:30 an old sourdough who lived all alone on the other side of the creek came in and said would I mind letting him have the two chairs he'd loaned me. He was expecting company, he said. I gave him the chairs. My dishes went next, when Elvira came up to me before she went home to lunch. "My father says could you give us back the set of dishes we lent you? We need 'em for our own use." She was all

117

red and blushing and I felt sorry for her. She was the nicest one in the whole family, but every time there was some kind of a dirty job to do she was the one who was sent to do it.

I tried not to let the way people felt bother me, but it did. I wanted to get along with everybody and have them like me. But here I'd been in this place no more than ten days and already I'd made people antagonistic over what I'd thought would have been the last thing I'd find on a frontier—prejudice.

Not everybody, of course. Along with some others, Uncle Arthur and Mert Atwood were on my side. Uncle Arthur said it didn't matter that much one way or the other, but Mert was hopping mad. He was in the classroom when Elvira took the dishes home and right then and there he made me go over to Mr. Strong's store with him and bought me a whole new set. I didn't want him to because I knew he didn't have much money. None of those old-timers did. They pulled maybe five or six hundred dollars worth of gold out of the ground in a season, which just about got them by, but Mert insisted.

Joan Simpson's parents invited me over for supper a couple of nights after it happened and they thought it was funny. A young couple out of Idaho, they'd built themselves a sturdy little cabin on Forty-five Pup. A pup was just a little creek that branched off a bigger one, and Forty-Five was so named because it branched off of Chicken Creek at a forty-five degree angle. They'd made a nice life for themselves. Tom Simpson had been a carpenter and his wife Elizabeth had been a seamstress, so they were pretty self-sufficient. I spent a nice evening with them.

"Don't pay it any mind," Tom said. "That Vaughn gink is just a blowhard. I heard that when he lived up at Fort Yukon he was all for forming a branch of the Ku Klux Klan, but he couldn't get any takers."

The one person who surprised me was Mrs. Purdy. "I think you have make mush trouble for yourself, Ahnne," she said when I was over at the house one night. "Many people not like what you have done."

118

"That's not the half of it," Fred said, smiling. "I can tell you in one word what they think—ugh!"

Mrs. Purdy frowned. "I do not see the joke, Frayd. It is bad for this Indian boy to be in the school."

"Why, Mrs. Purdy?"

"Can you not see, Ahnne? He is dirty, ignorant. What you call a . . . a . . ." Her hand fidgeted in the air as she tried to think of the word.

Fred leaned his cheek on his fist. "Bad example," he said.

"Yes. Thank you. It will be different, Ahnne, if Chuck is clean, neat. He is not. He is dirty and smells bad."

"That's simple," Fred said to me. "Tell him to take a bath."

"I've been thinking of it."

"Mary's got to pack water pretty far," Fred said, "but even if she didn't she wouldn't force him if he didn't want to. Indians are kind of easy on their kids."

"Think she'd mind if I gave him one?"

"Not at all. *He* would, though, I'd bet."

Mrs. Purdy shook her head. "It would be better, Ahnne, if you leave this boy Chuck alone. People look at him and think all native children are like him."

Fred groaned. "Ah, Ma . . ."

" 'Ah, Ma,' you say. *I* say I would like Mary Angus to go back to Indian village and take her children with her."

"Yeah," Fred said drily. "You want her to go back so bad you were the first one to say I ought to bring her over some wood. Tomorrow I'll go over and haul it all back."

Mrs. Purdy didn't think it was funny. "We must help those who need our help. We cannot let her freeze. But she does not belong here and the boy does not belong in this school. It was the same with Rebekah Harrington when she came to the school. That was not good," she said to me.

"How about the old-timers then? They drop in whenever they like. If they can do it, why can't Mrs. Harrington?"

"Rebekah is different," she said. "People do not respect her."

"If they don't, then what does it matter what she does—

whether she comes to school or anything else? As far as I'm concerned, as long as she doesn't disturb the class she has as much right to sit down in that schoolroom as anyone else."

Mrs. Purdy shook her head. "Ahnne, you are young. You do not know what is in the heart of people here. *I* know. My children know. You must be careful."

She was really upset, and it made me realize something. She wanted to fit in, be like everyone else, and any native who didn't was a reflection on herself. And suddenly I realized too why Mr. Purdy acted the way he did, never saying anything when I was around and just going off by himself. He'd done the same thing tonight. He was ashamed of Mrs. Purdy, ashamed that she was Eskimo, and Mrs. Purdy knew it. It was hard to believe, but I knew down deep it was true, and I felt sorry for him.

Later on Fred walked me home. The ground was as hard as concrete and slippery with leaves. The trees were so bare now that during the day you could see the game trails running through the woods. I put the hood of my parka up right away.

"Your mother really worries about what people think of her, doesn't she?" I asked Fred.

"Well, it took her a long time to make friends around here."

"I kind of felt bad arguing with her."

"You didn't say anything wrong."

I slipped on some leaves and he grabbed me. When he let me go we were both a little self-conscious. We kept trying not to bump into each other all the rest of the way. When we reached the schoolhouse we were walking a couple of feet apart.

"Anything you need to have done in the classroom?" he asked me.

"You've done so much I don't like to ask you."

"I've got plenty of time till trapping season."

I told him I could use some cubbyholes for the kids to put their stuff in, and he said he'd come by some time in the next few days.

Chuck stayed.

How he was able to put up with the way the other kids treated him, I didn't know, but he stayed. They made life miserable for him. The only thing I couldn't blame them for was not wanting to sit near him in class. He smelled something awful. It was partly my fault, because with everybody giving him such a bad time, I couldn't bring myself to tell him he smelled as bad as Ben Norvall.

If the kids talked to him at all it was just to make fun of him. They mimicked his accent and called him Ol' Man Yiss. "Are you half-baked or half-breed?" they'd ask him. "You got a siwash squaw for a mother and a father who don't even know your name." "Go back to Louse Town," they told him. "That's where you belong."

It wouldn't have been so bad if he could have held his own with them, but when they made him mad he couldn't think fast enough in English to talk back to them. He'd just stand there getting red in the face with fury and wind up stomping off.

No matter how many times I talked to them about it, it didn't do any good. Once they even waylaid him after school and threw rocks at him, chasing him all the way home to his shack. When I mentioned it to Mr. Vaughn and Maggie Carew they said they couldn't do anything about it. Mr. Vaughn hated him so much that sometimes I even thought he put the kids up to some of the things they did.

One afternoon, after Chuck had left the room, he dragged Chuck back in by the scruff of his neck. Chuck was terrified. His pants were open and he was trying to hold them up and keep from tripping at the same time.

"Here's your star pupil," Mr. Vaughn said. "He's so civilized he doesn't know enough to use the privy. I caught him squatting out in back."

He walked out leaving Chuck standing in front of the class, his own waste all over his pants and the class laughing. He looked so pathetic I didn't know whether to burst into tears or go out and tell Mr. Vaughn exactly what I thought of him. I took Chuck into my quarters and cleaned him up as best I

121

could, but he smelled awful—worse than he had before. I told him to stay in my quarters and when school was over I did what I should have done when he first came. I got all my pots out, filled them with water and put them on the stove. Then I took him over to the store with me. There we picked out a couple of good warm flannel shirts for him, two pairs of bib overalls and some socks. He loved them, but back in my quarters, when I told him he was going to have a bath before he could put them on his jaw dropped.

"Aw no, Tisha."

"You want those new clothes?"

"Yiss."

"You want to come to school?"

"Yiss."

"Then you're going to have to take a bath."

In he went, and while he was bathing I went over to the store and picked out a couple of pairs of long underwear. The pair he had on were shot.

When he was finished and all dressed up he looked like a different boy. I let him see himself in the big piece of mirror I had. "Like yourself?" I'd given him a shampoo and combed his hair.

He smiled. "Look too much good."

"We're going to do this once a week," I said. Even with scrubbing we hadn't been able to get all the dirt off him. Some of it was just too deep. The water in the washtub was black and scummy. After he helped me throw it out in back, we sat down and had something to eat.

"What bastid, Tisha?" he asked me.

"A bastard?"

"Yiss."

I tried to think of a way to explain it without hurting his feelings, but finally I just had to come out with it. "Well, a bastard is somebody whose mother isn't married. There's nothing bad about it. As a matter of fact a lot of famous people were bastards." That didn't come out the way I meant, but Chuck didn't care.

122

"Evelyn and Jimmy call me one bastid. Say I no got fodda."

"Sure you've got a father. Everybody's got a father."

"Why them kids they no like me?" he asked me.

"They don't know you yet, Chuck. That's the way kids are sometimes. You'll just have to give them time to get used to you. When they get to know you better and see what a fine boy you are they'll like you a lot."

"You know me?"

"I think so."

"I wait. Pretty soon them kids they know me too."

When the kids saw him the next day they almost didn't recognize him. It didn't make them any friendlier to him, though. When they found out I'd given him a bath and got him some new clothes they called him teacher's pet. But he kept coming. Whatever he had to put up with it was better than just hanging around that awful shack he lived in. I thought I'd been poor when I was a kid, but he didn't have anything. The lunches he brought were the worst I ever saw —stringy rabbit that was half-cooked, or fried bannocks that were little more than flour and water. After a couple of days I started making him sandwiches.

I had to admit that I was fond of him. I couldn't help it. There was just something about him that was so good and steady that it made me furious when the kids picked on him.

He dropped over to see me on Saturday and brought his little sister with him. She was a beautiful little thing, long black hair, delicate nose and big brown inquiring eyes.

"She name Et'el," Chuck said. He tried to get her to say hello to me, but she was too afraid. She hid in back of him. "She like too much you give brode."

I cut a slice of bread I'd baked that morning, smeared it with butter and honey and gave it to her. She gobbled it down so fast I was afraid she might throw it back up. She didn't though. Two more slices disappeared the same way.

Chuck brought her into the schoolroom and showed her some of his work, his leaf book, a couple of spelling papers and a picture of a moose he had drawn.

Before the two of them left I asked him where he liked it better—the Indian village or here.

"Indian village," he said. "Kids no play me here."

"I guess you'll just have to give it more time."

"I don' know, Tisha. I wait and wait and wait for them kids know me. They never know me."

"Sooner or later they will."

He sighed. "I hope maybe you be right. I wait too long I be old man like Uncle Arthur."

IX

"Is it time yet, Teacher?"

I looked at my watch. It was one minute to twelve. "Almost. Everybody's books and papers put away?"

They all answered yes, anxious to get out. The pack train was due in some time after lunch and this time I'd told them they could have the afternoon off. The first time Mr. Strong came in I'd kept school right up to the last minute, not wanting the school board to feel I was shirking my duty. But there'd been no point to it. All the class had done was waste time.

Mr. Strong hadn't been fooling when he said that the pack train coming in was a big day for the settlement. It was the only link we had with the outside world, with newspapers and magazines, mail from friends and relatives Outside, and supplies we'd ordered from the general store in Eagle. Everybody primped up a little, maybe not in Sunday clothes, but in the best and cleanest weekday ones, and the women put on a little rouge. Outside the schoolroom it was usually quiet during the day, with maybe just the sound of somebody sawing wood or doing some hammering, or a dog barking. But when the pack train was due in the miners for miles around drifted in starting about eleven o'clock, and the dogs all over the settlement had to take note of each arrival and try to out-howl each other about it. The whole settlement livened up and the class was too excited to work. Not that I blamed them. I was pretty excited myself. Today especially, because Nancy was coming in.

From now on I wouldn't have to eat supper all alone and I'd have somebody to talk to at night. I was getting lonely. She hadn't shown up the first time Mr. Strong came in and I was afraid that maybe she or her mother had changed her mind about her staying with me, but Mr. Strong had told me she'd be out with him on this trip.

"School's out for the day!" I yelled, and a minute later the classroom was empty.

The pack train didn't come in until late—almost three. By then it had started to snow again and it looked as though it might stick. Fred had come in to pick up his family's mail and he was playing softball with some of the kids, batting out easy flies to them. I was playing too, when all of a sudden the dogs all over the settlement began to bark and howl, raising a racket in their kennels. It meant that Mr. Strong was pretty near. We were having a good time, so we kept playing while everybody who'd come in from the creeks started emptying out of the roadhouse and others came straggling out of their cabins. I yelled for Fred to pop one over to me, and he hit one that went over my head. The ball hit the side of the Vaughn's storm entry just as Mr. Vaughn came out. He picked it up and the kids started yelling and waving for him to throw it to them, but he didn't. He walked over to me with it, his mackinaw collar turned up to hide his big goiter.

"What are all these kids doing out of school?" he asked me.

He knew as well as I did why they weren't in school, but he couldn't pass up the chance to let me have it.

"I gave them the afternoon off," I said.

"Who says it's up to you when they should have a holiday?"

"I'm sorry, Mr. Vaughn, I didn't think there was anything wrong in it."

"I suppose you don't see anything wrong in playing with them like a wild Indian either. I've seen you do it during recess." He turned to Angela Barrett and a few others who'd come up. "You ever see a teacher carry on that way?"

126

"Not in any school I ever went to," Angela said.

"Not in any I ever went to either," Mr. Vaughn said. "You'd better start watching your step."

I turned beet red, too embarrassed to say a word. He didn't like me and he didn't make any bones about it. Merton Atwood had come up, the black flap he'd made for his yachtsman's cap pulled down around his ears.

"What're you pickin' on the girl for?" he asked Mr. Vaughn.

"I'm trying to get her to act like a teacher."

Mert came to my defense. "What do you mean, act like? Girl's the best schoolmarm this place ever saw."

"The next time you want to take time off," Mr. Vaughn said, "you get permission from the school board."

Mert spoke right up again. "What're you talkin' about? Ever since I can remember, these kids been gettin' the afternoon off when the pack train's due in."

"You mind your own business. No little snotnose is going to decide how to run things here. We were here long before you arrived," he said, pointing a finger at me, "and we'll be here after you're gone. You're too darn smart for your own good."

"You don't have any right to speak to me that way, Mr. Vaughn."

"I'll speak to you any way I darn please." He pointed that finger at me again. "One more word out of you and I'll smack all that smartness right out of you . . . Go on," he challenged me, "let's see how fresh you can be now."

He was really working himself into a rage, and I began to feel weak in the legs. I was embarrassed too. Everybody was watching, and more and more people kept drifting over from the post office to see what was going on. I didn't know what to do. I didn't dare try to reason with him because he'd have slapped me as soon as I opened my mouth. I was even too scared to move.

Fred's hand touched my arm. "C'mon, Anne."

He started to lead me away and I went along willingly.

"Good thing your boyfriend has more brains than you have,"

Mr. Vaughn sneered. "I was just getting ready to take you over my knee."

He kind of sniggered, and Angela Barrett laughed too.

That did it. Fred whirled around. "You won't lay a finger on her," he said.

Mr. Vaughn looked as if he'd just heard something he couldn't believe. "What did you say?"

He walked over to us with blood in his eye. Fred was still holding the baseball bat and he drew it back without saying a word. All of a sudden I knew he'd use it if he had to. I heard Mert say, "Good boy, Fred," and I didn't know whether I felt more proud of Fred or scared of Mr. Vaughn.

"Are you threatening me?" Mr. Vaughn said.

"You touch her or me and I'll let you have it," Fred said.

He looked Mr. Vaughn straight in the eye when he said it and Mr. Vaughn knew he meant it. It made him swell up so I thought he'd burst his goiter.

He had a cruel wide mouth and teeth like one of those fish that swim way down in the deeps. He was a full head taller than Fred and he'd have chewed Fred up right then and there if he could. have. He was afraid of that bat, though.

"You dark-faced half-breed animal," Mr. Vaughn said. It seems to me I've seen your face around here an awful lot lately." He was still holding the ball, and suddenly he drew back and threw it. Fred ducked, but he didn't have to. It went wild.

Fred looked him straight in the eye. "Get out of here," he said.

My brain started working, and I found my tongue. "Mr. Vaughn, I didn't think anyone would think it was wrong for me to give the kids the afternoon off," I said. "I'll be glad to talk about it with the school board if you want me to."

That took the wind out of his sails. He gave Fred a contemptuous look just to show he was too puny to bother with, then he went on over to the post office. Fred and I drifted over along with everybody else and I tried to act as if nothing had happened, but I was so upset that the whole time we waited for the pack train I could hardly say a word to anybody. Even if he didn't like me he had no call to say what he did to me, especially in front of the class and everybody else, and he certainly didn't have any call to say what he did to Fred.

I felt a little better as soon as I saw Nancy. She didn't act too enthusiastic, though. All she gave me was a curt "How do." She gave even less than that to the people who said hello to her. She just mumbled something and then looked away. I figured she felt strange. As soon as she was settled down, she'd probably be more friendly.

Inside my quarters, while Nancy put away her things I sat down and read a note from her mother that Mr. Strong had handed to me. Along with a few other things Mrs. Prentiss had to say, she wrote that Nancy was usually sensible, "but keep an eye on her. Don't let her go off to any of those miner's cabins by herself. She's inclined to be lazy and stubborn. You make her toe the mark. I've warned her to be obedient and help out all she can. Otherwise you'll send her home and I'll whip the daylights out of her. Don't be afraid to tell her that." She'd also had second thoughts about her offer to pay me. "I heard you don't have an outfit," the note ended. "Since it won't cost anything for Nancy's room maybe we can work out something where I send you some grub for her keep."

I put the note in the stove, not thinking one thing or the other about it. Once I had a little boy in my class whose father wrote me that the boy was a liar and a thief, and he turned out to be one of my smartest and best pupils. So I knew better than to judge somebody from what somebody else said.

She didn't have much with her, just a few pairs of bib overalls and a couple of washed-out old dresses that looked as old-fashioned as the ones in Mr. Strong's store. After we found a place for everything I told her how much I'd looked forward to having her with me. She didn't say anything to that. Aside from being so lonely, I went on, the school was taking up so much time that I couldn't keep up with all the chores. "I guess it wouldn't be so bad," I said, "if there was running water.

I never realized how much water a person used until I started packing it up from the creek—water for washing clothes, for washing yourself, for cooking, washing dishes. That's all I seem to do all day is pack water and then dump it out." I started to laugh when I told her about the first bath I took. It was a major undertaking. Besides a five-gallon pot I'd had to borrow from Maggie Carew, the top of the cookstove had been crammed with every pot I owned. But when I poured the water from them into the washtub, even with cramping myself down in it, it came up about five inches. After I was finished I felt as dirty as when I started. On top of that it was another major job to dump all the water out back. "Ever since then I've settled mostly for sponge baths."

She didn't find anything funny about that, so I asked her about her schooling. "What grade have you gone through?"

"Eighth."

"Without being able to read?"

"I can read somewhat."

I gave her the nearest book at hand, a fifth-grade reader. Opening it, she studied it for so long that I thought she wasn't going to read. When she finally did she spat the words out like pits, but she did well enough.

"You read fine," I said. "I don't see why you need me."

"I know most of the words," she answered.

"That's what I'm saying. You read pretty well."

"You don't understand," she said. "I know how to read this book 'cause my ma tutored me with it."

"How long ago was that?"

"Two years ago."

She saw that I still didn't understand what she was getting at.

"I can only read," she said, "if somebody reads it to me first and shows me the words. Don't you see? My ma read this to me."

"But that was two years ago. That's a long time."

"I studied with it for a whole year," she said. "Try me with another book."

130

I showed her a book of fairy tales. "Have you ever read this?"

She shook her head. I opened the book to the beginning of a story. She studied the page for almost a minute before she began to read. Later I realized that she had guessed at the first few words. " 'Once . . . upon a . . . time . . .' " She paused before she went on, and what came from her next was gibberish. ". . . Three . . . was . . . a . . . title . . . tar . . ." I looked over her shoulder. "There was a little tailor," the words read.

She went on, the rest of it just as senseless, until finally she gave up. "I don't know what I'm reading," she said. I had her try again, but it was the same. She even mistook one letter for another—an *l* for a *t*, a *b* for a *d*. When I questioned her I found out she didn't know what a consonant or a vowel was, nor had she ever memorized the alphabet. To her a word was just a bunch of letters written down in a certain order. She didn't know that the letters made up syllables and that each syllable had a sound.

Now I understood what she meant when she said she could read something only after somebody read it to her first. She was able to memorize the key words, and guess at the rest. I'd never seen anything like it.

Her teachers had pushed her through to the eighth grade, I guessed, figuring it wouldn't do any harm and would make her feel good. She couldn't go any further, though, because in order to get out of the eighth grade she had to pass the territorial examination. And she wasn't able to read it. After quizzing her for a while I found that she had learned her school work pretty well. She was smart, there wasn't any doubt about it.

"We'll enroll you tomorrow morning," I said.

"I don't want to be enrolled," she said tightly.

I had to prod her before she told me the reason: she felt she should have been out of the grades already and couldn't face the idea of failing again. She became so upset that I agreed not to enroll her even though she would attend classes like the other pupils. At night, I promised her, I'd give her any extra help she might need.

For the first week I blessed Mr. Strong for advising me to take her. I'd fallen way behind in all my cleaning, washing and ironing, but Nancy pitched in with the chores so willingly that inside of a few days my quarters were spick-and-span. She did most of the cooking too, and even took the job of keeping the fire going. I didn't know what I'd have done without her, especially when it came to water. The snow that had started on the day she came kept up until it was two feet deep and the creek was running thick with slush ice. Then all of a sudden the temperature dropped to thirty below and the creek froze up. She was one step ahead, though, because she'd already piled snow high alongside the door, and there was our water supply. I didn't care much for the taste of it. It was flat, until Nancy dumped oatmeal in the barrel, and that improved it.

"We'll have to go easy on the water now," she told me.

"I thought I was going easy on it before," I said.

She said no, I'd have to go even easier. The trick, she showed me, was not to throw any water away until it was thoroughly used—first for personal washing, then for clothes. If necessary it could be used a third time to scrub floors. It didn't seem very sanitary to me at first, but after packing in snow and ice a few times I stopped worrying about hygiene. She also pointed out to me that Maggie Carew was not only shorting me on each cord of wood she had contracted to supply for the school, but that half of it was green instead of dry. "That's why the stove smokes so much."

After the first week or so problems began to come up between us. I'd told her that before she could learn to read she was going to have to learn how to recognize all her letters, printed and written, and learn the sounds they had. She buckled down at first, memorized the letters in no time, and even started to write simple three-letter words. But when a couple of the older kids saw what she was doing they made fun of her. That ended that. She told me she wasn't going to work in the

132

classroom any more, at least not on her reading and writing. I let her work in my quarters on those two things, but I wanted her to join the class for discussions, arithmetic, field trips and everything else. She'd sit in class, but she wouldn't say anything unless I called on her. She was bored. Pretty soon she wasn't even completing her reading and writing assignments. Either they were done sloppily or not at all. When I asked her what the matter was she said that she didn't understand why she needed all the drills I was giving her in syllables and sounding out words. She wanted to learn to read and write, and she couldn't see that she was doing so. I told her that she'd have to start from the beginning. "I know you think you're not getting anywhere right now, but once you catch on you'll be reading in no time."

It didn't do any good. She just didn't seem to be interested in learning the way I could teach her. If I asked her why she hadn't finished something, she'd say she didn't understand it, and no amount of explaining could get her to.

I started to think that maybe she didn't like me, but she didn't seem to like anybody else either—especially the old-timers. They'd been a big help to the class with our project, and had invited us over to their cabins when we went out on our field trips. We learned a lot from them about how they lived in the old days. Mert Atwood even showed us how they used to make butter. He brought over some caribou horns that he'd sawed up into lengths almost a foot long. We put them in a big pot and boiled them for almost three days, then we took them out and let the water cool. After a couple of hours, just as he said it would, a couple of inches of white butter formed at the top. It tasted good, too.

But Nancy didn't take to the old-timers. The only person she did like was Joe Temple. One time she went over to his cabin and stayed there for quite a while. I hadn't even known she'd been there until Uncle Arthur mentioned it to me. I spoke with her about it and asked her not to do it again. She said she wouldn't, but she was surly about it.

Mert came over after school one day, and after he'd visited

with us for a while he took off his yachtsman's cap and removed an envelope from it.

"Got this here letter th'other day," he said to me, "but I'm shipwrecked if I can find my glasses. Can't read a thing without 'em. Maybe you wouldn't mind readin' it for me."

I knew he couldn't read and didn't want to admit it, so I told him I'd be glad to. When I was finished Mert thanked me and put the letter back in the envelope.

Innocently, he asked Nancy how she was coming along with her reading.

"Heck of a lot better'n you ever did with yours," she said belligerently.

Stung by the remark, Mert smiled tolerantly. I tried to make conversation after that, but it didn't do any good. "Well," Mert said after a couple of minutes, "time to lift anchor and shove off."

"You really hurt that old man's feelings, Nancy," I said after he was gone.

"Well he hurt mine too."

"He was only trying to be sociable. He didn't mean anything."

"I didn't ask him to talk to me, didn't ask him to come here either."

"Nobody asked him. He just came because he's lonely and he likes to talk with us."

"Well let'm be lonely some place else. He's like all them other old windbags, dirty and smelly and always braggin' about how they're gonna get rich some day and the things they're gonna do when they are. They're not gonna do any of them things ever. They're just wastin' time jawin' and I'm not about to let'm waste my time."

She didn't like it either when I gave Chuck a bath, acting as if he was just about the lowest thing she ever saw. She didn't say anything the first time, but the second time she said that we ought to make him haul in the snow himself. "Unless you fancy waitin' on siwashes," she said.

I tried to kid her. "Ah, come on, he's only a little boy."

"You can't even turn around here without trippin' over 'im."

"He likes it here."

"Between him and all them other kids you'd think this was a roadhouse."

She didn't like the idea that the kids were always trooping in and out. Even after school they'd come over sometimes to work on something they hadn't finished in class or to play in the school room. I didn't mind it at all, but I could see how it would get on her nerves, so I tried to discourage them from coming into my quarters and get them to stay in the school-room instead.

But things kept going from bad to worse between us. I'd heard about some of the feuds that people who shared cabins sometimes got into and I'd always thought they were funny—like Harry Dowles and his wife moving into separate cabins and never talking to each other. I'd found out that even Uncle Arthur and Mert Atwood had been cabin-mates until one winter when they had an argument. They split everything up evenly and what they couldn't split they cut in half just for spite. They even cut their stove in half, Ben Norvall had told me, and the two of them nearly froze to death.

Now I could understand how that could happen. When you lived in close quarters with someone and you weren't getting along, everything that person did annoyed you. Sometimes it was all you could do to keep your temper. That's what was happening with Nancy and me. We finally got to the point where she wasn't even saying good morning unless I said it first.

A couple of weeks after she arrived Mary Angus came over one Saturday to bring me a pair of moccasins she'd made for me. She brought Chuck and Ethel with her. She didn't look well at all. Her cheeks were all flushed and there were dark circles under her eyes. I introduced her to Nancy, but Nancy just sat where she was at the kitchen table, sipping some hot cocoa, and hardly even looked up. Mary didn't want to, but I made her sit down and have some tea while I tried on the moccasins. As soon as she did Nancy got right up and went over to the couch.

The moccasins were beautiful. They were winter moccasins, with good sturdy moosehide below the ankle and caribou with the fur turned out up to the knee. She'd beaded them with dyed porcupine quills and trimmed the tops with rabbit fur. They fit perfectly too, but after I took a look at the beat-up moccasins on her own feet I didn't feel so good.

The three of them didn't stay long. While they were there, I gave Chuck his favorite—a slice of my "brode," as he called it, smeared with butter and honey. I gave one to Ethel too.

As soon as she bit into it Chuck started to bawl her out in Indian. She stopped with her mouth full, looking at him wide-eyed, while he pointed to me. Finally looking up at me she said something like "Oo." Chuck patted her. "Ver' good. She not got good manners, Tisha. I teach her say T'ank you."

"I'm proud of you, Chuck," I said. I was too. I'd been teaching him to say thank you when somebody handed him something or did something for him.

After they all left Nancy said, "You shouldn'ta done that, Teacher." I'd told her a couple of times she could call me Anne, but she wouldn't.

"Done what?" I asked her.

"Had 'er to the table."

"What was wrong with it?"

"People around here don't even let siwashes into the house much less sit down with 'em to the table."

"Then they ought to be ashamed of themselves."

She didn't say anything to that and I was glad she didn't. I was mad enough so that we'd have had a stem-winder, and things were bad enough between us already.

We both started to get petty. It was her job to see to it that we always had enough wood and water on hand. But when we ran low on them a couple of times, I had to remind her. After the second time she said it might be a good idea for us to take turns doing it.

"I've been leaving it to you," I told her, "because I figure you can do it better than I can." I also figured I was making up for it by tutoring her at night, but I didn't mention that.

136

She didn't say anything, but after I had to remind her a couple more times I got the hint. Finally we took turns washing the linens, sweeping, doing the dishes and everything else.

I hadn't planned it that way at all. I was in the schoolroom almost all day and I'd sometimes be working long after supper planning lessons and activities. I'd thought that Nancy would help me out the way I'd helped out Miss Ivy. But it wasn't working out that way. I had as much to do as I had before, and besides that I had to put up with someone I liked less every day. When I'd passed through her parents' roadhouse it was clean as a whistle, and so was Nancy at first. But after a while she was leaving her old dirty clothes hanging on nails or over a chair and didn't bother to wash them until they smelled as gamey as Ben Norvall's. If I mentioned it to her she'd put them all in a pile and keep them out of sight, but she didn't wash them any more often than she did before.

I mentioned the situation to Mr. Strong one day while we were going over the accounts in his store. "It's too bad," he said. "I was hoping that maybe getting away from her family would be of some help to her."

"What's the matter with her?"

"She's simply been worked too hard too long, madam. She's a good girl, but she's never had a chance. Her mother's been driving that girl ever since I can remember—made a slave out of her."

"If I could just get her to talk . . ."

"Can't get a word out of anyone in that family. All I can tell you is, she hasn't had it easy. You saw that roadhouse her folks run, the nice way they keep it. Well, they do it by making those kids of theirs hop. Nancy practically raised her two brothers by herself, and when she wasn't taking care of them she was working the garden or making beds or doing something else—but look, that's none of your affair. Send her on home if you can't take it."

I didn't want to do that if I could help it, especially after what he said. It made me understand why being able to read was so important to her, why even though she wasn't learning she still hung on. "I *gotta* learn, Teacher," she told me once. It was the only time she'd ever opened up. "I gotta pass that eighth-grade exam. If I do my mother promised I could go to high school in Fairbanks." It was the only chance she had to get away from her family.

But no matter how hard I worked with her it didn't do any good. I started to get surly myself. Everybody else in the class was working hard and having a good time, but Nancy couldn't seem to become interested in anything we were doing. She remained an outsider, never raising her hand to offer an answer, not wanting to answer even when I called on her. The class knew that I was tutoring her and they were jealous of the fact that she was living with me. They called her Miss Dumbbell and mimicked her by putting on sour faces when her back was turned. Once when I asked Jimmy Carew to read aloud, he did an imitation of her—slumping down in his seat and staring hard at his book, which he held upside down.

The situation came to a head one afternoon close to dismissal when Nancy rose from her seat, went over to Jimmy and smacked him hard across the ear. Then she walked into my quarters, slamming the door behind her. Stunned, Jimmy fanned his smarting ear and tried to hold back the tears. Then he put on a surly expression that made the other children laugh. Asking the class to be quiet, I went in to talk to Nancy, but she was already out the front door and didn't stop when I called her.

It was well after supper when she came back, leaving the door open a few more seconds than necessary while she wiped some mud off her shoes. I'd propped a piece of mirror on the table and was sitting by the stove marcelling my hair. There was going to be a dance in the schoolroom the next night and I wanted to look my best. I asked her where she'd been.

"Over to Joe Temple's."

"By yourself?"

"Uh-huh."

"You think that was a good idea?"

She shrugged and started to take off her parka.

138

"We're low on water," I said. Ordinarily I'd have gotten it myself, but I was feeling mean.

She made two trips, each time leaving the door ajar and letting the cold in. When she was done she sat down on the couch and stared into space, her eyes occasionally following the waving iron.

"I asked you once before, Nancy, not to go over to Joe's place alone."

"We just talked."

"I'm sure of that. But while you're here you're my responsibility. If I ask you not to do something there's a reason for it."

We were silent for a few moments, then Nancy said, "He's got Mary Angus for that, if *that's* what you're worried about."

"Why did you have to slap Jimmy?" I said, changing the subject.

" 'Cause he was taking me off, been taking me off for three days now."

"You could have told me. I'd've made him stop it."

"No need to now. He won't be making faces anymore."

I decided not to put the decision off any longer.

Finished with the iron, I started putting on a hair net, trying to think of a nice way to say what I was going to, but I couldn't. "Nancy, I think we've both tried as hard as we can and we're not getting anywhere."

She sat very still, her eyes meeting mine for a moment, then she stared down at the floor.

"Maybe it would be a good idea," I went on, "if you went home for ten days or so, give us both a rest. How would that be?"

She didn't answer. We both knew that if she left it would be permanent. An hour later I was studying my eighth-grade arithmetic, trying to figure out division of fractions, when she broke the silence. "You don't like me one bit, do you?"

"That's not true," I lied.

"Then why you sending me home?"

"I don't think we're doing each other any good."

"Just 'cause I slapped Jimmy Carew."

139

"No, that's not it."

"Well, then what is it? 'Cause I won't do all the scrubbin' and cleanin' you want?"

"Nancy—"

"Well, that's not what I come here for," she went on, deliberately using poor grammar. "I do enough a that at home. I come here so you could teach me to read and you sure ain't done it."

"No, I *ain't*," I said, beginning to lose my temper, "and the way you go around here I'll never be able to. Not the way you are. You're so busy being angry, you haven't got room for anything else inside of you." Nancy stared at me in surprise while the words poured out of me. "You've lived in this part of the country all your life, but when people stop by here to visit with us you won't say a word to them. You won't even look at them half the time. How do you think that makes them feel?"

"What'm I supposed to say to 'em?"

"Anything that comes into your head. It's better than glaring at them. And if you can't think of anything then just give 'em a smile. You've got a beautiful smile when you want to use it, you've got a beautiful face if you'd just wash it once in a while." I stopped, sorry I'd said as much as I did. I hadn't meant to. I calmed down. "When you came out here, Nancy, I was really glad to see you. I needed all the help you could give me, and you gave me a lot—at first. Now you won't do anything—you won't make the bed, you won't pack water, you won't even change your clothes unless I ask you. And when I do ask you to do something you look at me as though I'm being mean."

"My mother ain't payin' for me to cook and clean," she said stoically. "She's payin' for you to tutor me."

It was my turn to be surprised. "Nancy, your mother isn't paying me anything."

"What are you talkin' about? I heard 'er tell you when you first came through that she'd pay you for takin' me."

"Yes, she did. But I sent her a note back on the day you arrived. I told her she could forget about paying me."

140

She fought against believing me at first, but when I assured her it was true she went pale.

"Why'd you do that?" she said. Her voice seemed to come from far away.

"I was glad to have the company," I said honestly. "I was afraid being here all by myself." She looked so miserable that I wished I could think of something to console her. "I guess I should have told you," I said finally.

There was coffee in the coffeepot and I asked her if she wanted some. She shook her head. After I poured a cup for myself I sat down at the table again, feeling terrible.

"Nancy, if you'd like to stay, maybe we could try again."

She got up and went to the window. She slowly rubbed some moisture from a pane and stared out into the darkness.

Then she cried for a long time.

X

From then on Nancy changed. She hadn't been one to show her feelings much before we had the argument, and she didn't make any big display after it, but I could see the difference in her right away. Up to then I almost had to drag her out of bed in the morning. After that she was up when I was and sometimes even before. She was a dynamo, cleaning and washing, taking care of herself and doing so many chores that half a dozen times I had to tell her to slow down. She wouldn't, though. The way she acted towards me you'd have thought that my letting her stay with me without getting paid for it made me some kind of a heroine.

I kept complimenting her all over the place and she just glowed. She hardly ever looked me straight in the eye, and she wouldn't smile because of the cavities in her front teeth. I could tell she was pleased, though.

After a few days we sat down and had a good talk, something we'd never done before. I told her I appreciated everything she was doing, but I didn't want her wearing herself out. She said I wasn't to worry about that. "I just want to show you I appreciate what you did for me," she said, picking at some loose threads on her overalls. It was a habit she had that used to drive me crazy, always giving her attention to something else when you talked with her, as if she didn't really care what you were saying. She did, though. She just didn't know how to show it.

I tried to tell her I didn't do any more for her than Miss Ivy had done for me—a heck of a lot less, really, because I needed her help—but she wouldn't hear of it.

"You did more for me than anybody in my whole life," she insisted, "and I'm not forgetting it."

"If you really feel that way there's one way you *could* pay me back," I said.

"What's that?"

"Be a little more friendly with the kids in class."

"Won't do any good. They don't take to me."

"They would if you gave them the chance. They're a little afraid of you." I told her that she could act as sort of my assistant, like a helping teacher.

"Some helping teacher," she said, pulling out a thread she'd been worrying, "I can't even read."

"Nancy, you *can* read. All you have to do is give up that old crazy system you made up. Sit down and learn how to break words up into sounds and I guarantee you'll be reading inside of a month. Then you'll really be my assistant."

She didn't promise anything, and I didn't expect too much, so I was really surprised when she not only buckled down to work, but in her own way tried to be nicer to the other kids. Before, whenever she was in class she wouldn't budge for anybody. Now she started getting up to close the stove door whenever the classroom became too hot, or open it when it was chilly. When a few of the "books" the children had made started falling apart, she fixed them. She took them over to the roadhouse and sewed the pages together on Maggie Carew's machine, then shoved them at the kids with a gruff, "Here, I fixed 'em for ya." She was tops in arithmetic too, so one morning I asked her if she'd help Jimmy with his multiplication tables. She and Jimmy hadn't said a word to each other since she'd slapped him and neither of them looked too keen about the idea. I sent them into my quarters to work, and when I glanced through the door a few minutes later she was tutoring him as if she'd done it all her life.

After she helped Jimmy the class was less leery of her. She

even made up a game—a multiplication clock, she called it. It was a clock made out of cardboard with one hand on it, and she'd move the hand from one number to the next while the kids multiplied by two, or three, or five. After a while, we used a stopwatch to see how fast each of the children could do it.

She really blossomed. It didn't take more than a couple of weeks before some of the kids were taking a shine to her. During recess, when it was too cold for the little ones like Joan and Willard to go out, I let her supervise the older kids outside while the little ones played in the schoolroom. In private I told her that I'd appreciate it if she'd watch out for Chuck. The other kids didn't pick on him as much as they had when he first came, but once in a while they still reminded him he wasn't as good as they were, especially the Vaughn twins.

She watched out for him better than I could. During one recess I heard him start to cry outside and I went to the door. I opened it just in time to see Nancy give Eleanor Vaughn a shove that made her sit down on her behind fast. She'd have done the same with Evelyn if Evelyn hadn't danced out of the way. They must have washed Chuck's face with snow because it was all red and wet. None of them saw me, so I figured I'd let Nancy handle it. She was tougher than the two of them put together.

"You keep your hands off this kid from here on," Nancy said to Evelyn, putting a mitten on Chuck's shoulder.

"Since when you sticking up for siwashes?" Eleanor said, getting up.

"I'm not stickin' up for 'em anymore 'n I'd stick up for you," Nancy answered. "The teacher says you keep your hands off, so keep your hands off."

"You don't have any right to tell us what to do," Eleanor sneered.

"That's right," Evelyn said.

"I'm not tellin' you what to do. I'm just tellin' you that if you lay your hands on this kid again I'm gonna bash your head in."

They left Chuck alone from then on.

144

I guessed I was never so happy in my life as around that time. Everything just seemed the way I'd dreamed it would be—the settlement and all the country around hushed under a thick white blanket, the snow dry enough so you could walk around in moccasins and never get wet. Now I realized what the North was really like. It was made for winter, because winter was when everything went on. You could ski any place you wanted to and get there twice as fast and twice as easily as you could before there was snow. People went out and brought in the trees they'd cut for firewood and left lying until they could use sleds to haul them. The whole country just opened right up. You could hear somebody talking on the trail half a mile away, or dropping a pan on the stove a mile from the settlement. It was so quiet and open and free that it was like being let out of prison. It put everybody in good spirits and they went around looking the way the country did—clean and fresh.

Came lunchtime, the class was usually out of the room like a shot, and fifteen minutes later, after bolting their lunch, the kids were outside with sleds and skis. I learned how to ski in no time at all. I'd done a little when I was a kid, but that was just with barrel staves. It wasn't anything like real skiing. Once I learned I was as anxious as the class to get out and slide the hills.

The one thing I would have liked to learn was ski-joring— holding onto a string of dogs and letting them pull you—but I wasn't any good at it. Fred was expert at it and he tried to teach me a couple of times, but the dogs kept pulling me off balance. Finally, on the second try, he told me he was going to work something out where that wouldn't happen. "You be ready next Saturday morning," he said when I asked him what it was. "I'll be by around ten."

Almost on the dot I heard him call my name, and when I opened the door he was out there on his own skis, waiting. He'd brought his favorite lead dog, Pancake, and two others. "You ready?"

It wasn't that cold out, so I threw on a canvas parka with a warm sweater underneath. Outside on the porch I started to take my skis, but he said leave them. Then I saw what he'd done. He'd fitted an extra pair of straps on his own skis so I could stand behind him.

"You think it'll work?" I asked him.

"I don't know," he said. "I never tried it."

Nancy watched from the doorway while I got on, and I had the barest second to wave to her before he yelled "Mush!" and we were off.

We didn't go too fast at first because the dogs weren't able to dig into the packed-down snow of the settlement. Once we were on the trail, though, we speeded up. Then Fred began to sing *Sweet Rosie O'Grady* to them and they began to pull like sixty. Everybody had a different way of making sled dogs pull. Some used a whip. Others, like Angela Barrett, yelled and cursed at them all the time. Her dogs were so used to it that they wouldn't pull unless she swore at them, so you could hear her coming from a half-mile away. Fred sang to his and they loved it.

"No singing!" I yelled.

"Why not?"

"We're going too fast."

"We haven't even started."

"Fred, we'll fall!"

"No we won't!"

I held onto his parka as tight as I could, his skis crunching under us. The dogs were thirty feet ahead, the full length of the lead rope. If they geed or hawed all of a sudden I knew I was going to be dumped.

But I hung on. Skiing was fun, but it wasn't anywhere near as exciting as this.

After a while I started to congratulate myself. I was doing pretty well. I leaned into turns easily and could key my movements to Fred's, as if we were on a bicycle built for two. We must have gone half a mile before I got so cocky I didn't look where we were going.

The trail took a sharp turn. Fred leaned to the left, I dragged him off to the right, and we went flying.

146

Luckily we ended up in a drift, laughing. We didn't bother to get up right away, just lay back where we fell. "You all right?" Fred asked.

"Perfect. Maybe I'll take a nap." I propped myself up on my elbows, watching the dogs. They'd taken a spill too, and a couple of them were tangled in the lead lines. They were well trained, though, and didn't get excited about it. Pancake was a beauty, brown mask over a gray wolf face and slanted ice-blue eyes. Panting, he went to Fred as though he'd done something wrong, his tail down and his rear end moving from side to side.

"Look at that. He thinks it was his fault," Fred said. He sat up and started untangling the rope.

"Well, whose fault was it?"

"Yours."

"I knew I'd be blamed."

"Better than blaming Pancake." He rubbed the dog's head. "He'll feel bad."

"How about me?"

"You can take it."

I picked up a gob of snow and tossed it at him. He blocked it easily and it went to powder, then shoveling up a bigger gob, he hefted it high in the air. It plopped down on the hood of my parka and most of it stayed there.

"You look like a tree," he said.

"Nicest thing you ever said to me."

I looked up at the blue sky. It was still early, but the sun was low, skimming the distant mountain tops and sending out long blue shadows from the trees.

I watched Fred while he straightened out the harness. He'd been out on the traplines the week before and he was brown as a coffee bean. I'd really liked being so close to him on the skis and I wondered if he felt the same thing about me. I had a feeling he did. Even if he did, though, he didn't show it. It was the way he always acted with me. Careful. So far all he'd done was hold my hand once when we were alone. We never talked about it, but I knew full well why he was being so careful. He'd swallowed a lot of that halfbreed baloney people around here

147

were always slicing and it made him keep his distance from me, as if he wasn't as good as the next boy and I was something special. If he'd been pure white he'd have acted a whole lot different.

I wished there was some way I could show him how much I liked him, but I didn't know how. I'd tried just about everything.

The last time I was over at his house I'd let him beat me at carom checkers, and when we talked politics lately I let him convince me he was right even though he was a Democrat and I was for the Republicans. I'd even told him all about the junky places I'd grown up in, and how one summer I'd worked as a hired girl on a ranch, just so he wouldn't think my being a teacher made me a member of the aristocracy, but he still kept his distance.

I didn't know what more I could do. When I used to live with Miss Ivy she told me that boys didn't like it when a girl ran after them. There were ways to show a boy that you favored him, she said, ways you could encourage him—only she never told me what those ways were. I figured I'd given him all the encouragement I could, short of coming right out and being bold about it.

Fred got up now, brushed himself off and gave me a hand. Then we were off again.

A couple of minutes later we were in sight of Mary Angus' place.

There was smoke coming from the stovepipe, which meant she was all right. A couple of weeks ago when I'd seen her on the trail near Fred's house, I'd been scared she might die. She'd been pretty far away and it was almost dark. She was pulling a hand sled, and her little girl was with her. They were probably heading out for her trap line. We waved to each other, but before she went on she doubled over, coughing. A minute later when I crossed the place where she'd stopped I saw there was blood spattered all over the snow. Every time I thought about it I felt as sick as I did then. I'd written to the minister in Eagle to ask him if he could collect some food for her from the people there and he'd said he would. The Purdys saw to it that she had enough wood too, but there wasn't much else anybody could do. For a second I wondered if we should stop and see how she and her little girl were, but I decided against it. I'd just be bothering her.

A little later Fred and I were close to Lost Chicken when we started back for home. It was getting dark already, so we took a short cut across some fresh snow, figuring we'd pick up the trail again just past Uncle Arthur's place. The dogs had to break trail, leaping forward like fish breaking water, and it slowed them down, so we walked.

We found Uncle Arthur doing some "drifting" a little distance from his cabin. It was back-breaking work, especially for an old man like him, and he'd taken his parka off. He was all gnarled and twisted up from rheumatism and he must have been about seventy, but it didn't stop him from working with a pick and shovel. They were lying beside the prospect hole he'd dug, along with his coat.

Inside the hole, which was about two feet deep now, he'd piled kindling and logs. He'd put a match to them and was climbing out of the hole just as we got there. The fire would thaw the frozen ground so he'd be able to dig down a little further. Eventually he'd dig down to paydirt—anywhere from twenty to forty feet—and if he got some good pans out of it he'd spend the summer mining the surrounding ground. If the hole didn't pan out he'd prospect somewhere else.

"How you be, Missis?" he asked me.

"Fine, Uncle Arthur. You enjoying your cornflakes?"

"Hate cornflakes," he said. "Gave'm to Mert Atwood. That dumb bunny'll eat anything."

I knew he'd say that, but I couldn't resist asking him. Now that Mr. Strong was able to use his big sled he'd finally brought out the corn flakes Uncle Arthur had ordered—six cartons of them. But Uncle Arthur hadn't really wanted them. Like a lot of other people in Chicken, Uncle Arthur felt that Mr. Strong was making too much money on his mail contract, so they ordered as many bulky things by parcel post as they could.

The more space Mr. Strong had to give to parcel post, the less he had to use for freighting in the more profitable items that he sold in his store or that people ordered from Eagle. Uncle Arthur had hit on the perfect item to annoy him—cheap, bulky, and light enough so that the parcel-post rate was cheap, too. Now he had all the other old-timers ordering them. But Mr. Strong got back at them by not bringing them out until after the freeze-up, when he had plenty of room on his sled.

Uncle Arthur picked up his coat from the snow and put it on, throwing his head back so his beard wouldn't get caught as he buttoned up.

"Gonna have penmanship drill tomorrow?"

"Sure."

He never seemed to get tired of it, and if I didn't have it on the day he showed up he sulked and complained.

"That the way the two of you come out," he asked Fred, "on one pair of skis?"

"Yes."

"Makes it pretty cozy, I guess, but I don't know if it's somethin' the kiddies ought to see. Doesn't set a good example, if you know what I mean."

I wished he hadn't said that. It made Fred and me uncomfortable. It was hard for me to figure him out. Sometimes I thought he liked me. Other times, like now, he'd be cantankerous.

Fred talked mining with him for a couple of minutes, then we left. I knew he was still bothered by what Uncle Arthur had said. Instead of the two of us ski-joring out, he slung the skis over his shoulder and held the dogs on the lead.

Once we were out of sight I took his arm.

"When are you going to take me on that snow picnic?" He'd promised to a couple of times already.

"I was thinking we'd go in a couple of weeks."

"Why so long?"

"Have to go out on the trap line in a few days."

I was disappointed. He'd be gone for about a week. What was worse was that he hated everything about trapping. Most

150

of the time the animal was still alive when he got to it. Hissing and snarling with fear, it had to be clubbed to death, then skinned before the carcass froze. He'd told me all about it. The only reason he did it was because his family needed the money.

"I wish you didn't have to go," I said.

"Me too. I'm going to miss you."

"Will you?"

"Yes I will."

"I feel the same way. I'll miss you too."

If that didn't let him know how much I liked him, then nothing would. He dropped the skis on the snow and I got all tensed up wondering if he was going to kiss me. I could tell he wanted to because he looked very serious. Suddenly I thought of what he'd said about going out on the trap line. "Fred, you're not going to miss the dance, are you?" The Friday night dance was only a few days away.

"Don't you worry, I won't."

"Wouldn't it be nice if we could have midnight supper together this time?"

Uncle Arthur always brought his ancient gramophone to the dances and along about eleven o'clock the square dancing stopped and everybody danced to the scratchy records he put on. He always saved the *Home Sweet Home* waltz for last and nobody knew when he was going to play it. When he did, it was the signal for each man to run and grab the woman he wanted to take to the roadhouse for a midnight supper. I'd ended up with Mert Atwood one time and Joe Temple the other, but never with Fred. Uncle Arthur always made sure we were too far apart to get to each other.

"I'll keep an eye out," Fred said, "but I think the odds are against it. Wouldn't do for you to end up with a half-breed."

It was the first time he'd ever said anything like that.

"I know, but will you try anyway?"

"I have. I even know what color the label on that record is, but Uncle Arthur's pretty cagey."

"What color is it?"

"Green."

151

"You're really smart. I never thought of that."

I'd stayed as close to him as I could without stepping on his feet, so if he wanted to kiss me he had all the chance in the world. He looked at me in that serious way again and even before his arms went around me I knew he was going to. He was still holding onto the dogs' lead line, and I thought to myself that if one of those dogs pulled on the line now I'd kill it. But they all stayed quiet. And then Fred's mouth was on mine. I felt gawky and nervous at first and my heart was pumping like a steam engine, then all of a sudden I was feeling warm and wonderful, as if this was where I'd always been headed. After he kissed me he held me away from him a little and the way he looked at me I knew he'd always cared for me more than he'd let on. A lot more. Then his mouth was on mine again.

His parka was open at the neck and when I laid my head against his shoulder I could feel the heat coming from his body. He smelled of wood smoke. I wished we could go somewhere where we could be alone and sit and talk and hold each other.

"I shouldn't have done that, Anne."

"Why not?"

"You know why. There's a lot of difference between us."

"Does that mean you want me to become a Democrat?"

I don't know what made me say it. Usually I was the serious one between the two of us, but it made him laugh, and he took me in his arms and kissed me again.

We found a place to sit down on a small shelf of rock right over a creek bottom. Fred cut some spruce boughs for us to sit on and we leaned back, me in the crook of his arm. There was some scraggly brush right in front of us, so unless somebody knew we were there we couldn't be seen from the trail. It was a cozy spot and we snuggled together for warmth. After a while I said, "You still think you shouldn't be kissing me?"

"Uh-huh."

"How come?"

"Anybody sees us you'll be in for trouble."

"How about you?"

"There's nothing anybody can do to me."

I wasn't as sure as he was. "That day Mr. Vaughn picked on me I think he ended up more mad at you than at me."

"Probably," Fred said.

"Doesn't that bother you, people feeling that way?"

"No."

"It bothers me, makes me feel as if I'm in prison."

"Oh, maybe it bothers me once in a while," he admitted, "with people like Strong, or the Carews, but not with the likes of Vaughn. If somebody doesn't know me, what do I care what they think about me?"

"I was afraid he was going to beat you up that day."

"Not while I had that baseball bat he wouldn't."

"Would you have used it?"

He smiled. "Not if I could have run."

"You mean you *would* have used it?"

"If he'd really tried to hit you, I guess so . . . I don't know."

We started talking about what he wanted to do in the future. He'd worked for wages a few times and he hadn't liked it. What he wanted more than anything was to be on his own. He and his father had plans to buy a tractor. With it, he said, he'd be able to do ten times the mining they were doing with pick and shovel now.

"How would you get it in here?" I asked him.

"By airplane, have it shipped in piece by piece. It'd be expensive, but it would be worth it." Eventually he wanted to have his own airplane too, he said. There were a million things he wanted to do. He wanted to travel and he was thinking that if everything worked out the way he wanted he might even try farming. He felt it could be done, that anything that was done in the States could be done here. He loved it here.

"You just look out there," he said. "It's so big and beautiful it makes you feel wonderful just to be alive. I couldn't even think of living anyplace else."

I'd never heard a boy his age talk that way. The boys I'd known were all interested in going to work for some big com-

153

pany or other, getting an automobile and maybe buying a house one day.

We were still talking when all of a sudden a gust of cold air hit me. It was as if a giant box of dry ice had dropped on us. It took my breath away.

"We'd better get back," Fred said. "Temperature's starting to drop."

I couldn't understand what his hurry was. We weren't more than half an hour away from the settlement. Ten minutes later I realized what he meant, though. Ice fog was swirling around us and I could feel the cold nipping at my body, almost like teeth, trying to pull the heat out of me. It made me realize what it must be like for Fred to be caught in that kind of freee when he was out trapping in the middle of nowhere. The ice fog became so thick that we had to depend on the dogs to stay on the trail. If I'd been alone I'd have been scared, but as long as I was with Fred I wasn't. All the way back I felt as if I were part of him, his body pressing against mine, lean and strong.

By the time we reached my quarters the thermometer outside the window read thirty-five below zero. When he'd called for me it had been zero.

Nancy had a roaring fire going in the stove, but even so there was frost along the far walls. Fred stayed long enough to warm up, then headed for home. "See you Friday," he said.

I felt so good I wanted to sing out and dance around the room. I had more energy than I knew what to do with, so I washed some clothes. I sang *Row, Row, Row Your Boat,* scrubbing up and down on the washboard to keep time.

"Boy, are *you* happy," Nancy said.

"Happy? Of course I'm happy. I'm always happy."

"Not like you are right now."

"Fred and I had a nice time."

Fred was a kind of a taboo subject with her, so she didn't say anything. I could tell something was on her mind, though.

She waited until after supper to bring it up.

"You mind if I tell you something, Anne?" she asked me while we were doing the dishes.

154

"Go ahead."

"Sure you won't mind?"

"Is it that bad?"

She shrugged. "Well . . . There's a lot of talk goin' around about you and Fred."

"What kind of talk?"

"*You* know. That you and him are hangin' around each other too much."

"Let 'em talk."

"Some of it's pretty salty."

"For instance."

"Ah . . . you know what I mean."

"Who's doing the talking?"

"Mr. Vaughn, Angela, Harry Dowles—all of 'em."

"I don't care about them."

"They're not the only ones. A lot of other people don't like it either. A couple of 'em have already written to Juneau about you."

"I guess there's not much I can do about it."

She'd been washing the same plate for the past minute. Finally she dipped it in the cold water and handed it to me to dry.

"If he was any kind of a man," she said, "he'd stay away from you. He oughtta know how people around here feel."

"He does."

"Then why does he keep comin'?"

"Because we like each other."

She rested her hands on the rim of the washtub. "Anne," she said, turning to me, "you're so good you don't even realize what you're doing. That man's a breed. The way you act towards 'im is, well . . . *you* know, like somebody who's more than a friend."

"Is that the only way you think about him, Nancy—that he's a half-breed?"

"Well he is."

"Does that mean he's less of a person?"

"I never thought about it much."

"I'm pretty fond of him—and more than just as a friend."

She picked up a cup and started washing it. I couldn't read her expression, but she was unhappy.

"We could talk about it if you like," I said.

"No, that's all right," she said quietly.

For the next couple of days it stayed so cold that Nancy and I warmed up the bed with hot rocks before we got in. Even then we tossed a coin to see who was going to get in first, and when we woke up in the morning the blankets were stuck to the wall. On Thursday it dropped to forty below, and even though we moved all the tables in the schoolroom close to the stove, Willard, Joan and Lily couldn't work for their feet being so cold. We finally had to move the whole class into my quarters and let the little ones sit in the bed.

When Uncle Arthur showed up for school he said that if it was this cold and here it was only November, we were probably in for a three-dog winter. I asked him what that was and he said that a one-dog winter was nothing. You stay warm at night with just one dog in bed with you. A two-dog winter, now that was tough, but a three-dog, "Well, missis," he said, "it gets so cold the smoke freezes in the stovepipe."

That was an exaggeration about the smoke, but it was close. Up until the cold weather hit that week I never understood why Mr. Strong kept such a big supply of laxative pills in his store. I knew after it did, though: nobody wanted to go to the outhouse until it was absolutely necessary, so by the time you went you needed all the help you could get.

It was the outhouse that almost caused a tragedy of sorts at the end of the week. Ten minutes after I excused little Willard Friday morning he still hadn't come back to the classroom, so Nancy went out to see what was keeping him. Ordinarily I wouldn't have bothered because he was in the habit of running home sometimes and staying there a while, but this time I just thought I'd check. I was sure glad I did, because Nancy came back right away, trying not to laugh and looking worried at the same time. Willard was stuck to the seat.

Getting him off turned out to be a major undertaking. We

156

tried pouring warm water around him, but it froze almost as soon as it hit the boards, so finally Mr. Carew had to bring a crowbar and pry the boards off. The outhouse was a two-holer, so when we carried Willard into my quarters the boards were long enough so that he looked for all the world like a prince on a litter. It didn't seem to bother him, though. We propped one end of the boards on the stove and the other over a chair and he sat as calm as you please until he thawed off.

After that Mr. Vaughn loaned us a ten-gallon kerosene can with the top cut off. We put a toilet seat on it and put it in the cache. Since it was almost as cold in the cache as it was outside, somebody lined the seat with caribou fur to make sure nobody got stuck again.

The weather didn't keep anybody from coming to the dance, though. Just about everybody showed up. They were really something, those dances. Before everybody arrived the old-timers would sit around playing cribbage or rummy, and Fred would take out his banjo so that the rest of us could play musical chairs. By the time it was 8:30 the schoolroom and my quarters were jam-packed and we were ready. Then with Fred on banjo, his mother on accordion and Ben Norvall playing the fiddle and calling, everybody stomped and swung their partners so hard the dirt kept jumping up between the floorboards. And that Friday was no exception. It got so hot we didn't even need the stove after a while.

I had as much fun watching as dancing, especially when Rebekah Harrington was on the floor. She was almost as heavy as Angela Barrett, but she swung around and do-se-do'd like a young girl. Now that it was colder she wore about half a dozen skirts, and as the dance wore on she worked herself into such a sweat that she kept taking them off, one after the other.

She'd started showing up at school every so often again, but if the school board objected to it they didn't say anything to me, so I let her come. They didn't want to tangle with her husband Jake again. She must have been studying with Lily at home because she knew her letters. Whenever I gave my beginners drill with flash cards I could see her lips moving, naming the letters as I held them up. She wanted to learn to read, I knew that, but so far I hadn't tried to work with her. I intended to, though, as soon as I felt I could do it without getting into trouble over it. She was just about the happiest person in all of Chicken. It didn't seem to bother her in the least that the women in the settlement snubbed her. It didn't bother Jake either. "You know, boys," he told a bunch of miners in the roadhouse one night, "if you had the brains God gave you, you'd mush out to that Indian village and bring yourself back a squaw." Rebekah and his little girl Lily had been with him. Picking up Lily, he'd stood her on the table. "Take a look at that beauty, will ya—black as the ace of spades, but I love her! And that goes for my woman too. You want to look down your nose at me, you go on ahead. She ain't the Rose of Sharon, but by golly, I got myself the fattest, cleanest, hardworkingest woman any man here ever warmed up to on a cold winter's night!"

"Got biggest mouth in whole No'th country too," Rebekah had murmured. She hadn't looked too happy, and I didn't blame her, but Jake just laughed, crooked an elbow around her neck and gave her a fat kiss on the cheek.

She plumped herself down alongside of me and Maggie Carew right after the square dancing was over and Uncle Arthur was winding up his gramophone.

"How you doin', Tisha?" she asked me.

"Fine, Rebekah. How about you?"

She let out a long sigh of satisfaction. "Ah, I have lotsa fun me. Like dance too darn much. How you doin', Miz Carew?"

"Gettin' by," Maggie said.

"You make plenty money tonight," Rebekah said. "Everybody they too hungry when dance over, they maybe eat table and chair. What you think?"

"Whatever money I make you can be a darn sight sure I'll earn it."

"By golly," Rebekah said, sympathetically, "you tell truth. Not easy make cook for so much people."

Maggie got up. "I better get along. Gotta start preparin'."

158

Rebekah fanned herself with her hand. "Whew—too darn hot, I think."

I had to smile. "Too much dancing, I think."

"Ah, I like have good times. Life short. Today you here, laugh, tomorrow you go in ground, everybody shovel dirt on you."

Uncle Arthur had put on a waltz and the kids who were still awake were the first ones out on the floor. Two or three of them were already asleep on my bed along with Rebekah's Lily. Jimmy Carew was dancing with Joan Simpson, while one of the Vaughn twins was trying to wrestle Mert Atwood around the floor. As usual Fred danced the first waltz with his mother. They were so graceful that most people just stood on the side and watched them. He glanced over at me and we gave each other a quick smile. I'd looked over Uncle Arthur's records and made sure about the label on *Home Sweet Home*. It was green, all right.

As the evening wore on I kept looking over at Uncle Arthur whenever I could, hoping I'd spot that label. I saw him start to put it on once and so did Fred, but he took it off again when he saw the two of us head for each other.

It was almost two o'clock before he slipped it on. I was talking with Nancy and the next thing I knew Joe Temple was tapping me on the shoulder and grinning down at me. Except for the way he treated Mary Angus, I didn't have anything against Joe, but I was so annoyed I felt like going over to Fred and saying, "Why don't we let them all go over to the roadhouse and you and I stay here together?" It must have showed, too.

"Don't look so peevish," Joe said when we were waltzing. "You could have ended up with old man Vaughn."

That would have been something. Ever since the school-board meeting he hardly nodded to me.

"And you could have ended up with Angela Barrett."

When the waltz ended, I went to get my coat. I caught Fred's eye and we both kind of shrugged as if to say that's the way we knew it would be.

159

The roadhouse was so crowded it took almost an hour before everybody was served. Even Willard was carrying plates back and forth.

Joe had taken out a pipe and was smoking and I was almost finished eating when Maggie came over. "How's the grub?" she asked.

I told her the truth. It was delicious. Nancy and I had cooked up some salmon bellies and sauerkraut a couple of times, but Maggie's was the best I'd tasted. She'd saved Joe and me the little table against the wall, and had even put a candle on it.

"Good to see you two together," Maggie said. "You make a nice couple."

"That's a coincidence," Joe said, "we were just talking about getting married."

"Wouldn't hurt either of ya," Maggie said. "Keep you both out of trouble. 'Specially her," she added before she walked off.

I felt like telling her that if he married anybody he ought to marry Mary Angus. Back in Evansville once there'd been a boy who'd gotten a girl into trouble and there wasn't one woman in town who didn't think that the right thing for him to do was marry her. And he did, too. If Mary hadn't been an Indian everybody here would have felt the same, but because she was they didn't give a hoot. They even took Joe's side, which was worse. Maybe she wasn't right in doing what she did, but she wasn't the first woman who'd ever made a mistake like that and she wouldn't be the last.

I looked over to where Fred was sitting with his mother and I wished I was there with them. Everybody at the table was having a good time exchanging tall stories, and Ben Norvall's turn was next. He sat combing his moustaches with his fingers while people kept suggesting stories they wanted to hear him tell again.

The second time he'd showed up at school I'd had to take Maggie's advice and tell him that he couldn't come in unless he took a bath. Face black, hair matted, filthy pants held up by wire and string, he looked like he'd come out of a cave. Even

160

so, not wanting to hurt his feelings, I weaseled around a little, saying that I didn't personally find the way he looked and smelled offensive, but that I had to protect the health of the children. The truth was that, even keeping as much distance as possible between us, I still came near the edge of a dead faint a couple of times.

I'd brought him into my quarters to tell him in private, and he'd been very understanding. He'd had no idea, he'd said, that the children's health was endangered. Now that he did, he would take steps to remedy the situation. The next time he showed up he was a different man. Bathed, and dressed in clean clothes, he fairly glowed. He'd even bought a new pair of heavy duty suspenders to hold up his pants. The only drawback was that now that his face was washed you could see all his blackheads sprouting like potato eyes.

He was a good storyteller though. The one he told this time was about a partner of his who'd died on him in the middle of winter.

"I didn't know what to do with that sucker," Ben was saying. "I couldn't tell when the marshal'd be out to pick up the body and he was beginning to smell worse than a siwash fish stew. I couldn't leave 'im outside because there was a blizzard blowin' and he'd a been covered by drifts so high I wouldn't be able to find 'im till spring. Had an outside cache, but he was too darn heavy for me to lift him up to it."

"What'd you finally do?"

"Well, you're not gonna believe this, but it's God's truth. I just took 'im out and propped him against the side of the cabin, left him there for about two hours till he was frozen stiff, then I stored him up in the cache."

"I thought you said he was too hard to lift."

"Too hard to lift in one piece, I meant. But stiff like he was all I had to do was snap off his arms and legs, then throw 'im in the cache piece by piece. The marshal was a little peeved when he had to collect him, wanted to file charges against me for desecratin' a corpse, but I explained the situation to him

161

and he was as decent as you please. I heard later that after the undertaker got through with that sucker not a soul was the wiser."

Ben's story was followed by a few more from others, each one wilder than the one before. When they were ended I asked Joe if he'd seen Mary lately. He said no.

"I don't mean to stick my nose in, Joe, but she really needs some help. She goes out trapping and she shouldn't."

"I thought you said you don't mean to stick your nose in."

"I don't, but I just can't understand why you treat her the way you do."

"I don't treat her any way at all. I haven't even seen her in over a month."

"That's what I mean. Don't you care anything about her at all?"

"Why should I?"

"Because she's a human being." Because she had two children by you was what I wanted to say.

"Hey, are you a social worker or a teacher?" he asked sarcastically.

We didn't have much to say after that, and in a way I was sorry I'd said anything about it at all. He wasn't a bad guy. He'd made a pass at me once, but when he saw I wasn't interested he hadn't made a fuss about it.

We left a few minutes later. He was quiet all the way back to my quarters, so I knew he was irritated with me. I didn't realize how mad he really was, though, until we reached the porch and I thanked him for taking me to supper.

"Forget it," he said. "You taught me a lesson. I tried to help you out tonight by keeping you and that Purdy kid away from each other. Well from now on I'll mind my own business and you mind yours." Then he turned away from me and walked off.

162

XI

"Fred!"

"Hi, Anne."

"Come on in, it's freezing."

Nancy and I had just finished going over a math problem when he'd knocked. I'd heard he'd been back from the trap line for a couple of days and I was wondering when he'd be over. If Nancy hadn't been there I'd have given him a hug, I was so glad to see him. He'd lost a little weight from being on trail and eating and sleeping in rest cabins, but he looked wonderful.

He didn't stay long. I walked out with him on the porch before he went home.

"You ready for a snow picnic?" he asked me.

"Sure."

"How about Saturday?"

"That's swell. Where do you want to go?"

"We'll go over to West Fork," he said. "It'll take about two hours to get there, so I'll pick you up around nine."

He was going to kiss me, but he glanced over at the Vaughn cabin and changed his mind. "I'll see you Saturday," he said.

Before that Saturday came Mrs. Purdy paid me a visit after school. When I opened the door I couldn't have been more surprised to see her. She smiled up at me from under a beautiful hat of otter fur that made her look as chic as a Paris model.

She needed something from Mr. Strong's store, she said, but I had the feeling she wanted to talk with me in private.

Inside the store it was cold enough so that you couldn't smell the usual collection of musty odors. All she wanted, she said, was a can of peppercorns. She was going to make a pepper-pot stew and had just run out. She stuffed the pepper in the pocket of her fur coat, and as I was writing it down, she said, "You are going on snow picnic with my Frayd he tell me."

"On Saturday."

"He like you very mush, Ahnne," she said.

"I feel the same way about him."

"I understand why he likes you. You are attractive. Wear nice clothes. Yet I do not understand why you like *him* so much. He is only boy. He make no money, have no house, have nothing. Is that not so?"

"I never thought about that."

"Not wise. You are pretty, Ahnne. Many men like marry you. Some day you marry man who have mush money, give you *big* house, many things . . . Frayd, he give you nothing." She said it as if he were a dismal failure, and I almost had to smile.

"Mrs. Purdy, why don't you tell me what's really on your mind?"

She laughed, a lilting laugh full of good humor. "I see why you teasher, Ahnne. You are . . ." She stopped and tapped a mittened hand on the counter, searching for the word she was thinking of. She shook her other hand in frustration. ". . . Intelligent," she said, sighing with relief. "Someday," she added, exasperated, "I get new tongue. This one—agh." We both laughed at the face she made. Then she was serious.

"Please, Ahnne," she said slowly, "do not like him. It is not good . . . You savvy what I say?"

"Mrs. Purdy, do you think that Fred and I have done anything wrong?"

"No. I not say this. I say only that now there is mush trouble. Three days ago Mr. Strong come see me. He tell me of you and Frayd. Tell me Frayd like you too mush. People know, and it

164

is very bad. I am shocked he tell me this, Ahnne. I not know. When Frayd he come home I talk with him. He say it is true, and I weep. I am afraid, Ahnne. People will not talk with Frayd like before. Not talk with me, with my husband, and my Isabelle."

"Then maybe they're not your real friends, Mrs. Purdy."

She shook her head impatiently. "Ahnne. You are young, not understand. People here not like see white man, dark woman. Mush worse they not like see white woman, dark man. You like my Frayd too mush, Ahnne. Better to close book on that. Too many tears come your eyes, too many pains in your heart . . . I ask you—I tell Frayd you not like him anymore. Yes?"

I didn't want to hurt her for anything in the world. "Mrs. Purdy . . ."

"Ahnne, I beg of you."

"I'm sorry . . ."

She was angry, but it only lasted a few seconds, then she collected herself.

"I say good night to you, Ahnne," she said, "but first I tell you something make me sad almost to cry. You must come my house no more."

She started to say something else. Instead she turned and went to the door.

"Mrs. Purdy!"

She went out. I turned off the oil lamp I'd lit and went after her, locking the door as quickly as possible. By the time I caught sight of her she'd gone around the back of the store and was moving toward the shortcut home.

I called to her, but she didn't turn around. And as her tiny figure kept moving away I felt almost the same way I had years before when my Grandmother Hobbs had stood in the road and waved good-bye to me.

For the rest of the week I was afraid that when Isabelle came to school she'd tell me that Fred wouldn't be able to make it on Saturday. Knowing how much he loved his mother, I knew he'd want to hurt her even less than I did.

When Saturday morning came, though, he was outside with his sled almost on the dot of nine. It was still dark out—the sun wouldn't be up for a couple of hours yet—but it looked as if it was going to be clear.

As soon as I came out I saw that Pancake wasn't his lead dog this time. He'd put Pancake at wheel instead, directly in front of the sled, and harnessed all the malamutes up front with Shakespeare in the lead. Fred had taught me enough about sled dogs so I knew why. It had snowed again a few days before and the dogs would have to break trail part of the way. The heavier dogs like Pancake would be more likely to break through the snow and have tough going. The lighter malamutes would pack it down.

Shakespeare was really anxious to show what he could do, or maybe he knew Pancake was back there watching him, because as soon as I was tucked in the sled and Fred yelled "Mush!" that whole team took off as if it was their picnic they were going on.

Once we were out of the settlement, Fred launched into a chorus of *Oh, Susanna* and they really pushed into their collars. For the first hour we moved along at such a good pace and it looked so easy that I asked Fred to let me try driving.

"Might be a little hard for you," he yelled.

"No it won't."

"We'll be hitting some hummock ice soon, so maybe you better wait."

"I'll bet you I can do it."

"You sure now?"

"Positive."

We changed places and it seemed so easy at first I wondered why he'd hesitated. I started sing *Ta-ra-ra-boom-dee-ay* and all the dogs worked so hard that for the first time Shakespeare wasn't setting the pace. But between having to jump off to keep the sled from tipping and trying to manipulate the lead lines, I found out that it took a lot more strength than I thought to keep the sled on trail. I finally decided to give up when we hit the hummock ice. It was like going over slippery

166

rocks. Sweating and hardly able to breathe after a while, I said, "Fred, maybe you ought to take it."

"You sure you want me to? You're not doing bad at all."

"I'm getting a little tired." It was all I could do to hold onto the handles.

"There's only about another quarter mile before we'll hit the ridge, then it'll be downhill." He didn't turn around and I didn't realize he was trying not to break out laughing.

"I don't think I can make it."

"Sure you can."

"Fred, I mean it. My hands are killing me . . . Whoa!" I yelled to the dogs. It came out like a whisper and they didn't pay any attention. "Fred—"

He was trying to keep a straight face, but he couldn't.

I didn't see anything funny about it. "If you don't take this right now I'm gonna let it go."

He was laughing so hard he could barely yell whoa to the dogs. He stumbled out of the sled, trying to stop, but every time he looked at me he'd start all over again. Finally I started to smile in spite of myself. He took me in his arms and gave me a big hug, then he held me away from him. I couldn't think of anybody who ever looked at me the way he did then, unless it was Granny Hobbs. Only it was a lot different, and it made me feel a lot different. I had all I could do not to tell him I loved him right then and there. Because I did. Maybe I hadn't had that much experience with boys, but that didn't matter. I knew I'd never felt this way about anybody and that I never would again about anybody else. And I saw in his eyes that it was that way with him too.

Once the hummock ice was behind us we moved along fast, and finally we reached the crest of a hill from where we could see West Fork joining the Forty Mile River. Ahead of us stretched endlessness.

Months before the river below had been running, rushing along so fast that there didn't seem to be any force on earth powerful enough to stop it. But now something had. Something held it in a mighty grip, freezing it solid, freezing West

Fork all the fifteen miles back to where it began, freezing the Forty Mile all the way to Steel Creek and beyond to the Yukon. The sun was just coming up over the mountains—blood-red and cold. I felt as if I was standing in the mightiest cathedral that had ever been built. There was no end to it, and no beginning. All I could do was look at it and worship.

We found a picnic spot at the base of a soaring face of rock, and Fred tied the dogs. They were pretty well-trained, but they still had enough wildness in them so that if they spotted a rabbit or some other small animal they'd take off after it. In a little while, what with the fire and the bright ball of sun, it was warm enough for us to take off our parkas. I made some tea and we sat drinking out of tin cups.

"You think we'll ever get to go to the roadhouse with each other after the dance?" I asked him.

"No." He took my hand and held it in his own. There were cuts all over his from where the skin had been torn by the cold steel of the traps. My own hands were chapped and rough, but compared to his they were slender and soft. Most of his fingernails were broken off.

"Look at the difference," he said.

"Next time you come over I'm giving you a manicure."

"I meant look how light yours are—how dark mine are."

"I like your hands."

"You know what I'm talking about. We shouldn't even be here, together like this."

"What can anybody do to me, take back more pots and pans?"

"It's no joke. They can be a hard set, some of these people. When I told my mother we were going on this picnic . . . Well, I guess you know how she felt. She told me she went to see you. She's really upset."

"How about you?"

"I'm worried. About you and about my mother."

"You don't have to worry about me."

"Well, I do. If I had any sense I wouldn't have taken you out here all alone."

168

"Do you want to go back?"

"No."

He put some more wood on the fire and then I moved into his arms. After a while I didn't feel too well.

"What's the matter?" Fred asked me.

"I don't know," I said. "I think I'm dizzy from holding my breath every time you kiss me."

"Then what are you holding it for?"

"Aren't you supposed to?"

"I never heard of that."

"That's what I always thought."

"If you breathe through your nose a little it'll be easier. Try it."

I tried it and it made all the difference in the world. Up to then I'd been wondering why kissing someone had been so much trouble, but now I saw how much fun it really was. You learn something all the time, I thought. I could have kept on all day after that, except that my lips started to burn after a while. "I just learned something else," I said.

"What?"

"Why Eskimos rub noses. Their lips are always chapped."

"I don't rub noses."

"You're only half-Eskimo."

He smiled at that, then a moment later his eyes flicked to someplace in back of me. "We're being watched."

I tried to sit up, but he held me tight. "Don't move too fast," he said. "Just turn your head slowly."

I did what he said, but I didn't see anything.

"There," Fred said, "standing by that rotted spruce."

I finally saw him—a shaggy-coated moose. He'd been feeding on some willow, but now he was still, looking our way. He was tremendous, the racks on him wider than I was tall—maybe six feet and covered with white winter fuzz. He didn't seem to see us.

The sled was only about ten feet away, Fred's rifle slung across the handles. He started to ease away from me.

"Let him go, Fred."

"Anne, that's fresh meat—eight hundred pounds of it. Think of it," he said, "pickled tongue, braised kidneys, liver, heart, steak. You'll have enough for the whole winter."

"But we won't have a picnic." He'd have to butcher it right then and there and it'd be a mess of blood and entrails. He thought about it, then waved a hand toward the moose. "Have a good dinner," he said. The moose saw the movement, dipped his head and shambled off.

After we ate we took a walk out onto the river. It had frozen smooth in the center, but near the banks it was a mass of twisted shapes that looked like a sculptor had gone crazy. On our way back to the sled we were moving through a thick tangle of buckbrush when all of a sudden the whole brush came alive and exploded. I thought it was some big white animal jumping up and I screamed. The air churned with the flapping of wings—a whole flock of ptarmigan I'd flushed. In a moment they were gone.

When we got back to the sled I was all for building up the fire and staying there, but it was dark already and Fred said we should get back.

We hadn't seen another person the whole day, and on the way back I kept imagining we never would again, that we'd just go on and on through the moonlit night until we came to some magic place that we'd never have to leave. I leaned back in the sled and stared up at the heavens, imagining that we were on our way up to them, gliding into the stars on a trip to the Milky Way.

I came back to earth with a jolt, because suddenly there was an ominous crack from under the sled. Right after that the bottom dropped out from the right runner, the sled tipped over, and the next thing I knew I was tossed out like water from a dipper.

I thought I was going to land soft, but I didn't. There was a crust of ice under the snow. I crashed through it and landed with a jolt on bare ground about a foot below. Fred went tumbling too, but he got to his feet right away, waded across snow that cracked and gave under him like pie crust and

170

charged into the dogs. They were on solid ground, but they'd been jerked off their feet. As soon as they got up they started snarling and fighting with each other and tangling themselves up in the lines. Fred had to kick a few of them before they settled down and we were able to take stock.

We'd been lucky. We were shaken up, but aside from a few bruises we were all right. It could have been far worse. We'd gone through some "shell ice" that had formed over a shallow basin. Rain had probably filled up the basin, then frozen on the surface while the water below had seeped into the ground. It was one of the hazards of the trail.

The sled was on its side, but it wasn't damaged. The dogs' momentum had carried it to the edge of the basin and it hadn't gone through. We were able to right it fairly easily without even unharnessing the dogs, and then we were on our way again.

It was after six when we reached the settlement. Fred said good night to me on the porch. "See you at the dance Friday night," he said.

A few minutes later I'd changed into some slipper moccasins and Nancy and I were preparing supper when she told me we were going to have a visitor later on.

"Who?"

"I'll give you one guess." She acted as if I should have known who it was. "He's from Eagle."

"I can't imagine."

"Really? From the way he talked you'd think you were engaged to marry him."

"Now I have to know who it is."

"Cabaret Jackson."

XII

A little later on Cab stomped in, all dolled up in his Saturday-night cowboy clothes. He'd taken a bath at the roadhouse and pomaded his hair so that he smelled like a barber shop. He brought me a big heart-shaped box of candy, and just as Nancy had said, he acted for all the world as if the two of us were just one step away from the preacher if I'd just say the word. He was as loud and brassy as when I'd seen him in Eagle last, but he was such a good-natured grinning fool that I just had to like him.

He was leaving in the morning, he said, and he wanted to take me over to the roadhouse for some dancing. I told him that I had a headache and wasn't feeling too good, so he said in that case he'd stay over and take me for a sled ride the next day and supper the next night. I got out of the sled ride, but he wouldn't take no for an answer on the supper, so I said if he'd take Nancy too I'd go, and he settled for that.

I'd offered him coffee, but he said he was drunk on love already and didn't want to sober up. "Cab, I can smell what you're drunk on and it isn't love, I can tell you that," I said.

That made him whoop up a storm. "Ain't she somethin'?" he said to Nancy. "Ain't she really somethin'? Come on, Teacher, you gotta come over the roadhouse—just for a little while. I got all this money a-jinglin' in my belt, and if I can't spend it on the most beautiful gal in the Forty Mile what's it good for?"

172

"You must have struck it rich."

"I sure did," he said craftily. "What I got on that sled a mine's more precious than gold, grub or fire."

"What have you got?"

"Never you mind," he said. "Those delicate ears weren't meant to hear things they shouldn't."

He was running liquor, Nancy told me after he left. "He runs it all over the Forty Mile."

"Isn't he afraid of getting caught?"

"Not him. He's got the fastest dog team around, which is about all he's got. The deputy marshal went after him once when he started selling it in the Indian village, but that didn't stop him. He was so cocky he left notes for the marshal wherever he went, even told him where he was heading for next. The marshal kept on his trail for two weeks, then finally gave up. Cab's team was just too good."

I saw his team the next day, kenneled in back of the roadhouse. They were a mean bunch, but they looked fast: lean in the flanks and heavy in the shoulders. If Cab had wanted to make money honestly with them he could have. There were always people who were willing to pay top dollar for a man who knew the country and had a good team of dogs—metallurgists or businessmen who wanted to be mushed into the interior for one reason or another. It made me feel kind of sorry for him. He just didn't want to do things the right way, or maybe he didn't know how. All he was interested in was wasting his time drinking and bragging about how he'd been in every cabaret and honky-tonk from Dawson to the Bering Sea. I more or less told him that when he took Nancy and me over to the roadhouse the next night.

"Teacher," he said, "no truer words have ever been spoken. What I need is a good woman to keep me followin' my star. Somebody like you."

"Not me, Cab."

"I'd take a vow that nary a drop would I touch, and I'd build you a cabin that'd be a palace."

I told him thanks, but I intended to stay single.

173

"I tell you, Teacher, if you'd say yes, you wouldn't be sorry."

When he took Nancy and me back to my quarters he said he still wasn't going to give up. It was a game to him now and he was enjoying it. He was heading down toward Tanacross the next day, he said, and he'd be coming back through Chicken in time for the next Friday-night dance. He'd try again then.

We told him to come on ahead because that was going to be the Thanksgiving dance. We'd be having a party and everybody was welcome. It was due to start in the afternoon with the Thanksgiving pageant the class was putting on, then there'd be games and supper and finally the dance itself. Cab said he'd be there, "and if the answer is still no by then, Teacher, I'm gonna mush up to the Arctic and never come back."

"You better get an outfit together then," Nancy told him, "'cause your prospects don't look too good."

The Friday-night dances were fun, but the Thanksgiving party was the biggest blow-out we'd ever had. We'd planned it for weeks and by the time Friday rolled around we were ready. The schoolroom really looked festive. The class had cut turkeys and pumpkins out of colored paper and pasted them on all the windowpanes. Streamers and paper chains hung from the ceiling. "By golly, missis," Uncle Arthur said when he saw it, "you can hang me if this isn't the most Thanksgivin'- est lookin' place I ever saw in my whole life!"

By four o'clock there were so many people in the schoolroom that even though an icy mist rolled in every time someone opened the door, we hardly needed the stove. Except for Fred's mother, who was down with a cold, and his father, just about everybody showed up.

Nancy was the hit of the whole party, but before it started she didn't even want anybody to look at her. She and I had cut her hair short the night before, then marcelled it the next morning. She'd put on the dress we'd made for her and I'd helped her put on lipstick and rouge, just about the smallest amount you could wear and still have it show, but as soon

174

as she looked in the mirror it was all I could do to stop her from washing it off and jumping back into her bib overalls.

"Anne, I look like a flapper! Everybody's gonna laugh at me."

"You look beautiful," I told her. And it was the truth.

"The dress is so short," she complained.

"Nancy you've seen the pictures in the catalog yourself. It's no shorter than any girl your age is wearing now."

She was scared and happy at the same time and I couldn't blame her. I'd felt the same way when I wore my graduation dress. She was even more scared because compared to how she'd been dressing up to then she looked racy. Her old dresses had come down below her calf. This one had a sloping hemline that was about an inch below the knee. The only way I could finally get her to keep it on was to threaten to take off my own dress and wear bib overalls. It was one threat I didn't want to keep, especially since Fred's mother had made the dress for me and it was my favorite. A chemise with a flowered print, it had soft fur along the cowl neckline and insets of tatted lace along the bodice and the flounce. Mrs. Purdy had told me it was an old Eskimo design, but it looked smarter and more modern than anything I'd ever bought in a store.

When the first few people came in Nancy pretended to be busy at the stove and wouldn't even turn around. She couldn't get away with it when some of the children swept in, though. Jimmy Carew was in the lead and he stopped short. "Who are you?" he asked. He didn't even recognize her.

"Who do you think I am?" Nancy said grimly.

"Holy cow!" He stared at her, his mouth gaping. "Nancy, you look beyootiful!"

She was a hit all right. When Ben Norvall took a look at her, he rubbed his eyes in astonishment and started quoting Shakespeare. " 'But soft!' " he said, gesturing grandly, " 'What light through yonder window breaks? It is the east, and Juliet is the sun.' "

Nancy blushed beet-red, loving it. "Oh, now you get outta here," she said, slapping his arm.

175

The only one who didn't say something nice was Mr. Vaughn. Sure enough, he said she looked like a flapper. Nobody paid any attention to him, though. He was so old-fashioned that he wouldn't let his daughters dance the fox-trot.

As soon as we counted heads and found everybody was there the class put on the pageant. It was about the landing of the Pilgrims at Plymouth Rock and what they went through during their first winter.

After that we had early supper, and everybody dug in. We'd all saved our appetites, and with Maggie Carew's bear soup simmering on the stove to tantalize everybody, we were starved. Along with a whole load of oranges and apples, we'd had corn on the cob freighted in from Fairbanks, and everybody helped themselves to dozens of succulent moose spareribs, pickled caribou and dried king salmon. Willard Carew was sitting alongside me. He'd never seen whole corn before and was eating the cob and all.

"I sure don't think much of this," he whispered to me. "It's makin' me sick."

"Try eating just the yellow part," I told him. "Most people don't bother with the rest of it." He liked it a lot better after that.

We topped it all off with dried-apple pie and ice cream, but the best part of the whole meal were the apples and oranges. They'd cost us a lot—two bits apiece to have them shipped in, but they were well worth it. We hadn't seen a piece of fruit in a couple of months, and even though the apples were mealy and the oranges weren't the best, everybody sat around biting into them and making faces at each other as though they were in heaven. I'd almost forgotten how sweet fresh fruit tasted.

Once the supper was over we cleared the tables out of the schoolroom, and after the women did all the dishes Fred struck up his banjo and the square dancing was on. Filled up as everybody was it took a little time for them to get going, but inside of an hour Rebekah had three skirts off and the

176

lanterns all over the schoolroom were shaking as though there was an earthquake.

Cab didn't breeze in until about nine, stomping in with a bottle of whiskey in one hand and gin in the other. I asked him to please take them out again because besides its being against the law, I didn't think it was right to have drinking going on in the schoolroom. There were still plenty of people who you could tell were nipping from flasks on the sly, but at least they didn't come out in the open with it.

Cab laughed and took the bottles out, but he must have hidden them outside somewhere and wrapped them up in furs so they wouldn't freeze, because as the night wore on half the men in the place, and Angela Barrett too, kept making jokes about how they didn't know why, but they just seemed to have to go to the outhouse more than usual that night. The whole bunch of them smelled like a brewery after a while and started reeling all over the place when they danced, hardly listening to the calls.

Cab was the worst, bragging and carrying on about his dog team without a stop. He went over to Joe Temple and said he'd heard Joe had a good team of dogs and he challenged Joe to a race. But Joe saw right away how drunk he was and said he'd heard about Cab's team and wouldn't go a two-mile heat with him even if Cab gave him a mile-and-a-half lead.

"Good thing you wouldn't," Cab said. "That bunch you got wouldn't be no more match for my dogs then a string of asthmatic poodles."

After a while I didn't even want to dance with him, he was getting so wild.

The square dancing ended about ten o'clock, a little earlier than usual because it had been a long day. Everybody was hungry again, though, so we were still going to have midnight supper over at the roadhouse. I should have known something was going to happen when Uncle Arthur and a few other men started talking with Cab about how fast Fred's team was. Everybody knew Fred's dogs were not only good, but the best-

177

trained of anybody's around here, so I didn't realize that they were trying to start something. Cab buttonholed Fred and was all for having a race with him right then and there. "I just mushed 'em fifty miles to here and I'll put 'em up against yours right now."

Fred said no, he'd heard that Cab had come in second in the Annual Dog Derby at Fairbanks last year and he wasn't in that class. That should have settled it, but it didn't. Later on I found out from Nancy that Uncle Arthur and a few others had kept bending Cab's ear about Fred's dogs, leading Cab on and getting him steamed up. She said she thought they were telling him things about Fred and me as well, but she didn't know for sure. Whatever they said to him, Cab cornered Fred again just before the dance was over, but Fred wasn't having any of it.

"I'll make it over any distance you want," Cab said, "over any country you want."

"Thanks, Cab, but I'm not a racing man."

Cab had that stubborn look that said there was just one thing in his mind and he wasn't going to be talked out of it. "If you're scared you'll look too bad we can make it a fifty-mile mush and I'll give you an hour head start."

"Cab, I just don't want to race you."

"Well, I hear them's all Indian dogs you got anyway. Ain't worth the fish ya feed'm."

Fred walked away from him, but Cab was back to the same song again right after Fred and I danced a fox-trot. By this time his eyes were all bloodshot and he was getting mean. I was hoping that even if I didn't end up with Fred when the *Home Sweet Home* waltz went on, at least I wouldn't end up with Cab. He was willful when he was sober, drunk he was impossible. But when the *Home Sweet Home* waltz did go on I was flabbergasted: for the first time Fred was right beside me.

That was the loveliest waltz I'd ever danced with anyone. For the first time in my life I really felt beautiful. Just having Fred look at me the way he did made me whirl around that floor as if we weren't in a dinky little schoolroom somewhere out in the wilds, but in the grand ballroom of a palace.

Before the waltz was over a whole bunch of people had already left so that they could get to the roadhouse and be served before the crowd. Nancy had ended up with Cab and as the rest of us were leaving they came over to Fred and me. "You're pretty lucky there, boy," Cab said. "How about tradin' off partners? No offense, Nancy."

"No thanks, Cab."

Cab wasn't too happy about it.

In the roadhouse Fred and I sat at the end of one of the long tables. I wished we could have had the table for two, but I didn't care. Just having midnight supper with Fred was enough. We could hear Cab yelling all the way over on the other side of the room, still challenging anybody in the house to a dog race. Then I heard somebody say something about Fred and a few men laughed.

I didn't pay any attention to what was going on after that because Fred and I were talking, but when we were almost finished eating Nancy came over. She leaned down close to me. "Anne," she whispered, "if I were you and Fred I'd dog it outta here fast. Somethin's goin' on."

"What is it?"

"Trouble. You better go as soon as you can."

I told Fred what she'd said. We looked over at the other table. Angela Barrett was just about as drunk as Cab and she was staring over at Fred and me with hate in her eyes. There wasn't too much talk coming from where Cab was, just some murmuring, but there was something in the air, all right. Fred and I got up and he went to pay for our supper.

"Hey now, Teacher, you ain't leavin' so early, are ya?" Cab yelled out.

"Sure am, Cab. I'm dead tired."

He got up from the table and made his way towards us. "Hell, you don't have to go yet," he said. I said I did, but he had something in his mind and didn't even listen to me, just asked me the same thing over again. Fred brought my coat

179

over and Cab tried to take it from him. "You just give that coat to me and I'll take care of 'er. She can't go home yet. It's too early."

"Cab, I do want to go home," I said.

He understood, but he didn't care. Fred hadn't let go of my coat, and Cab tried to take it from him again. "Lemme have that," he said.

"It's all right, Cab," Fred told him. "I'll take her home."

"You will not, boy," Cab said. "Let it go." Fred looked at me, but before he could decide what to do Cab shoved him. Fred let my coat go and fell against the counter. "I said I'll take 'er home, 'n' I mean what I say!"

I was scared now. The whole place had gotten quiet, and everybody was watching to see what was going to happen. They weren't only watching, either. They were waiting, waiting like a pack of wolves for Cab to do their dirty work. They'd been wanting it to happen, planning for it to happen, and now they were licking their chops. Now I knew why Uncle Arthur had finally put the *Home Sweet Home* waltz on when Fred and I were close. Anything to get Cab riled up more. And Fred knew it. I could see by the way he was looking at everybody. He was cornered, being forced into a fight with Cab.

"Now you hightail it outta here, half-breed," Cab said to him. He was wound up like a spring. He wanted to fight bad, you could see it in the way his shoulders moved, as if he was going to shake himself apart any second if he didn't start lashing out. I felt sick to my stomach.

"I don't want any fightin' in here," Maggie Carew said. "The two of you want to settle it, go on outside."

"That's fine with me," Cab said.

"Cab, I don't want to fight with you," Fred told him.

"Thought so," Mr. Vaughn said. "He's going to crawfish."

"Sure is," Angela said. "Even an Arkansas Jew'd be fighting by now."

Cab wasn't listening to anybody anymore. He had blood in his eye and he kept moving his shoulders the way a kid does when he's excited about something and wants to get to it.

Fred moved away from the counter. He'd gone dead white

180

around his mouth and he was all tightened up, so I was surprised he could walk so easily. He went over to get his parka where it was hanging on a hook, and took it down. Cab rushed over to him and gave him another shove that sent him flying into a whole bunch of men. They pushed him right back and he went bang up against Cab. Cab must have thought Fred was coming after him because his fist went out and he hit Fred in the mouth. It was just a glancing punch, but Fred's lip started to bleed and it kind of stunned him. That did it for everybody. Mr. Carew and another man grabbed Cab, two others grabbed Fred, and they hustled them both out the door. I kept trying to get them to stop, and I yelled out to Cab that if he wanted to he could take me home, but nobody was listening to me.

So there Fred was, out in the middle of the snow, his parka still hanging over his arm and Cab staring at him wild-eyed, going into a slight crouch, telling Fred to get ready. And everybody was really having a good time now. "Slam'im in the mush, Cab." "Chew'im up!" "Paste 'im under the tab!" Not one of them was rooting for Fred.

I went over to Joe Temple. "Joe, get them to stop, please."

"And get myself slugged? No thanks."

Fred was still trying to get out of it, not raising his hands or doing anything but watching Cab. "Come on, boy," Cab said, "get 'em up."

"I told you, Cab. I don't want to fight with you."

Then Cab started to move in, all crouched up like an animal, his fists going as if he was winding up yarn, his eyes all wild. I was scared, really scared. I thought Fred would be too and I wouldn't have blamed him, but he wasn't. I almost didn't recognize him for the expression on his face. It was the strangest expression I'd ever seen on anyone, the look he might have had on trail when he was all alone and in trouble and it was only him against an enemy. At that moment I didn't know him at all.

I tried to go over to him, but Angela Barrett grabbed me. She was as strong as a wrestler.

"Let me go, Mrs. Barrett."

181

"You just settle down," she said thickly, "or he won't be the only one to get his brains knocked out."

What happened next made everybody jump. There was a big explosion and I caught a flash of flame out of the corner of my eye and smelled the sharp odor of burnt powder. It was Rebekah's husband, Jake Harrington, standing there holding Mr. Carew's thirty-aught-six over'n'under. Everybody froze and my ears were ringing so I could hardly hear what he was saying. He'd fired into the air, but now he was pointing that shotgun straight at Cab. "Go on back inside, Cab," he told him quietly.

Cab was drunk, but he wasn't so drunk that those two barrels staring him in the face didn't sober him a little.

"This is none a your business," he said to Jake.

"Only tryin' to do you a favor, Cab," Jake said.

"It's not him you're doing any favors," Mr. Vaughn said. "It's the breed." He was standing in back of Cab.

"It's him," Jake said. " 'Cause if he tries to hit that boy I'm gonna kill 'im. So maybe you better move outta the way."

You can bet Mr. Vaughn moved, all right. And he wasn't the only one. Everybody standing near Cab moved away too.

"What do you say, Cab? It's cold out here."

Cab said something he ordinarily wouldn't have said with ladies present, but he could be excused for it. Then he slouched back into the roadhouse and everybody else started moving back in too. I pulled away from Angela.

"C'mon, Fred." I took his arm.

"Anne," Nancy called after me, "I'll stay here a while."

All the way back to my quarters Fred was trembling so hard I thought he was going to fall down. Inside, he slumped into a chair. I built up the fire.

"Did he hurt you?"

"No. I'm trying to hold my supper down."

After a little while he picked his head up. "I could use an aspirin."

I gave it to him along with some water. His chin was smeared with blood and his lip was a little puffy. I got a wet

182

cloth and gave it to him. He went over to the mirror and dabbed the cut. I felt it was partly my fault. If he'd been badly hurt I'd never have forgiven myself. The thing that bothered me the most, though, was how everybody had really wanted to see him beat up.

"I'm glad you're not hurt too bad."

He almost smiled. "Me too. I just wish there was some way I could keep my mother from finding out about it."

"All she has to do is take one look at you."

"Well, at least she won't have to know what it was all about."

"What'll you tell her?"

"Oh, that Cab just got drunk and took a poke at me. This is a mess," he said. "Anne . . ." He started to say something else, but just then Nancy came in carrying my coat.

I went outside with him when he was ready to leave.

"I'm sorry, Fred."

"It's not your fault."

"I kind of feel it is."

I waited for him to say something, but he didn't.

"Why are you looking at me like that?" I asked him.

"No reason."

"Fred . . ."

"What?"

I wanted to say, I love you. Instead I said, "Can you kiss me good night or does your mouth hurt too much?"

He leaned down and his lips just barely touched mine. Then he hugged me so tightly it took the breath out of me. Before he walked off the porch, he stared at me in a way that gave me the most awful feeling, as if he'd pushed me away or shut me out. I wanted to call him back, ask him to stay a little longer. But I didn't. I just stood there, looking at all the cabins strung along the snow.

Far off to the northwest a flickering yellow glow appeared in the distance. Fred had told me it came from a peat fire that had been smoldering in the tundra ever since last summer. The snow had partly smothered it, but once in a while it burst into flame anew. It blazed up now, as if somebody had just lit a big collection of candles. Then it went out. I started to feel chilly and went inside.

Nancy was just slipping her nightie on.

"Thanks for trying to warn us," I said.

She murmured something, then pulled back the blankets and got into bed with her socks on. A little later when I climbed in beside her, her head was underneath the blankets. She poked it out while I was still curled up in a ball, trying to get warm.

"Anne?"

"Mm . . ."

"Jimmy told me that Mr. Vaughn told his father you're gonna have a baby by Fred. He said that come spring you'll be swoll' up like a poisoned dog. I told him it was a dirty lie."

I wondered why she was bringing it up now—then I realized she must have heard me ask Fred if he was able to kiss me goodnight. She'd probably been shocked. As good friends as she and I were, she still couldn't see how I could like Fred so much. She was waiting for me to deny what Mr. Vaughn had said. All of a sudden a picture came into my mind that made me smile—a little quarter-Eskimo baby toddling around the room looking exactly like Fred. It was so vivid I had trouble keeping my voice even. I said, "If it'll make you feel any better, Nancy—no, I'm not going to have a baby. I'll tell you the truth, though. If I was I'd want it to be Fred's."

Right after I said it I was sorry. I had no right to shock her like that on purpose. The silence was so thick you could have cut it with a knife.

"Nancy . . . try to understand. Will you?"

Her answer was a long time coming.

"I'm trying, Anne," she said, her voice troubled. "I'm trying. But it sure is hard."

XIII

"Fred went over to Steel Creek," Isabelle told me Monday morning. As soon as she'd showed up for school I'd asked her about him. Every time I thought of the look on his face when he left Friday night, I'd had a sinking feeling. I had the same feeling now.

"When did he leave?"

"Early yesterday morning. Did you know he was in a fight?" she asked me, wide-eyed.

"Yes, I did. When is he coming back?"

"As soon as he can, I guess."

I asked her what he'd gone for, but she said she didn't know. I asked Nancy if she had any idea why he might have gone to Steel Creek, but she said there was nothing she could think of.

His father showed up for the mail when Mr. Strong came into the settlement a few days later.

"How's everybody in the family?" I asked him while we were standing on line outside the post office.

"Fine," he said. "They all say hello."

"What did Fred go to Steel Creek for?" I asked him.

"See some people over there. He ought to be back in a few days."

I had the feeling he was holding something back and I wanted to ask him more about it, but I couldn't bring myself to pry any more.

185

There was a letter for me from Lester Henderson. He wrote me that he'd received the first monthly report I'd sent him at the beginning of October, and he was very satisfied with it. Then he went on to say that he'd received letters from a few people in Chicken.

> . . . The general tone of them is that you are a good teacher and have high moral standards. I've received two letters from parents, however, who object to your association with an Indian woman living there. One of them also mentioned that you have been teaching the children about the Indians and that you seem to be fond of a young man of mixed blood, Fred Purdy. (I've heard of the Purdys, by the way, and by all accounts they are a fine family.)
>
> I want you to know that I have the utmost faith in you and your abilities, and your personal life is your own. I do wish to advise you, however, to be as diplomatic as possible, especially if you wish to teach in Eagle next year . . .

His letter was dated November 6th, three weeks before, and it sounded as if he'd heard from plenty of people. They must have started writing him around the end of September, just about the time Mr. Vaughn and the school board came down on me. I could imagine what they must have written him since then about Rebekah, and about Fred too.

I wrote him back that I was going to do the best I could. More than anything else, I told him, I wanted to justify the faith he had in me. I told him all about Rebekah too, why I'd taken her into the school and what had happened because of it. If he felt she shouldn't be sitting in, I said, I'd tell her she couldn't come.

There was a letter from Cathy Winters too, inviting me up to the Indian village for a few days during Christmas vacation. She'd written to me right after the whole business about Chuck coming to school had happened and since then we'd written to each other a few more times. I wrote her that I'd love to come if I could arrange transportation. "If I can, I'll be there around Christmas day. That way I can come back with Mr. Strong when he comes through there on the 27th."

Those next five or six days just seemed to drag by. By the time Fred was due back, every time I'd hear footsteps outside I'd think it was him, and if anyone came up on the porch I'd feel that little jolt of expectancy. But it was always somebody else.

Uncle Arthur came over right after dark one afternoon. He wasn't his usual flinty self, and at first I thought it was because he knew I still wasn't feeling any too friendly towards him after what happened. "Mert Atwood asked me if you'd mind comin' over to see him," he said.

"Do you know what for?"

"He needs to see you, missis. He's feelin' poorly." From the way he said it and the hang-dog look he had I knew right away something was wrong. Mert had been sick for the last few days.

"You want me to go with you?" Nancy said.

"I think Mert wants to see 'er alone," Uncle Arthur said.

I got my parka, put on a couple of pairs of wool socks under my moccasins and we started out. "Is it very bad?" I asked him.

"It isn't good." He'd gone over to Mert's cabin a few days ago, he told me, when he hadn't seen smoke coming from the stovepipe. If he hadn't found him, Mert would have frozen to death.

"Darn fool," Uncle Arthur said crossly, "I alluz told him he don't eat right. Fries himself up them bannocks all the time. What good's bannocks do ya? Nothin' but flour and water. He don't eat right, don't do nothin' right. Don't even know enough to close 'is own door. Every single summer he leaves it open when he goes out and lets some bear wander in. Then you know what he does? Stands around cussin' and swearin' at that bear until the poor dumb animal's too scared to come out. So he comes over to my place and tells me to come on and bring my gun. An' I have to shoot it. Now isn't that just cockeyed dumb?"

"It's pretty careless," I said. He was feeling so bad about Mert that he had to get his anger out some way.

"Careless," Uncle Arthur scoffed. "He ain't careless. He's

187

crazy as a bedbug, that's what. Ever see all them ships in his cabin? Ships all over the place. If he likes ships so much why didn't he go to sea?"

He was talking about the pictures on Mert's wall—prints and engravings of everything from full-rigged schooners to the Queen Mary.

He kept on complaining so much all the way over that I knew he was scared Mert was going to die. They'd known each other almost forty years. At the roadhouse they'd sit and play checkers by the hour, arguing over which one of them knew more about mining or where the best fishing was, or how to cook a porcupine or dress a hen.

The ground around Mert's cabin was a junkyard of rotting sluice boxes and unused lumber. Like all the old-timers, Mert never liked to part with anything even though it was useless to him. Gear shafts and broken wagon wheels littered the ground along with a couple of pumps and an old steam engine, all of them covered with snow. And stacked in neat tiers was some heavy-gauge pipe that Uncle Arthur was always trying to get Mert to sell to him. Mert wouldn't do it, though. It didn't matter that the pipe was useless to him. It was part of his life.

"I'll get that pipe, you just wait and see," Uncle Arthur had told me once. "The day he dies it's mine. We made a deal when we split up—first one of us that dies, the other gets his outfit. And missis, I can't wait for the old fool to go."

"You don't mean that, Uncle Arthur," I told him.

"I don't, eh?"

He showed me how much he meant it when I was over at his cabin for dinner once. In a corner of the room was a coffin. "Cut the boards myself," he told me proudly.

"How long have you been working on it?" I asked him. There were carvings all over it, of spades and mattocks, gold pans and sluice boxes. The work must have taken him years.

"Too long," he said. "Every day the first thing I do when I go out the door is look to see if there's smoke comin' from his chimney, but the ol' fool just won't die."

Now that Mert was sick, he was heartbroken. He left me a

short distance from the door. Before he walked away he said, "Missis, I'm sorry about what happened t'other night. Don't blame it on Mert. He didn't have aught to do with it." I knew that without his telling me. Mert was just about the kindest and most harmless person in the area.

I had to knock a few times before Mert called out for me to come in. When I did I felt terrible. He lay on his cot, a couple of dirty pillows under his head. The stove was going full blast, and he was only a couple of feet away from it. When I said hello to him he shook his head, fighting off an attack of pain. I asked him if I could do anything for him but he shook his head again. His face under a few days' growth of beard was pasty, and his waist-long hair, usually tied with a string, flowed over the pillow and all around him. The blue yachtsman's cap that I'd never seen him without lay on the floor under his cot. His mouth kept falling open, and I could see by the way he'd clamp it shut that he was losing control over his jaw muscles.

The pain spasms finally passed, and after he took a couple of deep breaths, he said, "Like you to do me a favor—write somethin' for me if you will. There's pencil and pad in that top drawer . . . I'd write it myself," he said as I went to the bureau, "but my eyes are a-goin' bad."

Even though he was dying, he was still ashamed to admit that he couldn't read or write. I saw the letter he'd brought me to read a few months ago. It was tacked to the wall above the bureau along with some others he'd received in his lifetime. Some of them were so old the writing on them was yellow and the paper was shredding.

I got the pad and he told me to look inside of it. Opening it, I leafed through page after page of long division examples, some of them a whole page long. It's what he'd come to school for—to learn long division. All his life, he'd told me, that was the only thing he ever really wanted to learn, how to divide big numbers.

"I proved every one of 'em and they're correct," he said. "What do you think of that?" He was as proud as he could be.

"I think you really did it, Mert." I sat down at the foot of the cot and found an empty page. "What do you want me to write?"

"My funeral service," he said.

That hit me right between the eyes. Flustered, I said, "What for?"

"Cuz I'm gonna die." He waved away any argument. "I'm gonna die an' there's no gettin' away from it. Maybe tomorrow, maybe next week, I don't know. But it'll be soon."

He was telling the truth, trying to be offhand about it, even a little tough, so I wouldn't start pitying him.

"If you want to shed some tears you better go outside."

"I'm not going to cry," I said, "but if you don't mind my asking, why do you want it done now?"

"Cuz it makes me sick the way everybody carries on when they plant ya—sayin' all kinda lies, 'n' the poor sap they're plantin' can't say a word back."

"I'll tell you the truth, Mert. I don't really know anything about writing a funeral service."

"It's simple," he said. "I'll be a'lyin' in here, up on that there table. All you gotta do is write down some things about me an' Uncle Arthur'll say 'em. That's all there is to it."

"What kind of service do you want?"

"Good one. Want some honest things said."

"I meant religious, like a special psalm that you might—"

"Heck, no! Don't want any of that organ music junk. Don't believe in it. But you got the idea. I knew you were the one to do it."

"But I don't know what you want, Mert."

"You say some things an' I'll tell you if it sounds right to me."

"I wouldn't know what to say. It seems to me that if you really want an honest service you might know what's best to say. You know yourself better than anybody else does."

He thought about it. "That's a good idea," he said finally. "That's a humdinger of an idea." He paused, thinking. I kept pad and pencil ready.

"Say something like this," he said. "Say I been a good miner

. . . Say that all the time I been here in the Forty Mile I liked it here. Say everything's been A-one and that I didn't have no kicks at all."

He stopped and I scribbled it all down, then he thought again. "Say I wanted to mine an' I mined. Say the only thing I wished was I'd struck some rich pay 'stead of just makin' a livin'."

After I got it all down I asked him if there was anything else. He shook his head.

"We should have some particulars," I said. "When were you born?"

"Why you wanna know that?"

"I don't know. We'll have to put it on your gravestone . . . Or maybe for legal reasons," I added lamely.

"We don't need that. I won't be havin' no gravestone. Say this instead. Say when I come into this country—'97 I think . . ." His eyes lit up as he remembered. "Say that there was gold everywhere you looked in those days—poor man's gold, gold in the water you washed with, gold in the mud on your boots . . ."

By the time I finished putting it down he was staring past me vacantly, still thinking about the past. His mouth hung slack.

"Mert . . ."

His jaw clamped shut and he saw me again. "If you want to," he said, "you can put in what I done while I was here—minin', fishin', an' huntin'."

"Don't you think there ought to be *something* religious?"

"Fine with me," he said. "We'll take care of it right now. You put in there that I don't believe in church or ministers nohow. Don't believe nothin' about 'em. Say that."

"That's the way you want it?"

"That's the way . . . When I meet my Maker, I'll meet 'im the way I always did. By myself. Them church busybodies been gettin' in the way too long."

He was hit by pain again and when it was over he looked as if all the blood in his veins had turned to dust. "Say one

191

more thing." He spoke so softly that I could hardly hear him. "Say that everything I got goes to Art—Arthur Spratt—my friend these many years . . . He's to take charge of my funeral. He knows what I want."

I wrote it down and he scrawled his mark under it.

On the way back I couldn't help thinking how brave Mert was. He had next to nothing, a dirty old cabin out in the wilds someplace and nobody to take care of him in his old age. But he never complained, just kept on going year after year.

When I got back to my place, I almost missed seeing the skis leaning up against the wall on the porch. I had to look at them twice before I realized whose they were, saw the holes for the extra straps Fred had put on them for me. For just a second I couldn't believe it, but when I opened the door there he was, sitting on the couch having a cup of coffee.

He'd come back from Steel Creek a few hours ago, he said.

"Why'd you have to come over now?" I said. "I look terrible."

"You look pretty as ever to me."

"Can you stay for supper?" I asked him.

"No, I haven't been home yet," he said.

The three of us talked a while longer, and then he asked me if I'd like to go for a walk.

"Sure."

"If anybody's gonna take a walk it'll be me." Nancy said to me. "You already had your walk. I'll go on over to the road-house."

I almost asked her to stay. Even before she went out I could tell something was coming, something I didn't want to hear. "Feels like I haven't seen you for years," I said after she was gone.

"Feels that way to me too," he said. He was all tensed up and nervous.

"Want some more coffee?"

"Thanks."

"Since when did you get so polite?" I said it as a joke, but it didn't sound funny. It sounded stupid.

192

He got up from the couch and went over to the potbellied stove while I poured his coffee. I heard him open it up, then take a couple of pieces of wood from the woodbox and heft them in.

"Anne . . ."

I put his cup down on the edge of the cookstove. Somehow I had a good idea what he was going to say, and I didn't turn around. I braced myself, waiting for it.

"I'm going away," he said.

"Where to?"

"Steel Creek. There's some guys doing some winter mining there and they can use another hand."

"How long will you be there?"

"Till June."

Till June. I'd be gone then.

I still didn't want to turn around, but I picked up his cup from the stove and put it down on the table. I was as numb as if somebody had grabbed the back of my neck and was shaking me.

"When are you going?"

"Tomorrow."

That hand on the back of my neck felt tighter than ever. The gas lamp threw our shadows on the wall. I was almost surprised to see mine there. I felt as if I'd faded away to nothing.

"I don't want to go, Anne. I don't want to go at all. But I have to."

"Why?"

"I don't want to see you hurt."

"I can take take of myself."

"Not once these people turn against you, and that's what they're doing. Come spring you won't have a job in Eagle or maybe anywhere else in Alaska. They can write letters to the commissioner that'd curl your hair."

"They already have. I'm not scared of them."

"I am. Not for me. For you. For you, for my mother and my sister."

193

I think I must have groaned then, I felt so awful. "Oh Fred . . ."

He was as miserable as I was. "Don't you see, Anne? There's nothing else I can do. I've thought it over and over. I can't do you anything but harm. I don't have a thing right now. I can't give you anything, I can't take care of you."

"That's what your mother said to me."

"There was a nurse up at Fort Yukon. About a year ago. She was white. She fell in love with an Indian minister, a really fine man. Everybody liked him, but once they found out that he and that nurse were in love with each other they made life so unbearable for the two of them that she finally went Outside and the Bishop had to transfer him to another parish. You see what I'm trying to say?"

"No." I knew he was doing it for me and that he thought it was the right thing, but he was wrong. And yet I didn't know how to make him see it.

"I'd better go," he said finally.

I moved over to him and my arms went around him. "Please, Fred. Don't."

"I have to."

"You don't have to."

I knew he'd made up his mind and I kept trying to think of a way I could change it. Maybe he didn't know how much I loved him, I thought. Maybe if he did—if he really knew—he wouldn't be able to leave.

"Hold me . . . ?" My mouth searched for his and I pressed myself against him, hoping it would tell him how much I loved him, hoping he'd realize there wasn't anything I wouldn't do to make him stay. At first I thought he was responding, reaching for me. Then he gripped my arms and held me away from him. "Anne, will you try to understand . . . !"

"You don't have to go right now," I said desperately. "We can talk a while. Just stay until Nancy gets back."

He hesitated. He didn't want to leave, and for a moment I thought maybe he wouldn't. But then he let my arms go and he was moving to the door. I didn't want to beg him, and

194

I guess I should have had more pride than to do it, but right then I didn't care about pride or anything else. I didn't care what Miss Ivy or anybody else had ever told me about what was right for a self-respecting girl to do and what was wrong. All I cared about was him, holding him and having him close to me. If I could just keep him close to me now, I thought, he'd stay.

"Please, Fred," I asked him, "don't go. I love you so much. It isn't fair."

"Anne, don't let's do it like this," he said, his voice hard. "I'm going."

That stopped me almost as if he'd slapped me. I was acting cheap. I let him go. He said something else before he went out and closed the door behind him, but I didn't listen. I heard him walk off the porch and move off around the back and I kept thinking it wasn't fair. I'd never loved anybody as much in my entire life as I loved him and now he was going away from me for the stupidest reason in the whole world.

"It isn't fair," I said, starting to cry. "It isn't fair at all."

It wasn't until later on, long after Nancy came home and the two of us went to bed, that I realized what he'd said before he went out. He'd said, *I love you.*

When I remembered it I almost started crying all over again. He thought he was doing something noble and good, when all he was doing was showing he didn't think he was as worthwhile as anybody else. And that made it even more unfair.

XIV

The next morning I was so bleary-eyed when I woke up it seemed as if I'd slept only a few minutes. The blankets were frozen to the wall, as usual. I tugged them free and lay back, glancing at the clock. 7:30. I dived back under the covers and tried to go back to sleep, but it was no use.

Wearing a couple of heavy sweaters, Nancy was sitting alongside the stove, a book open in front of her, studying some arithmetic. So as not to wake me she had lighted the oil lamp instead of the Coleman lantern. As soon as I pulled the blankets off I felt the cold. The stove had a roaring fire in it, but there were dots of white all over the walls from where the nails were frost-covered. Nancy called them frost buttons. When my feet touched the floor, I jerked them back. It felt icy, even through my socks. Nancy got up and pumped the Coleman lantern, then lit it and the room became bright.

"Morning, Anne," she said.

"Morning. What's it down to?"

"Fifty-four."

Fifty-four below zero. Getting some bib overalls and a shirt, I hung them over the stove to warm them, then dressed quickly and brushed my teeth. Pouring a cup of coffee, I went to see the temperature for myself. Nancy had already rubbed a hole in the thick layer of frost that covered the window. I rubbed again and peered through. It was dark outside, but I could read the thermometer.

"It *was* fifty-four. It's fifty-six now."

I washed in silence, thought about breakfast, but had no appetite.

Pouring another cup of coffee, I sat down for a minute on the unmade bed, trying to think what I should do next. Instead I thought of Fred, thinking that maybe he would come over and tell me that he had changed his mind, that no matter what anybody said or did he loved me. Over and over again I imagined all kinds of romantic scenes, but deep down inside I knew he wouldn't be coming. He'd made up his mind and I knew him well enough to know he wasn't going to change it.

I did some washing just to keep busy, but I couldn't shake off the feeling of being trapped. I kept wanting to go somewhere, anywhere, just to get out, and every fifteen minutes I'd look at the time, hoping that somehow another hour had gone by. In a couple of days I'd be leaving for the Indian village, and it helped a little to think about it. I'd be catching a ride with a freighter who'd passed through the day before with two big rowboats and a load of pipe on his huge double-ender sled. He was headed over to West Fork with them and wouldn't be back for two more days. After I hung the wash in the schoolroom I did some ironing. Then finally I couldn't stand being cooped up any longer. I started to get dressed.

"Where you going?" Nancy asked me.

"For a walk."

"Want me to go with you?" She knew how I was feeling. I'd told her last night that Fred was leaving. Even though she was glad for my sake, she was still trying to be sympathetic.

"No."

"It's pretty cold out there."

"I won't go far."

I started to walk without even thinking about where I was going. A couple of times it crossed my mind that maybe I could go far enough so that I wouldn't be able to get back and I'd freeze. Or maybe I could get caught in a blizzard. It was mean enough out so that it wouldn't take long to freeze to death if I did. Gray and still, it was so cold that my parka was white with the frost from my own breath.

After a while I found myself near Mary Angus' shack. It looked so lonely and forlorn I almost started to cry. For the first time I really understood why she was staying here, how even though she was sick she could keep on living in a place like that. If you loved somebody enough you could live anywhere.

From there I went towards the Purdy cabin. I stayed far enough away so nobody inside could see me, wishing I had the courage to go and knock at the door. I hung around hoping that if Fred hadn't left yet I might see him and talk to him, but after an hour my feet began to sting and I headed back home.

The next day I took a long walk over to the Forty Mile River. I was feeling so sorry for myself that I went out on the ice hoping I'd find a spot thin enough to break through. All I managed to do was stay out so long that I wound up with frostbite. I didn't even know it until I got back and realized my toes were numb. Nancy had to help me bathe my feet in snow and then warm water. They were so badly frostbitten that the pain was agonizing before circulation came back, and I knew I'd never do anything like that again.

Finally the freighter came back from West Fork and it was time to leave for the Indian village. Nancy came along. She was going to visit her family. She wasn't anxious to, but she didn't want to stay in Chicken all alone.

It was a nice trip, easier than going by dogsled. The double-ender was fourteen feet long and built for carrying heavy cargo. Compared to a dogsled it was a luxury liner. We piled hay inside of it, and when it was too cold to sit up front with the driver Nancy and I scooted down under the tarpaulin cover and bundled up in fur robes. We followed the same route Mr. Strong took down the Forty Mile River, and we made it to the Indian village in a day and a half.

It was dark when the sled pulled in, dark and windy. The

cabins strung along the frozen river bank were black silhouettes against a bleak gray landscape. Cache doors banged in the wind and empty fish-drying racks stood like trembling skeletons.

Cathy was as glad to see me as I was to see her. Neither of us had talked with a girl near our own age since the last time we saw each other. The first night we stayed up until almost three in the morning and she told me why she had come here. She was writing a thesis on the Athapascan Indians of the Forty Mile for her doctorate. She was on her second year here and would have liked to stay on for another. But a lot of white people had written letters to the Alaska Native Service about her, saying that she was "spoiling" the Indians, so she had a feeling this was going to be her last winter.

She was from upstate New York, a graduate of Columbia University. I felt like a hick next to her. Not that she put on the dog, she was as natural as could be, but she'd seen plays on Broadway, read everything Sinclair Lewis wrote and had even met people like John Barrymore and Katherine Cornell.

That first night turned out to be practically the only chance we had for a really good talk. A flu epidemic had started a week before, and from the next morning on, Cathy didn't have too much time to herself. She'd taken in two little girls whose parents were down with it. Caring for them and keeping up with all the other things she had to do didn't leave her much time.

I didn't think I'd be affected by the village the way I'd been the first time, but I was wrong. When I made the rounds with Cathy the next morning I was horrified. In one cabin after another families huddled around small stoves that smoked and sputtered with green wood, or else they lay in tiered bunks, shivering under thin blankets. And everywhere there was coughing, eyes that watered, cheeks flushed crimson.

In one cabin there were seven children, the oldest about eleven. Every one of them was hollow-eyed and needed a bath and a good meal. Cathy went in to change the bandages on a little boy who'd burned himself. I flinched when I saw the burn: his whole forearm was raw. It happened to kids a lot,

199

Cathy said. They huddled too close to the stove in their sleep, and sometimes they'd let a hand or arm fall against it. In the same cabin she changed the dressings on a little girl's neck. The ones she had on were filthy, and her long hair clung to running sores.

Cathy really gave it to the father, Arthur Jack. He was sitting on the bottom tier of a bunk, glassy-eyed and smelling of whiskey even though it was only about eleven o'clock. She asked him in English what he was going to do about getting some grub and some wood. "Soon. Soon I get," he said thickly.

"When?" Cathy asked him. "After all your kids are dead?"

"Tired now. Sick."

"Drunk you mean."

"You no mind business," he warned, making a fist, "get good beating."

His wife, a little hunched-up woman, sat in a corner mending a snowshoe. She had a black eye and one side of her mouth was all puffed up.

Cathy didn't bat an eye. "You touch me and Titus Paul will hit you so hard you'll never lay a finger on a woman again."

He glowered at her, but that was all. Back at her place I told her that for a few seconds I was afraid he might have hit her.

"He wouldn't dare. He knows what Titus would do to him if he tried anything."

Titus had lunch with us that afternoon, and from the way Cathy acted around him I could see she was pretty fond of him. I couldn't understand why, though. He was a tough customer. With that tight-skinned face of his and eyes that bored right through you, he reminded me of a lizard. The scars all over his neck didn't help either. He hardly said a word the whole time he was there. He didn't speak English very well, and when he did speak it you'd have thought he was Moses the way he made pronouncements. About halfway through lunch Cathy asked him if he was going out trapping soon and he barely nodded. I asked him what kind of dogs he had.

"McKenzie River Husky," he said.

The McKenzie River Husky was supposed to be the true Northern dog. It had a strong wolf strain. You could see it in the long slanting eyes, the muzzle, and the coarse short hair. I told him that Fred favored the Siberian husky and the malamute.

"McKenzie River Husky better," he said flatly. "More smart. On trail, take harness off McKenzie River dog, he run for timber, not come back till feeding time. Good strong dog. You have dogs?"

I said no and he didn't bother to look at me again. Cathy told him about her visit to Arthur Jack. "He's beating up Minnie again and drinking too much. Will you talk to him?"

"Why?"

"Because if you don't those kids of his are going to die."

He didn't say he would and he didn't say he wouldn't.

After he left I asked her if he was the chief and she said no. "He swings a lot of weight, though. I used to go the Council about people like Arthur Jack. All they did was have a meeting and tell them to change their ways and then they'd do whatever they wanted. Titus Paul'll tell him he'll break his neck if he doesn't get out and do some work. He'll listen to Titus, for a while, anyway."

Titus was sort of the unofficial head of the village, she told me, one of the few Indians the whites couldn't boss around. When he was little he'd gone to a boarding school for Indians at Carcross, in Canada. The school had been run by whites and was finally closed when the authorities found out that the kids were starving. Some of them had even been beaten to death. Titus was lucky to be alive. The scars on his neck were from glandular TB, the running sores that so many children in the village had. His were especially bad because the way the people at the school had treated the sores was to plaster them over with plain adhesive tape. "By all rights he should hate whites," Cathy said, "but he doesn't. He's not fond of them, but he doesn't hate them."

"Honest to God, Cathy," I told her. "I don't know how you can bear to stay here."

"Somebody has to do it."

"I wouldn't."

"Oh yes you would. From what I hear you've stuck your neck out a few times already."

"That's different. What I can't see is doing things for people when they won't do anything for themselves."

"Anne, I told you when you first came through here," she said sharply, "that you couldn't judge these people by white standards."

That got my Irish up.

"Cathy, you have to have *some* kind of standards. Can't they go out and just cut enough wood to keep warm, or put up meat for the winter?"

"They're doing the best they can. They just don't think about the future the way white people do. They did fine before the white man came along. Look at this." She took a stone ax down from a shelf. "This is what they used before the whites came—stone, stone tools, stone weapons. And they survived. So don't try to tell me they can't do things for themselves."

"That's what I'm trying to say. Now they've got more—axes and hatchets, knives and rifles. They have everything you can think of, so how come they just sit around and starve?"

"Because they're weak. Before the whites came these people were hunters. Their diet was almost all meat and that practically raw. They had the strength to go out and take some game. Now they eat the white man's grub—flour, sugar, canned goods, junk. And they drink his liquor . . ."

I dropped the subject, but I still didn't understand. When I'd gone out with Cathy in the morning the first thing I'd noticed was the empty space alongside so many cabins—an empty space that should have been filled with cords of wood. Alongside Cathy's place and the church and a few other places the wood was neatly ricked up, but at least half the rest had almost none. Yet nobody stole wood from anybody else. I could remember how, when I was a kid, my brothers and I used to slip down to the railroad tracks at night with burlap

202

sacks and pick up whatever coal had fallen off the cars. It was stealing, but everybody did it. And I knew that if I were living here—or any other white person for that matter—and my kids and I were freezing to death, *I*'d sure have stolen wood from somebody. Yet nobody did. As far as I could see they were practically committing suicide. It just didn't make sense; if these people made out all right before the whites came, how come they couldn't do it now when things should have been easier for them?

I didn't find out until the next night, after the dance in the church.

It was the last night I was there and I wasn't looking forward to the dance. I figured that with all the hunger and sickness around, it wouldn't amount to much. I couldn't have been more wrong, though. The church was packed, with pews pushed back against the walls and a huge oil drum heater that sent out enough heat to bake everybody twice over. The Indians cured their leather with urine, so what with all the parkas and the moccasins, the air took getting used to at first. Once the dancing started, though, there was so much noise and fun I forgot all about it. Most of the men wore bib overalls and a shirt, but the girls were really gotten up, bright combs in their hair, plenty of bracelets and colorful kerchiefs around their necks.

Cathy looked lovely. She had on a dress that I wouldn't have dared to wear, but on her it was exquisite. Made of caribou skin that was as soft as chamois, it had a fox collar that showed part of her back. It was almost like a long parka, except that it was split to the thigh, and the hem, trimmed with beadwork and fur, came to a point in front and back.

The dance itself was less rackety than the ones at Chicken because hardly anyone wore boots or shoes. The men were better dancers, too. In Chicken the men used to get so rough at times that I'd be scared of getting knocked out by an elbow. Here, even though there was plenty of whooping and floor-stomping, there wasn't anything rowdy about it. I didn't see any of the men ask a woman to dance. They'd just go over and lead her out on the floor and that was that. The people who weren't square dancing stood on the sidelines tapping their feet and clapping in time to the music, some of them chanting *Little Brown Jug* or *Turkey in the Straw* in their own tongue.

I danced the first couple of sets with Ben Norvall. He'd left Chicken a couple of weeks ago to come here, where he was living with Mary Magdalene. Face flat as a pie, and a lump of snuff always tucked inside her lower lip, Mary was strong as a football player. When she didn't have a lip full of snuff she smoked a smelly old pipe. Ben wasn't any prize package either, so they were about even. Besides beginning to smell bad again, he was full of mischief and was always stirring up trouble. Once I sold him a gallon of kerosene and he went around to everybody asking how much they'd paid me for a gallon; then he said I'd charged him ten cents less. It wasn't true, but it brought three or four customers down on my neck before I straightened it out. Ben was always doing things like that. He especially enjoyed getting people mad at each other by telling them what other people had said about them. In every place that he'd lived he'd eventually get on people's nerves so much that they'd finally threaten to burn down his cabin if he didn't get out.

Between sets he told me that he was going back to Chicken when I went back. "These people just don't appreciate me," he said, "so I'm gonna siwash it back to my own people." It was the exact same thing he'd said when he left Chicken, which probably meant he'd worn out his welcome here fast.

After the second set was over I was sitting down for a rest when someone came over and stood in front of me, his moccasin tapping the floor in time to the warm-up music. I looked up. It was Titus Paul. He didn't say a word, just held out his hands and kept that one foot tapping. Up until then I wondered what Cathy saw in him, although when he walked in earlier all dressed up in beaded leather vest and broad-brimmed leather hat he looked kind of dashing in an ugly way. The way he was looking at me now, though, I automatically gave

204

him my hand and let him lead me out on the floor. He was as
good a dancer as Fred, maybe even a little better.

After I danced with him, no sooner did I sit down than
there was another Indian standing over me, smiling and tapping
his foot. It was that way for the rest of the night.

The dance didn't break up until after two. Ben Norvall
and Titus came back with Cathy and me to her house, the four
of us fighting a wind that blew down the frozen river so hard
we had trouble keeping our feet. The moon was out, bouncing
off the parts of the ice that the wind had polished. We sat
around with our parkas on until the fire that Titus built up
in the stove was going strong.

"How'd you enjoy the dance?" Cathy asked me.

"I liked it . . . You're a good dancer, Titus."

He didn't say anything, just glanced at me with those
lizard's eyes of his.

Ben was sitting back in an overstuffed chair that was leaking
cotton padding, his feet in front of the open stove door. "That
all you can do is grunt when a lady pays you a compliment?"
he asked Titus.

There was a long pause, then Titus said slowly, "Thank
you."

"That's the trouble with you Indians," Ben said, needling
him, "you don't talk. If you did you wouldn't be in the fix
you're in."

"What's talking got to do with it?" Cathy said.

"White people like a man to talk, say what's on his mind.
That's the way they get to know him. With Indians it's the
other way round. They get the feel of you by just sitting
quiet. If they don't like what they feel they walk away. Isn't
that right, Titus?"

Titus nodded.

"What's wrong with that?" Cathy asked.

"Nothing at all if this was an Indian world, but it isn't.
It's a white one. The trouble with these people is they don't
understand that. That's one reason they're goin' under."

205

"They're going under, as you say, because they've been used."

"Used! Aw now, Cathy, where do you get that stuff from? Only person who ever used an Indian is another Indian. You don't use these suckers. Bulldoze 'em maybe, but you don't use 'em. What do you say, Titus?"

"I listen what *you* say," Titus said gruffly.

"See what I mean?" Ben said.

"I'd like to hear it too," Cathy said. "What do you mean 'bulldoze'?"

"What I mean is that if it was the other way around, if the white man hadn't bulldozed these people, they'd've bulldozed the whites."

"That's some way to look at things," Cathy said.

"It's not the best, but what are you gonna do when there's no cop on the corner and it's every man for himself? Heck, when I came into this country you didn't mess around with the Kutchins—none of them—the Vunta, the Natche, the Tutchone. They were tough as they come. They'd walk right up to your cabin and tell you they wanted to make a trade with you, give you so much for so much. Nine times out of ten you got the worst of the bargain, especially if you were all alone. They didn't threaten you if you didn't trade their way, but when there's just you, or maybe you and a partner, you weren't about to tempt Providence. No sir, I'm telling you, they were tough. They didn't steal—still don't. If they wanted something they went and took it. That was their way." He looked at Titus. "You tell me if I'm lyin'."

"You tell truth," Titus said.

"You betcha it's the truth," Ben went on. "They were a strong bunch. Why you couldn't hammer a nail through the muscles on some of those braves."

"Then what happened?" I asked.

"I don't know," Ben said. "They got soft, I guess, lazy. Never thought much about it. *You* know?" he asked Titus.

Titus thought it over, then he said, "Nothing."

"What does that mean—'nothing'?" Cathy said.

"Nothing. We are same as always."

"But you're not," Cathy said, "that's just what we're talking about."

"We are same," Titus insisted. "We think same as before. Before white men came."

"What kinda thinkin' is that?" Ben asked him.

"Like hunter. Something turn up. Today hungry. Tomorrow big cook."

Cathy didn't understand and neither did I, but Ben seemed to. "Huh!" he said. "I never thought of it that way. 'Something'll turn up.' Darned if it isn't the truth."

"How about letting us in on it?" Cathy said.

"Think of it this way," Ben said. "Before *we* came these people lived in sweathouses. They're like igloos," he said to me, "a wood frame with snow built up around it. The Indians weren't any more sociable than they are now, so there was just maybe two or three families traveling together—one family to a sweathouse. They just drifted from place to place. Well, imagine living out there in all that wind and ice and the only thing between you and starvation whatever game you can take. Half the time they starved. Sometimes they'd go so long without eating they'd chew the rawhide off their snowshoes. They had a tough time of it even before the white man came—the women in particular. These people never did think too much of women. The squaws had it so miserable that sometimes if they had a little girl-baby they'd kill it so it wouldn't have to suffer like them."

"They really did that?" I asked Cathy. She nodded.

"They sure did," Ben went on. "Now you ask yourself something—if them suckers had it so hard there must have been *some*thing kept 'em going, something that kept 'em alive. And they did. They had faith."

"You mean like faith in God?"

"*Their* gods, the Spirits. Same thing, maybe. Anyway, they had faith, real strong faith—kind of faith the wolf has."

"What do you mean?" Cathy asked. "*Animal* faith?"

"I mean hunter's faith," Ben said, "any kind of hunter, man or beast. Wolf's got it. No matter how much his ribs are

207

stickin' out, he's got the courage to go on, the faith that somethin's gonna turn up. White men, they don't think that way. They think like the beaver, put somethin' away for tomorrow. The real hunter, and again I'm talking about man or beast, he doesn't do that. That's what the Kutchins were—hunters. They were born to it. Why they hunted moose by runnin' 'em down on snowshoes. They could run all day, most of 'em. Try to put people like that to workin' for wages, doing manual labor and they're no good at it. That's why white people think they're lazy."

"What does all this have to do with faith?" Cathy asked.

"Everything," Ben said. "You've heard that faith moves mountains. Well, it does. Gives people strength. And it gave those Kutchins strength too. Faith. 'Today I'm going to bed so hungry I could eat my dog,' they'd think, 'but tomorrow I'm gonna come across a nice fat caribou and the whole bunch of us'll have a big cook and eat till we're sick. Something'll turn up.' Something always did, too. And one day something else turned up—the *unjyit*, the white man. Yep, the white man. And by golly, here was the answer to a hunter's prayer. 'Behold!' that Indian said, 'Just look at that white critter, will you? Comes into this country out of nowhere and before you know it he's building himself cabins ten times bigger than a sweathouse. And grub? Great Spirit, look at it all! He's got it stacked in tin cans, in sacks, in boxes, shoots it without the least trouble.'

"So the Indian went to this white man and he said, 'Bud, I like your style. Want to live the way you do. How do I do it?'

" 'Bring me furs,' the white man says, 'all kinds—lynx, muskrat and marten, black fox, red fox and wolf. I'll take 'em all.' 'Easy,' says the Indian. And he did it—stopped hunting food and started hunting fur, started trading for axes and traps and guns, flour and tea.

"He stopped traveling from place to place and settled down where the white man was. For a while he didn't do too bad. Missionaries came around and taught 'im all about Jesus Christ, which was fine with him, because the one thing he

208

wanted to know more about was the God that had made this white critter so rich and powerful.

"Well, I tell you, for a good many years that Indian was like a bear in a blueberry patch. He did real fine, kept them furs comin' and lived better than ever he did before. Until the day came when it all went bad. The price of fur went down. Where maybe it took a stack of fur halfway up a man's shin to buy a sack of flour, one day it took a stack up to his waist, then up to his shoulder. Then for a while the white man hardly wanted any furs at all. That Indian was stuck. From living in one place and eating the white man's food, he'd gotten weak. Flour, sugar, biscuits—none of that stuff can keep you going for long. You need meat in the winter, good fresh meat with plenty of fat on it. But there wasn't any meat around, at least not nearby. The white man had chased it away and the Indian, not being a hunter anymore, didn't have the strength to go any long distance for it.

"He was stuck all right. Every winter things got worse for 'im. Weak as he was, he picked up all the white man's diseases—influenza, whooping cough, TB. The only thing that made him feel good for awhile was liquor, so he drank that whenever he could get enough money to pay for it. He got weaker and weaker, sicker and sicker. But no matter how weak or sick he got, he still held onto the faith that'd kept him going when he was a hunter—'Something'll turn up. Somehow I'll make it through the winter.' And that's what keeps all these people in this village going even today—the faith that something's bound to turn up. And that's the awful part of it. This time it looks like it's not going to. These people are on their way to the big El Dorado up in the sky. They've hit the sunset trail and they're dying. All because of faith."

When he finished we were quiet. Even Cathy was moved.

Titus reached over and touched Ben's arm. "You tell story good," he said, and when Ben remained silent he pointed a finger at him. "Why you no say thank you?" He broke into a big smile and it made us all laugh.

I couldn't get over what Ben had said, though. "Does it have

209

to be that way?" I asked him. "Isn't there anything that can be done about it?"

Ben shrugged. "I don't know. Schoolin', I guess."

"It's not doing it so far," Cathy said, "at least not here. The only reason most of these kids come to school at all is because it's the warmest place in the village and I give them a hot lunch."

"Well then what *can* be done?" I said.

"Raze this place to the ground," Cathy said. "Burn it and move everybody up to the Chandalar country."

"Where's that?" I asked.

"Northwest of here," Ben said. "There's a tribe up there won't even let white men come near 'em except to trade once a year. They mushed up there to get away from the white man. Doin' pretty well too."

We all looked at Titus. He shook his head.

"No. We live here. We stay here."

"And die here," Cathy said. "Maybe I'm pessimistic, maybe I'm wrong, but I don't see how this village is going to make it. We've got two children and a new-born babe dead so far, and the worst part of the winter is yet to come. And when it's over, when spring is here again, what'll happen? The old people and the women and children will go to the fish camp and some of the men will go to Eagle to find jobs. They'll cut wood for the riverboats, work on the boats as deckhands, then they'll all come back here and go through another winter. What you said is true," she said to Ben. "Almost everybody here is living in the past."

"Not everybody, Cathy," Titus said. "Some, they learn. Little children get educate, every year learn more. Read. Write. We *learn*," he said emphatically. He went on to say that the Indians had never had it easy, that for them to go north and try to live the old way wouldn't accomplish anything. Their life was here.

Listening to him talk, slowly, confidently, and thinking about what Ben had said, I finally realized what Cathy meant when she'd told me I couldn't judge these people by white standards. They were doing the best they knew how, and the last thing in the world they needed was to have people look down their noses at them. They had guts.

The next day, when Mr. Strong and Nancy came through to pick me up I was almost looking forward to being back in Chicken. I'd left there hoping I'd never see the place again, but staying with Cathy made me realize that my troubles just weren't that big. When the two of us said goodbye and I thanked her for letting me stay with her I meant it. I'd learned a lot.

XV

We arrived back in Chicken on New Year's Eve, and Maggie invited us to a party at the roadhouse. I didn't feel like going. Instead I stayed home and wrote a letter to Fred. I told him exactly how I felt. I missed him badly, I wrote him. I never knew it was possible to miss somebody so much, and all I did was think about him. I told him that I was mad, too—mad because he was wrong. "You may say you did it for me," I wrote, "but I wonder. I wonder if maybe you just didn't really care about me that much. Maybe you were just trifling with my affections, and when it really came down to it you just took the easy way. If you did then I want you to write and tell me. I can take anything as long as it's the truth . . ."

When I finished the letter I felt better. I put it in an envelope and stamped and addressed it before I could change my mind about sending it.

I sat and read for a while after that. Occasionally I'd hear whoops and hollers and square-dance music from the road-house. I didn't have any desire to go over there, though. Nancy had tried to get me to come, but I'd told her there wasn't anybody there I wanted to see. It wasn't that I hated them, because I didn't. Not now, anyway. For a few days I had hated them with all my might. Now I didn't know how I felt towards them—indifferent, probably. All I wanted was for school to open so I could get busy again and not have time to think.

I was still up when twelve o'clock came and everybody started hooraying and whistling and banging on pots. Then they started singing *Auld Lang Syne* and that almost started me bawling, it made me feel so lonely. Someone came running towards the schoolhouse just as they got towards the end. It was Nancy. She burst in and there were tears in her eyes. "Anne," she said, "I just wanted to come over and wish you . . . wish you a—" That was a far as she got before she rushed over and threw her arms around me and then we both started bawling. She kept saying over and over how bad she felt for me and I kept saying she shouldn't, the two of us crying so hard I couldn't tell whether I was consoling her or she was consoling me. We had such a wonderful cry that when it was over we almost smiled. "Please come on over, Anne," she said. "Everybody wants you to—Uncle Arthur and Joe and Maggie Carew, everybody."

I said no, I was too tired. And I was—all kind of cried out and empty. "You go on and have a good time," I said. "You deserve it." She did, too. She'd been looking tired lately and I was worried that she was pushing herself too hard at school.

After she left I took out the letter I'd written to Fred and thought about whether to send it or throw it in the stove. I almost threw it in before I made up my mind I'd send it. After that I made a New Year's resolution that from now on I wasn't going to think about anything but teaching school and doing my duty, and I was going to do the best job I knew how. It made me feel better right away.

When school opened again I could feel almost from the first day that something was different about me. I wasn't short with the children or anything like that—we still sang in the morning and had as much fun as before—but I made them work harder. They only had till June to get all the schooling they could, I figured, and they were going to get it. And that went for Rebekah too. I'd been kind of pussyfooting around with her, scared to come right out and teach her for fear of what people might say. Knowing it, she never asked any questions and just picked up what she could, but she was dying to learn. From then on I treated her like everybody else, called on her for answers, gave her assignments and let her know she was expected to learn as much as she possibly could. It was just what she'd been waiting for and she loved it.

Not one person said a word about it to me either.

People must have noticed I'd changed, because they acted differently towards me, as if I wasn't a kid anymore—or a cheechako either for that matter. They stopped asking me things like whether it was cold enough for me or not and what I wanted to be when I grew up. When Uncle Arthur and Ben Norvall came into class a couple of days after school opened they started kidding around right away. I usually let them get away with it, but this time I told them that I'd appreciate it if they'd calm down until recess when we could all have fun. They did it too, without even looking at me cross-eyed. I felt a little bad about it when it came to Uncle Arthur because Mert Atwood had died the day before and he wasn't feeling too good. They both stayed, though, and just to please Uncle Arthur I gave penmanship drill.

I couldn't put my finger on what it was, but I felt different, all right—as if all my life I'd been trying to be what other people like my parents or Mr. Strong or all the people here in Chicken wanted me to be. Now I was going to be myself. I wasn't going to be hard to get along with, or go out of my way to say anything mean, but from now on people were going to have to take me for what I was. It was the way Cathy Winters felt, I realized. I knew now why she'd answered Mr. Strong the way she had. I still wouldn't have answered him like that myself, but I'd care just as little as she did about what he thought of me personally. It was as if I'd grown up all of a sudden, as if up to then I'd been a girl and now I wasn't anymore.

A couple of weeks after school started I got a letter from Fred. He hadn't been trifling with my affections at all, he wrote. He cared for me more than he'd ever cared for anybody in his life.

I did what I thought was right, Anne. I didn't do it because I was scared of anybody. I can't tell you how much it turned me inside out to come here, but I did it because I love you so much that there was nothing else I *could* do.

Oh, how I wish I was on my own and could do just what I want! That's the thing that really hurts—that I love you so much and there's nothing I can do about it. I keep thinking that some day maybe I'll be able to, and then I also think that when that day comes you'll probably be married to somebody who loves you as dearly as I do.

If I can take it, I'll be staying here until summer, so I won't be seeing you for a long time. Maybe never again. I don't know. I just want you to know that I love you deeply, but I am not going to take up any more of your time. Come the summer you'll be going to Eagle to teach and then you'll probably forget all about me. And maybe that's the best thing.

I read the letter over and over, and every time I saw the words *if I can take it* I winced. On the way back from the Indian village I'd asked Nancy how Fred was doing at Steel Creek and she'd told me he was lonely. "The other miners aren't too friendly to 'im," she'd said. "They don't like to work alongside natives or halfbreeds. They won't even let him bunk with 'em."

"Where is he staying?"

"Ma and pa rented him the workshed back of the roadhouse." She was embarrassed. "It's not too bad, Anne. It's a pretty good place. I mean it's nothing like Mary Angus' place. It's got a wood floor and it's clean."

Every time I'd thought about it I wanted to kill somebody. Fred lived in a workshed all by himself when here he had the most beautiful home of anybody and a family that loved him. And it was all my fault. He hated working for wages, and on top of it he had to work with men who didn't even want him.

He must have been miserable, but all he'd said about it was *if I can take it*.

I wrote him a letter telling him I thought he should come back. "We don't have to see each other at all," I ended it.

> I promise you that. I won't even say hello to you if I should see you. I'll act as if I don't even know you. I know how you feel now and I'll respect your feelings, so please don't stay there just because of me.

I signed it "Your friend (and I mean just that), Anne."

In a way that was the most peculiar time I ever went through. I'd never felt more alone in my life, and yet at the same time I felt more whole than I ever did. I didn't seem to need anybody, as if there was a protective shell around me that made me so sure of myself I couldn't say or do anything wrong. I didn't know what it was, but I took everything in stride. Not that I didn't feel things. I did. I just felt them in a different way. The night that Nancy finally accomplished what she'd set her heart on, for instance, I was so composed I hardly recognized myself.

We were just sitting around not doing much of anything that night. Nancy was looking through a Third Reader and I was practicing on the harmonica. As long as I didn't have a piano I figured I ought to have a musical instrument to play when we needed music for songs and games, so I'd taken it up at the same time Jimmy had. When Nancy and I had been feuding she'd always asked me to stop while she was studying. Now nothing seemed to bother her. I was playing *Home on the Range* and not doing bad at all when I heard her say, "Anne?"

I looked over at her and there was just no way to describe the wonderful smile on her face. Even before she said a word I knew what had happened.

"I can read," she said.

"You sure?"

She nodded.

"Go ahead."

216

" 'Once upon-ay-time,' " she read, " 'ay-crab-left-thee-sea-and-went-out-upon-thee-beach-to-warm-himself-in-thee-sunshine . . .' " She went on, sounding out each word the way a little kid would. Once or twice she almost got stuck, but she kept going. It was the first time she'd ever read anything without my help, and she read it perfectly. I didn't know anything about psychological blocks. I did know that if that was what had been holding her back up to now, it was all gone. When she finished she was glowing.

"Was that reading?"

"That was reading."

We tried her with a newspaper just to be sure, and she read some headlines from the Fairbanks *Daily News–Miner*. She didn't do too badly with a few paragraphs from *Collier's* either. She was so happy about it she almost started to cry. A couple of months before I'd not only have joined her, but I'd have wanted to run out and yell the news up and down the length of the settlement. Not that I wasn't as happy as she was. I felt wonderful for her, and we stayed up late talking about plans for her future. I just wasn't surprised. It was as if I'd known all along it was going to happen and accepted it that way—as something I'd expected.

Too excited to sleep, she sat up reading long after I turned in. The next morning she told me she'd been up till two. She wasn't the least bit tired either. She could barely wait for the class to show up to tell them all, and before the day was over everybody in Chicken knew she was able to read.

Maggie Carew invited us both over to supper to celebrate. It was the first time she'd had me over in quite a while, and it meant she wanted to bury the hatchet. Now that Fred was gone she felt more kindly towards me, or maybe she was even feeling sorry for what had happened. I didn't know and I didn't care. I liked her. At least she was honest and straightforward. She'd been about the only one in the settlement that really said what she thought and she hadn't made any bones about it.

After supper she asked me if I was looking forward to teaching in Eagle next year.

217

"I don't know," I said.

"Whattaya mean ya don't know," she said. "You got a contract, ain't ya?"

"Yes, but I hear the school board has some doubts about me."

"Well, I oughtta have something to say about that," she said. "End of next spring we're movin' there. I bought the roadhouse right alongside the dock. I'll put in a good word for you —unless a course you got other plans."

"No, I don't," I said.

I didn't have any at all.

I'd always kept a scrapbook of poems that I liked to read over and over. My favorite was "Waiting" by John Burroughs. When I reread it it seemed as though it was almost written for me.

> Serene, I fold my hands and wait,
>   Nor care for wind, nor tide, nor sea;
> I rave no more 'gainst time or fate,
>   For lo! my own shall come to me.

It was exactly the way I felt. I was just waiting—for what I didn't know. Something. There was an empty space inside of me, but what was going to fill it up I couldn't say.

Came February I almost wondered if I wanted to teach anywhere in Alaska at all because suddenly the weather turned so mean it felt as if God had gone away from this part of the world. Day after day the sky stayed so dark you couldn't tell whether it was day or night. For almost a week the temperature dropped to fifty and lower and stayed there. Even if there'd been no thermometer we'd have known how cold it was: all the moisture was sucked out of the air, leaving everybody thirsty all the time—no matter how much tea or water we drank we still felt dry.

People began to get as mean as the weather. With the holidays over everybody had cabin fever—aggravation from staying indoors day after day—and they started quarrels with each

218

other over everything. Uncle Arthur swore Ben Norvall had stolen a pick from him and just for spite went out and sprang all of Ben's traps. Then, in a drunken rage one day, Angela Barrett threw a pot of scalding water over one of her dogs when he barked too long. Maggie Carew's husband had to put it out of its agony by shooting it.

Maybe if I hadn't had the class to keep me busy I'd have felt the same kind of aggravation. Sometimes I'd find myself getting annoyed over small things, but most of the time I was calm—not hard or cold or anything like that—just kind of detached, as if I was still waiting for something to happen.

When it did finally, it was a day I'd never forget.

It was just after the class came back from lunch. It was sixty below that day and the little children were using my bed again. I was beginning to think the bed was the most important article of furniture I had. Besides the kids using it when the floor was too cold, Nancy and I had had to put our sack of potatoes in it because it was the only place we could be sure they wouldn't freeze.

We were tidying up in my quarters when I heard Evelyn Vaughn start up with Rebekah in the schoolroom. "Hey, Rebekah—how much two and two?"

"Fo'."

"How much one and two?"

"T'ree."

"How much t'ree and two?" she mimicked.

"Fi.' "

"Rebekah, me think you one verry smart woman," Evelyn said, "right Eleanor?"

"That's right."

At first I used to interfere when anybody made fun of her, but by now she could take care of herself.

"Oh no," she said to Evelyn as I walked into the room. "You not think Rebekah smart, little lady. You think *you* too much smart. Think you not speak good English and Rebekah not know."

Evelyn looked as though she was sorry she'd started, but

Rebekah wasn't going to have any mercy on her. She was as tough as Evelyn anytime, and a lot smarter. She opened her eyes wide and pointed a finger at her. "You not be nice I make bad medicine. Send Brush Man get you at night."

"Who's the Brush Man?" Evelyn asked, uncertainly. Rebekah's expression was so horrible the whole class was spellbound.

"You not know Brush Man?"

"No."

"He live all over—in tree, in hole, anyplace—only come out when dark."

"I don't believe it," Evelyn said. She was afraid of the dark and everyone knew it.

"Aagh!" Rebekah cried. The sound was as terrible as her expression. "You say this, Brush Man get you for sure! You know how when too much cold you see little blue light in bushes?" I'd seen it myself once in a while—static electricity. "That tell you Brush Man near. But you never see him till he grab you—*then* you see him, ha ha."

"What's he look like?" Evelyn asked. She was trying to make out that she didn't care, but she was worried.

Not taking her eyes off Evelyn, Rebekah raised her hands over her head and bared her teeth. "Ten feet big," she growled, "maybe more. Much hair. Face all black from cold and long teeth like grizzly. Yellow eyes like punkin. My father big medicine man, tell me how bring him. You make more fun me," she warned Evelyn, "I send Brush Man for *you!*"

In the silence that followed we heard three distant rifle shots, one right after the other. We all knew what they meant. Someone was calling for help. I asked the class to sit quietly while Nancy put on her coat and went outside to see if anyone knew where they'd come from. She came back a few minutes later. "The Carews think they came from somewhere over towards the Purdys," she said. "Your mother and father's goin' over," she told Jimmy. "They said you and Willard could go along."

After that there was no keeping the rest of the class in, so I let them all go, with the exception of Joan Simpson. Three more shots came as they all ran out.

"I think maybe come from Mary Angus, Tisher," Rebekah said.

"You feel like going over?" I asked Nancy.

"If you want."

Outside, even though I had a scarf over my face the first breath I took caught in my throat. Before we could head over to Mary's we had to take Joan Simpson home. She was too young to let her go alone. For the first few steps our warm moccasins slipped on the snow, but then the bottoms coated up and we were able to walk. Joan lived in the opposite direction. It took us fifteen minutes to get to her cabin, and then we started back for Mary Angus' place. A gray-black mist hung over everything, and the cold made it impossible to talk, so we trudged all the way in silence, moving fast enough to stay warm, slow enough to avoid perspiring.

The kids were playing outside the shack when we got there. A couple of them were riding in Mary's hand sled while Robert Merriweather pulled it and Jimmy pushed from behind yelling, "Mush!" As soon as they saw Nancy and me they came running over.

"Mary's dead, Teacher!" Jimmy yelled.

"Dead as a doornail," Willard chimed in.

"And there's blood all over the place. They won't even let us come in. Ask 'em if they will, Teacher? We wanna see."

Jake Harrington was standing outside the door with Rebekah.

"Is it true?" I asked them.

Jake nodded. I pushed the door open. There were a lot of people inside, but only a sputtering candle for light so at first I could only make out Angela, the Carews and Joe Temple. "Close that darn door before this candle goes out!" I heard Angela yell.

I closed it.

"Well, it's our little teacher," she said sarcastically. She was drunk, smiling at me in a way that made it plain she didn't have any use for me. She'd been drinking more than ever the past few weeks and getting worse every day. A few days ago in the roadhouse Ben Norvall had said something she didn't like and she went after him and gave him a couple of good wallops before anybody could stop her. He was in a corner with Chuck, the two of them bending down over what must have been Mary's body. Ben was covering her up with a wolf robe.

"What happened?" I asked Maggie.

"She musta hemorrhaged," Maggie said. "When they get as far gone as she was they go fast."

Mr. Vaughn was there too. "Take a slant at her," he said, jerking a thumb towards the corner. "See what a good siwash looks like."

"There's no need for that kinda talk, Arnold," Maggie said. "We're tryin' a decide what to do," she said to me. "Joe here's gonna get his sled and mush the body over to our place. We'll keep it in the extra cache till Strong can tote it up to the Indian village, but we ain't figgered out what to do with the kids yet."

Now that my eyes had adjusted to the darkness I saw Ethel. She was sitting on a box, with nobody paying attention to her. She was wide-eyed and scared from all the commotion. I went over to her.

"How about it, Joe," Angela said. "You gonna take the kids?"

"What am I supposed to do with them?"

"All you gotta do is keep 'em a week or so," Maggie said. "Then Strong'll mush 'em outta here."

"I don't know anything about taking care of kids," he said.

"That's what they all say," Angela said. "They can make 'em, but they don't know how to take care of 'em."

Ben and Chuck got up from Mary's body. I was glad Ben had covered it with the wolf robe. I didn't want to see it. There was blood on the edge of the mattress and a big pool of it on the dirt floor that was all frozen and blackened. Chuck was in shock. I put an arm around him and he just let me hold him without making a sound. "This one had it the worst," Ben said, putting a hand on Ethel's head. "I was going by and didn't see any smoke coming from the chimney. Came in and she was sitting alongside Mary there." He patted her head. "If ol' Ben hadn't happened by," he said to her, "you'd liable to have froze to death."

"Maybe she'd of been better off," Maggie said.

"That's sure as shootin' true," Angela said. "She certainly ain't got nothin' to look for'ard to in that Indian village." She took out a flask and drank a couple of mouthfuls.

Mr. Carew spoke up. "Unless we're gonna stand around here jawin' all day, let's decide what we do with the kids."

Chuck was limp against me. I put a hand on his shoulder.

Angela said, "I vote Joe takes 'em. Teach 'im a good lesson."

"That's not funny. I told you before I wouldn't know what to do with them."

"How about you, Maggie?" Angela asked. "You got the bunkhouse."

"I got my own to look after."

"I'll take them," I said to Joe.

"*You*'ll take 'em!" Angela said.

"Yes."

"How are you going to take care of them and teach school too?" Mr. Vaughn asked.

"I can manage it."

"That's fine with me," Joe said, relieved. "Thanks, Anne."

"I don't think it's right," Mr. Vaughn said.

"I agree with 'im," Maggie said. "She's just a kid."

"Then why don't you take them?" Joe snapped at her.

She looked as if she was considering it and for a few seconds I held my breath. I wanted them. I wanted them badly.

"I got my own," she repeated.

"They're all yours," Joe said to me.

I picked up Ethel. "You take Chuck," I said to Nancy.

"Sure." She was a little surprised.

Nobody made a move to get out of the way. They just stared at me as if I was some kind of a circus freak.

"Anybody else want them?" I said.

Nobody answered.

"Then if nobody minds, we'll take these children home."

223

XVI

Ethel was quiet until we reached the door. Then she realized that I was taking her away and she began to scream. By the time we were outside she was fighting me tooth and nail and I had to let her down. Even then I could barely stop her from running back inside the shack. She was just too young to realize her mother was dead.

If it hadn't been for Ben Norvall I don't know how we'd have gotten her home. He went and got Mary's hand sled from the kids, then helped me tuck a blanket around Ethel and tie her into the sled. It was the only way we could get her out of there. She wouldn't even pay any attention to Chuck when he tried to talk to her.

Harnessing myself to the sled, I started pulling, but I hadn't gone twenty yards before my lungs felt as though I were breathing fire. I was so rattled I'd forgotten to put a scarf over my mouth.

It was hard going, the snow so dry that it tugged at the runners like sand. After ten minutes Nancy took over, and all the way back to the house Ethel kept screaming and struggling. When she threw her head back the first time and I saw her face I thought for a second something terrible had happened to her—until I realized it was her tears. They'd frozen all around her eyes.

By the time we were inside the house, Nancy's cheeks and

nose had turned white, and from the numbness I felt I knew mine had too. Ethel ran straight under the table and sat there crying. And no sooner was Chuck inside than he started crying too.

Nancy put the kettle on for tea while I tried to console him. It took a while before he was able to stop, and then he wanted to know when his mother was going to wake up. I had to tell him that she wasn't going to, that she was dead. Even though he knew what the word meant he couldn't accept it as meaning he'd never see her again. "Who take care me now?" he asked me.

"I'm going to take care of you."

"When my mudda come?"

"She's not going to. You're going to stay here with me and Nancy. Chuck—" He looked as though he was going to start crying again. "I need your help. Can you help me? The first thing we have to do is explain to Ethel that she has nothing to be afraid of here. She doesn't understand what's happened. You're going to have to tell her. Can you do that?"

He went over to the table and kneeled down beside his sister. She was still sniffling, but she listened to him. She almost started crying again at one point, but he made her stop. They exchanged some words, and when they were done she looked kind of lost. She let Chuck lead her out from under the table. My sense of smell had been frozen up to then, but it came back just as Ethel stood up. The worst odor in the world hit me. Her parka was covered with grease and old food, but that wasn't what it was coming from.

Nancy wrinkled her nose. "She must have done something in her pants."

"We'll have to give her a bath."

"The sooner the better," Nancy said. "Pee-yew."

While the water was simmering on the stove there was a knock at the door. It was Maggie and her husband with Chuck's and Ethel's things, some moccasins and clothing, a .22 rifle and a couple of pairs of children's snowshoes.

After we had enough hot water in the washtub I took off

Ethel's parka, but when I tried to take off her clothes she pulled away and began to cry. I asked Chuck what was wrong.

"She not like take off clothes," he said. "Nevuh take off."

"She has to have a bath."

Chuck explained to her in Indian, pointing to the washtub. She shook her head. It was no.

"You better tell her she's going to have to," I said. "There's no two ways about it."

That did it. He explained, she took one look at Nancy and me and the next moment she dived under the bed. There was nothing else for it but to go after her, which we did. I got a bite on the hand and Nancy a good healthy kick before we dragged her out screaming to high heaven. Chuck put his fingers in his ears, and while Nancy held onto her I took off her clothes—knee-length moccasins, a light jacket, and a calico dress with another cotton dress underneath. Her undergarment had me stumped when I got to it. It was tight-fitting, like a union suit. It even had a drop seat, but there were no buttons up the front.

"What is it?" I asked Nancy.

"Indian-style underwear. The mothers sew 'em up in it around October and it stays on till April."

"How do you get it off?"

"Cut it off."

I got a pair of scissors and Nancy held her still, but as soon as I started to cut Ethel panicked. She struggled and screamed so loud it made my eardrums ache. It scared Chuck, and he began to cry in sympathy. I stopped, not knowing what to do.

"She's gotta have a bath, Anne," Nancy said.

I knew that, but I couldn't help feeling like a villain. The best thing to do, I thought, was get Chuck out so he wouldn't have to watch.

"Ugh," Nancy said, trying to hold Ethel away from her. I didn't blame her.

"Chuck, are you hungry?"

He said he was, and as soon as he stopped crying I got him

into his parka and brought him over to the roadhouse. After I explained what was going on to Maggie, she said she'd give him something to eat and keep him until I came over for him.

When I got back, Ethel and Nancy were just as I'd left them. Ethel was still in tears. As soon as I came near her with the scissors again she was so terrified she tried to climb Nancy.

"Maybe if we gave her something to eat first she'd calm down," I said. "She loves bread and butter and honey."

"C'mon, Anne," Nancy said, "we gotta do it. Give 'er somethin' to eat now, she'll throw it right up."

"But suppose she gets a heart attack or something?"

"If anybody's gonna get a heart attack, it's gonna be us," Nancy said. "You ready?"

"Would you rather I held her?"

"If I thought you could I'd let ya. She's a wildcat, this one. I'll hold, you cut." She got Ethel in a good strong grip. "Start cutting," she yelled.

I started, shearing both sleeves up to the neck, then cutting and ripping down to her ankles, peeling the garment as I went. Finally it was all off. Naked and screaming, she looked more animal than human, her hair matted, her whole body just one mass of caked dirt and excrement.

Nancy picked her up, and together we brought her over to the tub. I tested the water. It was just right. We lowered her into it. As soon as we did, all heck broke loose. If she was frightened before, she was horrified now. I'd never have believed that a little child could have had as much strength as she did, but she went into a rage. As if we'd dumped her into a tub of ice cold water, she let out a shriek, started striking out and clawing at the two of us, and before we could stop her, water was flying in all directions and she was out of the tub. I managed to grab her wrist and the next thing I knew she was trying to bite me. If anybody had walked in just then they would have thought Nancy and I were a couple of white savages bent on killing and cooking a little Indian girl. Ethel must have thought just that, because she dodged around the room as we went after her, overturning chairs and screeching

227

horribly. Before we were able to grab her finally, I nearly fell in the washtub and Nancy almost got a black eye.

In she went finally, fighting and clawing in a berserk rage. We didn't dare try to wash her. It was enough just to hold on to her. There wasn't but half the water left in the tub. What wasn't on Nancy and me was all over the floor, and some of it near the wall was already frozen. Ethel kept struggling to get out, thrashing around and fighting so hard that I was almost ready to give up. Until suddenly Ethel just sat back, choking out sobs, all the fight gone out of her. Nancy and I looked at each other in relief. I didn't know anything about the way I looked, but if I looked half as bad as Nancy I was a mess.

We started to wash Ethel and she let us do it. She'd done all she could and now the battle was over. She whimpered and talked to herself in Indian, even tried to tell us a couple of things, but she didn't lift a hand to stop us when we used the washcloth. She was a little scared when I added some hot water after about ten minutes, but it was only to look at me with soft liquid eyes, silently pleading with me not to hurt her.

She'd looked pretty bad when we started washing her, but once we'd shampooed her hair and washed her face even Nancy was taken with her. "Gee, Anne, if you didn't know she couldn't speak English, you'd think she was like any other kid. She's a beauty."

She was too, with skin like a dusky rose and shining black hair. By the time we were ready to take her out she was playing with the water, trying to poke holes through the layer of scum on the surface. When we stood her up and started to dry her she looked so frail and helpless I'd have given anything to be able to tell her she was safe and that we weren't trying to hurt her.

We put her in bed to keep her warm, then rummaged through the stuff Maggie had brought, but there were no clothes for her. Whatever she owned she'd had on.

"I'll have to go over to the store and see what I can dig

228

up," I told Nancy. Ethel had disappeared under the blankets and crawled down to the foot of the bed right alongside our sack of potatoes. I went over and listened.

"Sounds like we have a gopher," I said to Nancy. "Can you eat potatoes raw?"

"I don't know. I never tried 'em."

Not wanting to take any chances I pulled the blankets back. Sure enough, she'd gotten into the sack and was munching away on one. I took it away from her and she cursed me roundly before she dived back under the blankets.

I couldn't find too much in the store to fit her, a pair of bib overalls that were a little big, some long underwear, socks and a corduroy shirt, but at least she had clean clothes.

On the way back I picked up Chuck. He watched without saying anything while Nancy and I dressed Ethel. We had to roll up the bottom of the overalls and she looked lost in the shirt I'd bought, but she really looked cute. Even Chuck thought so. "My gosh, Tisha," he said. "She one pretty girl, I t'ink." He went over to her and examined her carefully, then sniffed her. "Smell good, too," he added approvingly.

"Maybe you ought to introduce us," I said.

"Dis Tisha," he said pointing to me. "Tisha. An' dis Nancy." He said something to her in Indian, then pointed to us again, but Ethel didn't say anything. Chuck nudged her impatiently. "Tisha . . . Nancy," he said warningly.

"She's a little scared, Chuck. Give her time."

"No no. She say." He said something to her in Indian again and stabbed a finger at me. "Tisha."

"Tisha," she said.

"An' Nancy."

"Nassy," she mimicked.

Nancy and I applauded. "That's wonderful. She's very smart, Chuck."

"You bet," Chuck said. "I tell her she no say I give one big smack."

One thing we didn't have trouble with was getting her to

229

eat. She wolfed down two thick slices of bread for supper and a good helping of moose roast and beans. She didn't like having her face and hands wiped, though. That made her cry.

Maggie Carew came by right after supper. "Joe brought the mother over," she said. She looked at Ethel admiringly. "Kid doesn't look half bad now. Havin' any trouble with 'em?"

"None at all."

She put a paper sack down on the table. "Some of Willard's old clothes. They might fit the girl."

I thanked her and before she went out she said. "If the two of 'em are too much of a handful maybe I could put the girl up in the bunkhouse."

"They're no trouble at all, Mrs. Carew."

"Nice of you to keep 'em here."

"I don't mind a bit."

The clothes came in handy. There was a small flannel nightie in the sack and even some diapers and rubber pants. When it came time to put Ethel to bed, though, she raised a howl and wouldn't let us. We asked Chuck to explain to her about pajamas, but he didn't understand the idea himself. He and Ethel had always slept in their clothes. She had to have the diapers, though, because she'd be sleeping between Nancy and me.

"Maybe if Ethel saw you change your clothes she wouldn't mind so much," I told Chuck. He said it was all right with him, so back I went to the store for a pair of pajamas to fit him. He was fascinated by them, liked them "too much," but Ethel was still suspicious, so we made a compromise for her—diapers under outer clothing. Before we put the diapers on her we had her go to the toilet in the cache. She was afraid of the toilet seat, though, and we finally had to settle for letting her do her business on newspaper.

We put them both in the big bed so that Ethel wouldn't be scared. When Nancy and I were ready for bed a little later we'd transfer Chuck to the couch. We'd built the fire up in the schoolroom so we could work in there and let them sleep, but as soon as we went inside and started to close the door Chuck wanted to know where we were going. I told him we'd be in the schoolroom, but he said he'd be scared if we went, so we stayed. Nancy worked away on a reading comprehension test I gave her while I drew some outlines for hand puppets the kids wanted to make. Chuck and Ethel tossed and turned for a while, murmuring to each other, then they were quiet. I thought they were both asleep, but Chuck wasn't. He called to me, and I went over to him. He was still trying to understand what had happened.

"My mudda, she catch die," he said.

"Yes."

"She all by herselfs in cabin. Priddy lonely, I t'ink."

"They've taken her out."

"Where they take?"

"They put her in the cache—in back of the roadhouse." I tried not to get choked up, but it was hard.

"Still priddy lonely." He started to get up. "Maybe I go see. She not be lonely."

"She's not lonely, Chuck. She's sleeping. And she's very happy."

"You t'ink so?"

"I know it. She'll sleep forever now. And she'll never again be cold, or hungry, or sad."

"You no tell lie? She never be hungry, be cold?"

"Never. That's the truth. Her spirit is up in Heaven now. She's very happy."

"She have big cook?"

"What's big cook?"

"Kill big fat moose. Have big cook. Eat."

"Oh yes. She has everything there."

"I like dat. She one good mudda me. You good mudda me too, Tisha. You take care me like real mudda."

"You're a fine boy, that's why. Now you go to sleep. Good night."

"Night."

My eyes were so wet that I could hardly see when I sat down. I looked over at Nancy. Her face was all twisted up and she was trying her best to hold back her tears. Finally she got up and went into the schoolroom. I went in right after her and the two of us stood like fools, crying silently so that Chuck wouldn't hear us.

Later on we transferred him to the couch, then we both got in on each side of Ethel. We'd left the oil lamp on so they wouldn't be scared if they woke in the middle of the night. Ethel was in a deep sleep, a lock of long black hair curled across her cheek. I pushed it back. She was lovely.

Outside a wind rose and little drafts of freezing air nipped in. I thought of Mary lying cold and alone in the dark cache. There was nobody to take care of Chuck and Ethel now, nobody at all. They were all by themselves. Back in the shack, when everybody had been standing around trying to decide what to do with them I'd wanted them right away. The longer I'd stood there listening to the whole bunch of them talking about Chuck and Ethel as if they were dirt, the more I wanted them. Maybe it was because nobody had ever wanted me either when I was a little kid—nobody except Granny. They needed somebody to take care of them, and I could do it.

"You awake, Nancy?"

"Uh-huh."

"What do you think about keeping Chuck and Ethel here?"

"For how long?"

"I don't know. But I don't want to send them back to the Indian village. Not now anyway."

"How long do you want to keep 'em?"

"As long as I can."

"Yeah, but I mean how long?"

"I'll give you one guess."

When what I was getting at finally dawned on her, she still couldn't bring herself to believe it.

"Anne—you saying you want them for your *own?*"

"Yes." Up to then I'd had doubts about it myself, but saying it out loud made them all disappear. "What do you think?"

"I don't know . . . That's up to you," she said.

232

XVII

I asked Nancy not to tell anybody about it. Besides the fact that it was going to start a ruckus, they were still Joe Temple's children and I'd have to talk to him before I could go ahead and keep them. If he said no, there wasn't anything I could do. I wanted them, though, I knew that for sure.

For the first few days Ethel never let Chuck out of her sight. Everything was new to her and she was scared, but you wouldn't have known it from the way she acted. Not that she didn't cry. It took hardly anything to set her off. She'd start crying as soon as Chuck left the room, or when school was over and the kids left, things like that. But otherwise she was about the most self-possessed little girl there ever was. She was timid, but she had every right to be. She couldn't understand a word of all the English flying around her head.

One thing that helped was that the kids in class were nice to her—much nicer than they were to Chuck. It was partly because she wasn't any competition for them and partly because they knew she was an orphan. They didn't make fun of her or try any of the nasty things they'd tried with Chuck. In fact they all went out of their way to get her interested in something.

She and Willard took to each other from the beginning. The first morning she came in he wanted her to sit at his table. She sat down alongside of him and he started babbling to her right away, until I finally had to tell him to be quiet. By afternoon he had her coloring with crayons and making paper chains. He also had her eating the flour paste and licking the window. The first one I didn't mind too much, but the second was dangerous. It was his favorite sport, getting his tongue to stick to the window just enough so he could still pull it away easily. He'd lost a sliver of tongue doing it once and there'd been blood all over the place. I stopped it fast.

Ethel wandered around so calm and quiet most of the time you'd have thought nothing in the world bothered her, but it wasn't so. After a couple of days we started finding bits of food hidden all around. One time I found a piece of bread in my sock. Chuck explained to her that there would always be plenty of grub, but it didn't stop her. She kept stashing bits of meat and everything else here and there.

I'd always heard that mothers had a lot of trouble getting their kids to eat, but with Chuck and Ethel there wasn't a problem in the world. The only time Ethel didn't have an appetite was at supper the first day. She just stared at her plate until the rest of us finished, then right after that she threw up chunks of every color in the rainbow—all the crayons she'd been coloring with.

Having the kids around all day helped her a lot, and in a few days she was repeating words all over the place—book, sandwich, eat, dish. She was as fastidious as they come, too. Chuck always gulped his food so fast I had to keep telling him to slow down, but Ethel ate like a little princess. After we finished supper one night she put her hands out and said, "Hello?"

"Well, hello," I answered. It was the first time she'd ever said a word by herself.

She looked at Nancy and repeated it, so Nancy said hello to her too. She shook her head, got down from her chair and went over and pointed to the cupboard. "Hello?" she piped.

I went to it and looked inside. She wanted jello, I finally realized.

The fourth night she woke up screaming, throwing her arms around my neck and holding on as if there was a devil after

234

her. Even after Nancy lit the gas lamp she was still too terrified to go back to sleep and she wouldn't let me go, so I got up and sat in the rocker with her, until an hour later her eyes closed.

I had almost a full week to go before I'd have to talk with Joe Temple about my keeping her and Chuck, and I kept putting it off. I was shy about doing it. But finally, a couple of days before Mr. Strong was due in, something Chuck did forced me to.

He'd been trouble that whole day, knocking into the other boys on the sliding pond, talking out of turn and even deliberately tearing a drawing of Isabelle's. It wasn't like him. Yet when I tried to get him to tell me what was wrong he said it was nothing. Then, just before dismissal, he threw a pencil at Evelyn Vaughn. I told him to go into my quarters and he stomped through the door and started kicking chairs around. By the time I went in after him they were all over the place. As soon as he saw me he ran out minus hat and coat and headed for the outhouse.

I left him alone, figuring he'd be back as soon as it got too cold for him, but when ten minutes went by and he was still gone I threw on a jacket and went out after him. It was dark outside. A kind of sinister gray pall hung in the air, erasing even the near hills. I pushed on the door, but Chuck had braced a foot against it. He was crying.

"Chuck?"

He didn't answer. Mr. Carew called to me from the roadhouse.

"Somebody stuck again?" He was holding an armful of wood.

"No. It's all right, thanks," I called back, then I lowered my voice. "Chuck, I wish you'd come out of there."

He didn't answer me, and I waited to hear the roadhouse door slam before I said, "Chuck?"

"Go 'way."

"It must be terribly cold in there . . . Won't you come out?"

"I never come out. I catch die, you no see me no more."

235

"I'd feel terrible if that happened."

"Oh, no. You no care. You be happy." I could hear his teeth chattering.

"Chuck, if anything happened to you I don't know what I'd do. I love you very much."

He was furious. "You lie. You one lousy white woman tell big lie!"

"You must be awfully mad at me . . . What did I lie about?"

"You say you take care me. You no take care me. You make me go 'way Indian village." He could hardly talk for shivering.

"Chuck, I didn't lie to you. I want you to stay with me. Don't you know that?"

"Ev'lyn, he say when Mr. St'ong come he take me 'way."

"Can I come in, Chuck? Please?"

There was a long silence, then the door moved. I pushed on it and it bumped against him. He was huddled on the floor, in the corner. I sat down between the holes. All I could see was the top of his head in the dimness, his breath misting up around it.

"Could you come up here and sit with me?"

He stayed put.

"Please, Chuck. I want to tell you something."

He had trouble standing up, his legs were so cramped. He sat down beside me, trembling, and I put an arm around him. What a place to talk with somebody you cared about, I thought, sitting and freezing in an outhouse. The only consolation was that it was too cold to smell.

"What Evelyn told you wasn't true. I'm not going to send you away—not if I can help it. I want to keep you and Ethel with me, but I have to talk to your father first."

He relaxed a little. "Why you talk with my fodda?"

"Because it's going to be up to him."

He looked up at me and he almost smiled. "My fodda no care, Tisha. He say yes. I know he say yes."

"Whether he cares or not I still have to talk to him. I'm

236

going to tell him what a fine boy you are and that I want you to stay with me. I want it very badly. You believe me?"

His arms went around me and he hugged me with all his might. "I believe, Tisha. Oh, I believe too much." He straightened up, happy. "I gonna tell that Ev'lyn he lie."

"Don't tell her anything. Not yet. Let me talk to your father first, all right? Not a word. Now for Pete's sake let's get out of here."

After supper I skied over to see Joe. I'd never been over to his place, but I didn't have any trouble finding it. He lived about a mile from the settlement on Stonehouse Creek. All I had to do was follow a sled trail till I reached the creek, then follow the creek up the hill to his cabin.

As many times as I had gone out at night alone it still scared me a little. There was no wind, and a bright crescent moon shone down. Everything was so still it was like being alone in a big wax museum. Nothing moved. Every twig, every bush that pushed up through the whiteness stood out in the pale moonlight. By the time I reached Stonehouse Creek, slung my skis over my shoulder and started up the hill I felt almost like two people, one of them breathing hard and making all kinds of noise, the other out there watching me moving along, a tiny speck in a big white sea. The hill was steeper than it looked, and before I was halfway up I was sorry I'd brought the skis. They weighed a ton.

Joe's dogs began to howl and act up before I reached the top. He came out to see what was going on and I waved to him.

"Tea or coffee?" he called.

"Tea!"

He disappeared inside and came out again just as I reached the top. The racket from the kennel made it impossible to hear, so he didn't say anything until we were inside.

"No chaperone?"

"I couldn't get her to climb that hill."

He held out his hands. "I'll take your duds."

I slipped off my parka and plopped down into a chair. He

237

had a nice place, just the kind I'd have expected. There were a few guns on the wall—a high-powered rifle with a telescopic sight, a shotgun and a revolver—and they all were clean and gleaming with oil. He took as good care of his things as he did himself. He'd made a built-in basin for the kitchen counter, and on the shelf over it all his toilet articles were lined up neatly—hairbrush and comb, shaving brush and mug, shaving lotion and straight razor. The whole place was so neat and clean compared to mine I felt like a slob. With all the kids trooping in and out, my place was always a mess.

He had a good library too. Some painted boxes nailed to the wall were filled with books: Dickens, Sinclair Lewis, Fitzgerald, Milton. A can of tobacco and a rack of pipes sat on a crate beside a rocking chair. His cot was made army-fashion and was pushed against the wall. There were some nice furs he'd hung on wooden hoops. I couldn't tell what they all were, but I recognized the silky rust-gray, almost topaz color of lynx, and two soft, shining pelts of silver and black fox.

The only thing I didn't like was the odor of all the furs that were piled on newspapers. They smelled rank. It was only too bad that the women who were going to wear them couldn't see the whole sickening process of trapping, killing and skinning the animals they came from. They'd never wear them again.

A few burlap sacks already crammed with furs were piled by the door.

"That's some catch," I said.

"Half of it's last season's." He handed me a steaming cup of tea. "The price wasn't that good, so I held onto them."

"That was smart."

"Same thing anybody would do if they could afford it, but most of these old-timers can't. That's how you make money in this country—have enough money so you can hold out for your price."

The cup felt nice and warm. Joe poured himself some coffee, then took a bottle of Canadian whiskey down from the shelf.

"Mind?"

"No, go ahead."

Just to be courteous he offered me some. I said no and he poured some into his cup. "Skoal," he said, taking a sip.

"Joe—"

"Don't say a word. I want to see if I can guess what this visit is all about. You didn't come for my company, I'm sure of that. Or for supper—it's too late. I guess I give up."

"It's about Chuck and Ethel."

"What about them?"

"Can I have them?"

"Are you serious?"

"Of course I am."

He laughed. "What do you want them for?"

"What's the difference?"

"You're asking me to give you something. I want to know why you want it."

"Joe, I just want them."

"Good enough. Take them."

I'd expected him to say no and I had a dozen arguments all ready. Now I hardly knew what to say. "You mean it?"

"Sure. You know you're going to get people all riled up, though, don't you?"

"I guess so."

"Doesn't that suggest anything to you?"

"Like what?"

"Like the fact that ever since you've been here you've been getting them riled up."

"Is that my fault?"

"Whose else is it? You're a genuine card, let me tell you."

"I don't know what you're talking about."

"You mean it doesn't seem peculiar to you when a young single girl decides all of a sudden that she's going to play mother, especially when she knows that everybody isn't exactly fond of the offspring she'll be playing it with."

"I'm not playing anything."

"Then why not avoid a whole mess and let those kids go to the Indian village where they belong?"

"Joe, you know what that Indian village is like. It's not a

place for a dog, much less for children. Don't they mean anything to you at all?"

"No."

"How about Mary—did she?"

"What's she got to do with this?"

"You're asking me questions. Why can't I ask you?"

"Mary and I were finished over a year ago. I didn't ask her to come out here. She came on her own. I tried to get her to go back a half a dozen times. I told her I'd give her enough money to tide her over the winter if she would, but she wouldn't."

"She must have loved you an awful lot."

"That was her hard luck."

He knew how cruel that sounded, but he didn't apologize. He took a long swallow of coffee, finishing it. Then he got up. "Why'd you come into this country?" he asked me while he poured himself some more.

"To see it."

"No wonder you go around like Little Miss Muffet. Everybody took bets the day you arrived. Half of them bet you'd last about a month after freeze-up and the other half bet you'd stay and freeze to death."

"Sorry to disappoint everyone." I started to get up.

"Don't get so insulted." He made a motion for me to sit down and poured some more whiskey into his coffee. "It's about time somebody told you a couple of things. The first is that it wouldn't be a bad idea for you to get your nose out of the air and stop judging people so much. Maybe you came here for the fun of it, but nobody else did. They came to make a strike, get rich and move on, because that's all this country's good for."

"You sound as though you don't like it here," I said.

"You're beginning to get the idea."

"Then why do you stay?"

"For the same reason everybody else does," he answered. "I can't afford to go. Two kinds of people live here—the ones that have investments, like me, and the ones that don't have enough money to pack up and get out, like these old-timers who have it in the back of their mind that they're gonna hit a big pay streak one of these days. That's why they hang on even though their bones ache and they'd like nothing better than to hightail it for California and forget this place ever existed."

The whiskey had relaxed him, or maybe he simply needed to talk. He stopped long enough to take a deep breath.

"Maybe you don't like the way I treated Mary, but what do you know about her and me? She knew what she was doing. I never told her I was gonna marry her, even though there were times when I thought about it. But all I'd have to do was think to myself, what happens when I go Outside—when the two of us go Outside? What could I say to people when I introduced her? 'Here y'are folks, meet the wife. She knows everything there is to know about curing fur, making jerky, drying fish, chopping wood or sewing mittens. Just don't talk to her about politics, literature, current events, art, mortgages, or anything else like that.' "

I tried to interrupt him, but he wouldn't let me. "Well, the problem never came up, because we broke up. I didn't want her to come out here, but she made up her mind she was gonna do it and that was that. I gave her just enough grub to keep going, hoping she'd go back to the Indian village. She wouldn't. So I thought if I simply didn't give her anything she'd be forced to go back. Well, it didn't work. She made up her mind she was gonna stay, and when an Indian gets it in their head to do something, nothing gets it out."

I got up and asked him to let me have my parka.

"I've got a couple more things to say," he went on, "then if you want I'll walk you back to your place."

"I can make it on my own," I said.

He took my parka down from the rack and handed it to me. "Have it your way," he said. "You stepped on a lot of toes since you've been here and if you weren't as nice a kid as you are you wouldn't have gotten away with it. Or maybe it's just that you're a kid and so everybody looked the other way. If people don't like Indians they don't like Indians and that's their business. I've got nothing against Indians myself, but I'm not about to start lecturing other people on how to feel toward 'em, and that goes for half-breeds too. Fred Purdy did you the biggest favor in the world when he pulled out of here, only you don't have enough sense to see that. This is his home. He has to live in this country. He's not about to make it tough on himself by messing around with a white girl. He did the right thing by you. You ought to be grateful. Instead you have to go ahead and stick your foot right smack in people's faces again and take these kids. Well I'm telling you you're making a mistake."

"You all done?"

"All done."

"You asked me before why I came into this country. I'll tell you the truth. I thought I was going to find something wonderful here—everything I ever dreamed about. Maybe that's stupid, but that's what I thought. Well, I found out one thing. People here aren't much different from the ones back in the States. The only difference is that here they can do anything they want, which means acting just about as mean and selfish as they can."

"You want a soapbox?"

"I'm just telling you how I feel."

"Oh, for Pete's sake, Anne, put on some rouge and lipstick, have some fun, and stop worrying about the underprivileged."

He looked so smug and superior I felt like gnashing my teeth. "Joe, honestly, I'd really like to give you a punch. All you've told me so far is that you don't like the country and people around here don't like Indians. Well, if I want to like both of them that's my right—and I'm getting sick and tired of people looking at me as if I'm a nut because of it."

He smiled. "It hasn't stopped you so far. Go ahead, take the kids. Do what you like with them. Just remember they're still part savage."

"If they are it's probably the part they got from you."

242

I thought he'd get mad at that, but he didn't. "I'm sorry," I said.

"Forget it."

I started to go. "I can still have them?"

"They're all yours . . . Wait a minute."

He walked over to one of the burlap sacks and ripped it open. Peering inside, he pulled out first one, then another black fox pelt. They were perfectly matched and worth a lot of money. He fluffed them out, then clamped the snouts together and draped them around my neck.

"Peace offering," he said.

The way he was smiling made me feel sorry for him. His cabin was neat, and he was pretty well off, but when it came right down to it, all he had was a comfortable place to be lonely in.

"Thanks, Joe." I said. "Will you do me one more favor? Don't say anything to anybody. There's no use in anybody knowing until Mr. Strong comes in."

He said he wouldn't.

Outside, when I got to the edge of the hill and looked down, I couldn't bring myself to push off. I was scared I'd run into a tree.

"What's the matter?" Joe asked.

"It's pretty steep."

"That it is."

I put the skis together and sat down on them. "Don't laugh," I said. "Give me a push."

He pushed me off. Halfway down the skis separated and I went tumbling. The skis went on down without me.

I could hear Joe laughing. "Still in one piece?" he called. He didn't have to raise his voice. It carried clearly.

"Just divine." I did a quick dance step that made him laugh even more, then I collected the ski poles and the furs and walked and slid down the rest of the way. He was still in a good mood when I reached bottom and started strapping on my skies.

"So you think we're all mean, eh?"

"Sometimes. Not most of the time." It felt strange to be talking with him as if we were in the same living room and not a quarter of a mile apart. "How about you? You really think this is such an awful place?"

"Sometimes. Not most of the time . . . Sometimes I stand up here and I look out over everything, and then I think, it's all mine. All of it. I don't have to buy it, pay taxes on it or worry about it. It's mine." He was quiet a few seconds and I thought he was going to go on. Instead he just said, "Well, goodnight kid."

"Goodnight, Joe."

I felt good all the way home.

Ethel was asleep, but Chuck was still up. When I told him the news he let out a yell and hugged me. "I know you make him say yes, Tisha, I know you make him say yes!" He was so excited he didn't fall asleep until after ten.

"What do you think Mr. Strong will say?" I asked Nancy later on. He'd be expecting to take Chuck and Ethel back to the Indian village along with Mary's body.

"He'll be speechless," Nancy said.

"Be nice if everybody else was too."

"Don't you worry, they won't be."

244

XVIII

On the days Mr. Strong came into the settlement I always let the class out about fifteen minutes before he arrived. On those days there were always at least one or two visiting dog teams tied up by the roadhouse. They belonged to miners and trappers who'd mushed in either to pick up goods or to send stuff out. One minute they'd be lying in the snow all quiet, maybe sleeping, the next they'd be lifting their heads, then getting up and stretching. After that, between them and the local dogs it was pure pandemonium—barking and howling that kept getting louder and louder until owners and drivers put a stop to it. Sure enough, if it didn't happen to be a stray animal or a stranger that had started them off, fifteen minutes later Mr. Strong's horse-drawn sled would come rumbling into the settlement. How they could tell he was on the way nobody knew, but they could.

This time they started barking right after lunch. As soon as the class heard them everybody stopped work and listened, waiting to make sure it wasn't something else. Even though it was just about the right time there was no guarantee it was Mr. Strong. There wasn't even a guarantee he'd come in at all on the day he was supposed to. Too many things could hold him up: heavy drifts, a sudden storm or an accident. Now that it was February the weather was especially freakish. The past few days you couldn't even hang out wash. No sooner would you get it on the line than it froze, and then the wind would bang it up against you hard enough to hurt.

So we were quiet, listening as the barking became more and more excited. And finally someone down by the roadhouse yelled out exactly what we wanted to hear: "Wahoo-o-o-o! The dogs say he's a-comin'!"

After I let the class go I threw a sweater around my shoulders and went out. The air was flying white and it was colder than it usually was when it snowed. I ran across the road to check the fire in the stable. I always started it in the morning when Mr. Strong was due in, then kept it going all day. After the long, miserable trip his horses had, the least they were entitled to was a warm stable. After I put another log in the stove I filled the feed bags, then ran back to my quarters. There were a lot more dog teams tied up near the roadhouse than usual, I saw. The word was out that prices at the Seattle Fur Exchange were at their highest now and everybody was shipping their catch out.

Fifteen minutes later everybody including me was waiting outside the post office, stomping around to keep warm.

Jimmy and the rest of the kids were busy piling up snow at the edge of the settlement. They did it every time Mr. Strong was due in, built a barrier a few feet high just so they could watch Mr. Strong's horses kick it to pieces when they went through it. Chuck and Ethel were with them, making their contribution. As soon as we heard the jangle of the bells in the distance the kids came running over to the crowd. Ben Norvall leaned down over Chuck. "Been happy staying with the teacher, have ya?"

Chuck said, "Yiss. Tisha make good grub me."

"That's the way to a man's heart," Ben said. His moustache was peppered with snowflakes. "Bet you'll sure be sorry to go back to that Indian village now."

"I no go back," Chuck said. "I stay here."

"Is that so?" Ben looked at me inquiringly, but I pretended not to be paying attention.

246

Uncle Arthur was on the other side of me.

"Lemme say, missis, it was good of ya to take care of the little tykes. I ain't the marryin' kind, but if I wuz I'd ask for your hand and take these two to boot."

"Then they could all go up to the Indian village and live happily ever after," I heard Angela say to somebody.

Jake Harrington came over with Rebekah and Lily. "Howdy, Teacher."

"Hello, Mr. Harrington."

"How's my woman doing in school?"

"Fine."

"Hope so." He smiled. "I can't get a lick of work out of 'er these days with all the studyin' she's doing. Next thing you know she'll want to go to college."

We heard the bells and everybody got quiet. A few minutes later the sled materialized, rocking and tinkling and crunching its way toward us.

Mr. Strong was standing up looking like a big bear, furred from head to toe, cracking his whip and urging the two horses on. He didn't have to, they wanted to get here as bad as he did, but it made a good impression on everybody and showed he was on the job. As soon as the horses smashed through the snow barrier the kids had built, they tried to head over to the stable, but Jake Harrington and a couple of other men ran out and shied them back towards the post office. They'd had a rough trip, you could see that. The corners of their mouths dripped blood from where the frozen bit had torn them up and their blankets were hung with icicles. The two of them were just one big cloud of steam.

There was somebody sitting up front alongside Mr. Strong. As soon as the sled stopped he jumped down and yelled at the men who were crowding forward. "Just hold on, all a you! Lemme get my wife and baby out."

It was Elmer, Maggie Carew's son-in-law. He moved to the back of the sled where somebody was already pushing up the covering canvas from underneath. When he pulled it back,

247

there was Jeannette, swaddled in a cocoon of furs. She started to hand Elmer a little bundle wrapped in blankets, but Maggie was already alongside of him and said, "Give 'er to me!"

While he helped Jeannette down all the women crowded around Maggie to have a look at the baby. She wouldn't let them see it though. She headed right over to the roadhouse with it, not even taking a peek herself. If they wanted to see it, they could come over later, she said. She wasn't about to let it catch its death out there in the cold.

I got all my mail, then went back to my quarters with Nancy and the children. There was a letter from Lester Henderson, and he didn't have very cheering news. It wasn't that he didn't like my work or think I wasn't doing a good job. "Your reports are thorough and your pupils seem to be making excellent progress," he wrote. "Personally, I'm more than satisfied with your work, especially since this is your first year."

> However, there may be some difficulty in my placing you in Eagle next year. At this point I can't say for certain, but please don't let it concern you. I have any number of other schools I can place you in, and you may rest assured that I'll do so with pride . . .

I knew what that meant. People had written to him about me, and the chances were that the school board in Eagle wouldn't want me teaching there. I tried not to let it bother me too much, but it did. I wanted to teach in Eagle. It was close by and I knew what it would be like. On top of that Maggie Carew was moving there, and even if she wasn't crazy about me, she was somebody I knew. I didn't relish the idea of going to some strange place where I'd have to start all over again.

After supper, Nancy started to get dressed up to go over to the roadhouse. What with everybody coming in from all over to send out their furs it was kind of an occasion and there was going to be a dance and partying. I had to go over to Mr. Strong's store to go over all the accounts with him and give

248

him the cash I'd taken in, but I kept putting it off until Nancy was all dressed, then I couldn't put it off any longer. "I'll be back soon," I told her.

Joe Temple was banging away at the piano when I went by the roadhouse and everybody was singing *Yes, Sir! That's My Baby*. I was hoping the store would be empty, but Mr. Vaughn, Harry Dowles and a couple of other men were sitting around the oil-drum stove when I walked in. The place was suffocating with heat and tobacco smoke. Harry Dowles shifted his quid of chewing tobacco and asked me if I was coming over to the roadhouse.

"I don't think so," I said. I didn't want to drag Chuck and Ethel over there, tonight of all nights.

"Too bad." He spat into the big tin can sitting by the stove. "Fred Purdy's liable to show up." Harry's wife was the one who'd taken back the washboiler from me when I threatened to quit if Chuck didn't stay in the school. Because he and his wife weren't on speaking terms, they were always asking other people to relay what they wanted to say to each other. Once they trapped me between them, and for over fifteen minutes they drove me crazy repeating to the two of them what they could have told each other in a third of the time. They were both peculiar people, and it made me nervous to be around them. Him more than her. With a pale pudgy face, some missing front teeth, and eyes like little pieces of black coal, he looked like an evil snowman. He was always acting as if he knew something you didn't, and I thought he was just being smart now, so I didn't pay him any attention. But then he said, "I'm givin' you the straight goods, Teacher—ain't I, Walt?"

Mr. Strong was leaning over the counter going over some figures. He nailed one of them with his pencil and looked up at me over his glasses. "Fred came in with me," he said.

"How come I didn't see him?"

"He jumped off at Stonehouse Creek and siwashed it from there."

Harry Dowles chuckled. While I went over the accounts with Mr. Strong I knew they were all giving each other know-it-all looks in back of me, but I just pretended I wasn't any more affected than if I'd just been told it was snowing outside. I wouldn't give them the satisfaction. I kept hoping they'd leave before I talked with Mr. Strong about Chuck and Ethel, but they stayed put. After we finished tallying up I was about to mention it, but Mr. Strong beat me to it.

"Too bad about Mary Angus," he said.

"Yes, it was."

"We all have to take the sunset trail sometime or other," somebody said.

"That's the truth," Harry Dowles said.

"I'll be bringing the body back to the Indian village," Mr. Strong said. "I won't be paid for it, but it's my duty. It was commendable of you to look after the two youngsters."

"I didn't mind at all."

"You may bring them over here tonight if you wish. I can give them a couple of sleeping bags. Or if you don't mind I can pick them up before I leave tomorrow."

"You won't have to do either," I said. "They're going to stay with me."

He peered at me over his glasses again. "I don't understand."

"I'm going to keep them for a while. I don't think they ought to go back to the Indian village just yet."

Mr. Vaughn made a snorting noise and Harry Dowles spat. He must have missed the tin can because I heard the squirt sizzle against the stove. "Kinda got your hands full as it is, don't ya, Teacher?" he asked.

Mr. Strong frowned at him. "I'm having a conversation with this lady, Mr. Dowles. I'd be pleased if you wouldn't interrupt." He turned back to me. "Madam, I'm sure your intentions are good, but those children belong among their own people."

"I want to keep them with me, Mr. Strong."

"I believe that you are all of nineteen years old—"

"No, I'm twenty now."

"Since you have not reached the age of consent, I don't see

how you are entitled to take charge of children that do not belong to you."

"I already spoke with Joe Temple about it. He said it's all right with him."

"For how long do you intend to keep them?"

"I don't know."

"I asked you a simple question because I am afraid you are on the verge of making a grievous error. How long do you intend to keep them?"

"For quite some time."

"Quite some time," Mr. Vaughn mimicked. "You're crazy." He got up without another word, took his parka from the wall and walked out. He'd be headed for the roadhouse to tell everybody. The others stayed put.

"I'd suggest, madam, that you bring those two children here tonight."

"I've pretty well made up my mind."

"I would be doing you a service if I were to go over to your quarters right now and take them forcibly."

"And I'll help you out," Harry Dowles said.

"I don't think you'd do something like that, Mr. Strong," I said. I was pretty upset by now, scared he'd do it. He shook his head a little and his mouth tightened up. "Goodnight, madam," he said finally.

I walked out shaking. I'd wanted to stop at the roadhouse and see Maggie's granddaughter, but with Mr. Vaughn inside spreading the good news about Chuck and Ethel, I wasn't about to.

Nancy asked me right away how it had gone and I told her what Mr. Strong had said.

"Well, if he did come over for 'em he'd have plenty of help. You want me to stay?"

"No. You go on and have a good time. I'm not worried," I lied. I didn't mention the news about Fred.

After she left I played tic-tac-toe with Chuck for a while, then after he and Ethel were in bed I sat down to write to

251

Mr. Henderson. I told him that if he could manage it I'd prefer to teach in Eagle, but that if he couldn't I'd take another school. I also wrote him about Chuck and Ethel, explaining who they were. "I'll be keeping them with me at least until June," I wrote, "and I have the feeling you'll be getting some letters about them from people." I tried to kid about it to take the edge off a little.

Ethel, the little girl, sleeps with Nancy and me, so between the three of us and the potatoes you might say I have about the most crowded bed in the Forty Mile. It will be emptying out a little pretty soon, though. We're getting low on potatoes.

While I was addressing the envelope there were quick footsteps on the porch and the door was flung open. I was scared out of my wits, thinking it was a bunch from the roadhouse come to take the kids, but it was Nancy. She had tears in her eyes and a big red welt on her cheek. Maggie Carew was right in back of her, fuming mad. She hadn't even bothered to put on a shawl. "Just what the heck are you up to now!" she yelled before I had a chance to say anything.

"What happened?"

"What does it look like?" Maggie said. "She nearly got her head knocked off on account a you."

"The kids are asleep, Mrs. Carew."

I brought the lamp into the schoolroom and we closed the door behind us. "Are you crazy?" Maggie hissed at me.

"What happened?"

"She sassed Angela and Angela walloped her one and it's all your fault."

"It isn't her fault," Nancy said. "Nobody asked Angela to hit me and if you'd of just let me alone—"

"She'd of really given it to ya, so shut up." She turned to me. "Are you keepin' those kids?"

"Yes, Mrs. Carew—"

"I don't want to hear any blabber. All I wanna hear is that

252

those kids are goin' outta here. Otherwise there's gonna be lots of trouble."

"Mrs. Carew—"

She wouldn't let me talk. "Do you have any idea what you're doing? You got half the people in this place thinkin' you're nuts and the other half ready to lynch ya."

This time she let me talk. "Mrs. Carew, I'm doing what I think is right. If those two kids were white nobody would think twice about my keeping them here."

"If they were white they wouldn't *be* here! Look, I'm try'na tell you somethin' for your own good. You keep those kids and you're askin' for it. Goin' daffy over that half-breed was bad enough, but this takes the cake. Do you realize you're lousin' up your whole future?"

"I'm not worried about it."

"Well you better. You better worry about a lot of things from here on in. There's talk over to the roadhouse about some a them comin' over here and takin' those kids whether you like it or not."

That did it. I saw red. I was so mad that if I'd had a lightning bolt I'd have thrown it at that roadhouse and everybody in it. "I'll be right back," I said.

I went into the cache and put a box by the wall. Getting up on it, I felt around for the nickel-plated revolver, my hand finally closing around the holster. It was freezing cold, and if I hadn't been so mad I'd have realized I was in for a shock.

"What are you gonna do with that?" Maggie said when I marched back into the schoolroom.

"If I have to I'm going to use it." I took the revolver out of its holster. "I'm going to keep this out until I go to sleep tonight, and when I go to sleep I'm going to put it under my pillow. Please do me a favor. You tell anybody at that road-house who has a mind to set foot in here and take those children from me that if they try to, so help me God I'll shoot 'em. I will shoot them dead."

"You'd be crazy enough, wouldn't you?"

"You are absolutely right."

"I'll tell 'em. But I'll tell you one thing too. Maybe you don't know it, but I been stickin' my neck out for you. Come spring I'm leavin' here for Eagle as you well know and buyin' the Adkins's roadhouse there. That Adkins woman is on the school board and she wrote me to find out if you were as crazy as she's been hearin.' Well, I wrote her back, sayin' you were just a cheechako and didn't know the ropes, but that you were a darn good teacher and if she could swing it, to see that the school board didn't turn you down. She came back to me and said she'd do it. Well, I'm gonna tell you here and now that I'm about to change my mind and tell her you're as crazy as a bedbug and that compared to you that Mrs. Rooney is a patron saint. Now are those kids leavin' here tomorrow or ain't they?"

"They're staying with me."

"Then that's the blow that killed Father. I wash my hands of the whole thing. I'll tell you one more thing, young lady. This ain't over yet—not by a long shot. As for you, dummox," she said to Nancy before she left, "you stay out of Angela's way."

As soon as she was out the door I let out the yelp I'd been holding in and rushed over to the stove. Throwing open the door, I shoved the revolver in as far as I could without burning my hand.

Nancy was wide-eyed. "What's wrong!"

"It's stuck to my hand."

I kept hopping around in front of that stove as if I had to go to the outhouse. A few seconds later the metal warmed up enough. I dropped the revolver on the table with a sigh of relief and started blowing on my hand.

"What'd you hold onto it for?" Nancy said.

"Just to make a point."

My hand was all right. A couple of blisters, that was all. I asked Nancy what happened between her and Angela.

"Aah," she sneered, "Angela was saying things about you, about how you and Fred carried on and that he'd probably lived with you a couple of times. She said she had a good mind to come over here and wipe the floor with you and feed Chuck and Ethel to her dogs. I told 'er she oughtta mind her own business and she walloped me.

"We better stay out of her way."

"I'm not afraid of 'er."

"I am."

"You heard about Fred bein' back, I guess," Nancy said a little later.

"Yeah."

"I guess they musta given him a real bad time."

"I'll bet they did."

We didn't sleep too well that night. Every time I heard somebody go by I expected them to come charging in. But nobody bothered us.

XIX

"Cargo," I said to the children I was giving a spelling test to the next morning. "The riverboat carried a cargo of provisions and supplies."

"Willard's licking the window again, Teacher," Joan Simpson said.

"Willard," I called, "I've told you for the last time to cut that out." Yesterday under his expert guidance Ethel had finally left part of her tongue on the window. She'd literally gushed blood for a while and it had frightened her into a screaming fit. It almost did the same for me.

"If you were busy doing your own work," I snapped at Joan, "you wouldn't care what Willard was doing." Joan gave me a hurt look and went back to doing the simple sums I'd given her. I shouldn't have snapped at her but I was nervous. I could hear Mr. Strong swinging open the doors to his stable across the road. He'd be leaving in a few minutes, and even though I didn't think he'd try to take Chuck and Ethel by force I was still a little worried. I hadn't slept much last night. I'd kept having weird dreams that I was a little girl again, sleeping on a cot in the kitchen, and I'd kept waking up all night, thinking that any minute Angela and the other vigilantes might come charging in.

Rebekah was aggravating me too. For some reason she was in a bad mood when she came in this morning, especially with Chuck and Ethel. Ethel had sidled up to her while she and Lily were copying letters together out of the alphabet book. Putting her finger on the open page Ethel said, "Book?" Rebekah shoved her away. She gave her such a hard push that Ethel started crying and Nancy had had to take her into my quarters. A little later when I asked Rebekah to let Chuck work with her and Lily at their table she said there was no room for him. I let it go and sat him alongside of Joan, but it had irritated me.

"Through," I went on. "The train went through the tunnel."

"That's a hard one." Isabelle said.

"Nah, it's easy," Jimmy Carew said happily. He started to write and Evelyn Vaughn tried to peek at what he was doing, but he cupped a hand around his work.

"Yah!" I heard Mr. Strong yell to the horses. Everybody looked up as the jangle of bells sounded outside and the sled was on its way. I sat back and relaxed. I looked at my watch. It was 10:30. Nancy was taking the test also, so I asked Rebekah to take the little ones out for recess.

When the test was over nobody else wanted to go out, so I left Nancy in charge and went outside myself. Chuck and Willard were busy terrorizing the girls by throwing snowballs at them and Rebekah was shouting at Chuck in Indian. *"Awnee!"* she yelled to him: Come over here!

He didn't listen. Instead he threw some snow at Joan. Rebekah stalked over to him, grabbed a handful of his parka and shook him viciously.

"Rebekah!"

She let him go and he fell on his behind. He got up and was about to kick her when I grabbed him. "Stop it!"

"She hurt me. I not like her one stinkin' bit," he said. "What a dirty black Injun!"

"You will not use that kind of language!"

"She call me same, say me dirty black Injun I say same her."

"Go inside. I'll talk with you later."

He stomped in, slamming the door behind him. The other kids were watching and I told them to go ahead and play, we'd be going inside in a few minutes. "Rebekah, why are you picking on him?" I asked her.

"He one dirty mean kid, that kid. Him and sister. Dirty and ugly them both."

"They're not dirty and they're certainly not ugly."

"You not tell me!" She huffed. "I see lotsa Indian kids and I tell you you make one big mistake not send Indian village. Chuck, he no good and Ethel same thing."

"You still haven't told me why you're picking on them."

"I *tell* you, no? Kids no darn good. Both ugly like Uncle Arthur."

"From now on keep your hands off them."

I walked away from her and started the kids playing *Ring Around the Rosie*. Ethel didn't know what it was all about, but she joined in anyway and they had a good time. Rebekah came up behind me.

"Tisha . . ."

"What is it?" I didn't bother to turn around.

"I no like you be *sahnik* me," she said.

I'd heard Chuck use the word, so I knew that it meant angry. "I'm not *sahnik* with you," I lied.

"You *sahnik*."

"All right, I'm mad," I said, turning. "It just seems to me that you're going out of your way to be nasty to Chuck and Ethel and I don't like it. I don't like it at all."

She looked so contrite I felt bad.

"You A-number-one fine lady, Tisha, I have good feel in my heart for you. Like you too much. Want you be happy."

"What has that got to do with Chuck and Ethel?"

"You no savvy lotsa things in No'th country. You catch big troubles you keep this kids. Everybody hate—not like see Tisha-no-husband be motha for dirty Injun kids. I try help you. Be mean. Tell you kids no good, maybe you send Indian village. You see?"

"Yes."

"You not be *sahnik* no more?"

"No, but try to be nice to them, will you? They need it badly."

"You keep for sure?"

258

"For sure."

"You no worry." She patted me on the shoulder. "I treat nice."

Before we went back in she said, "I make one big lie, Tisha. They good little children. Smart. Ethel, she pretty like Mary. Chuck, he pretty like Joe Temple. I tell you truth now."

"Thanks, Rebekah."

"You welcome."

After lunch the weather turned so cold I had to put the little children in my bed again, and at dismissal time I kept Isabelle and Joan in. They were both too young to let them go home alone in this cold.

Joan's mother picked her up a few minutes after school was over, but no one came for Isabelle until a half hour later. Somehow I had a feeling it was going to be Fred, and sure enough, it was. I'd kept preparing myself for when I'd be seeing him again, and I'd made up my mind to be level-headed and poised. The last thing I was going to do, I'd said to myself, was act as if the world had come to an end just because things had worked out the way they had. As soon as he walked in, though, I felt the kind of lurch you get when you walk downstairs in the dark and think there's one more step where there isn't. He came in, bringing the sharp tang of cold air with him, and any poise I thought I'd have turned to mush.

Not that he did much better. No sooner did he say hello to me and Nancy than he let Chuck buttonhole him and show him a couple of things he'd made in school. He looked through the book of minerals Chuck had made as if every page had a special message for him. Finally Nancy took the kids into the schoolroom so we could talk by ourselves, and at first we just sat there like two blocks of ice.

"I guess you're glad to be back," I said.

"I sure am," he answered.

"You back to stay?"

"Uh-huh."

We both started to say something at the same time, then like Pierre and Gaston we told each other to go ahead and talk

259

first. We were so polite you'd have thought we were the king and queen of England. "I was just going to say," I said, "that I guess you heard about my taking Chuck and Ethel."

"Me and everybody else in the Forty Mile," he said.

"What did you think?"

"That it was just the kind of thing I'd expect you'd do."

He meant it as a compliment, but I couldn't help kidding him. "Oh you would, would you?"

"Yes, I would. That's the way you are." The way he said it made me feel like glowing, but then I had to go and put my foot in it.

"Why'd you come over?" I blurted out, and as soon as I did I was sorry. I should have kept things light. Instead I had to open my big mouth and force things.

"I wanted to see you one more time," he said.

"You going away again?"

"No."

"Oh."

"I just came over to say good-bye."

"That's stupid." There I go again, I thought, saying exactly the wrong thing. "I mean I told you in my letter that I wouldn't act any way around you but like a friend. Didn't you believe me?"

"Yes I did, but—"

"Well, then why do we have to say good-bye? Can't we even be around each other, be friends?"

He shook his head as if he was tired. "I shouldn't even have come over," he said. "I just can't make you understand."

"No, you can't," I said, trying to get angry. If I didn't I was afraid I'd start crying and I wasn't going to do that. I'd cried enough already. "I can't understand why two people who like each other aren't even entitled to look at each other . . . Fred, you're the one person around here who really means something to me. . . I love you. I love you very much. I don't want you or anybody in your family to be hurt, and I swear that none of you will be because of me. Can't you believe that?"

His elbow was resting on the table. Impulsively I put my

hand on his. "Oops, wrong thing," I said, pulling it back. "See, I'm learning already."

He almost smiled, but not quite. "Do you know why I left Steel Creek?"

"Because they treated you lousy there."

"That was part of it, but not the whole thing. I knew when I went that the men wouldn't be too friendly. The only reason I was hired in the first place was because the foreman is a friend of my father, so I got what I expected. But I finally realized that there wasn't any point in staying there. The reason I went was to take the pressure off you and my mother, but after a while I realized that I could do the same thing even if I came back. All I had to do was make sure that you and I stayed away from each other. That way everybody'd be happy."

"Except you and me."

He shrugged, then he got up.

"I guess you won't be at the next dance, then."

"I'll be out on the trap line."

I got up too. "How about the one after?"

"Same thing."

He hadn't taken off his parka. It was untied at the throat and his neck was the color of coffee and cream, his face darker. I remembered how he'd smelled of wood smoke every time he held me.

Inside the schoolroom we could hear Nancy and the children tossing rope rings onto the wooden post. Chuck must have made a ringer because he shouted excitedly.

Fred said, "Anne, if you ever need me, if you ever need me for anything at all, I'll be here. That's what I came over to tell you."

"Thanks. Should we shake hands now or something?"

He just stared at me without saying anything for the longest time. "I didn't mean that," I said finally.

"I know. But I meant what I said."

He went past me to the schoolroom door. Opening it, he told Isabelle it was time to go. A couple of minutes later they left.

"What did he say?" Nancy asked me.

"Good-bye."

A few days later, when it rained, Mr. Purdy showed up for Isabelle. The following week Mrs. Purdy came over for her. Like Fred, it just wasn't in her nature to stay mad at someone. We had a cup of tea before she took Isabelle home. She didn't pay any attention to Chuck and Ethel at all except to glance at them once in a while, then her eyes would go right past them as if they didn't exist. But she knew they were there. Chuck was working on a spear and doing a beautiful job on it. He'd found a piece of metal somewhere, cut a groove in the end of the spear and fitted it in and tied it with rawhide, then he'd painted it and added some ptarmigan feathers. It was turning out to be a work of art. When he showed it to Mrs. Purdy, she managed a grudging compliment.

"How long you take care them, Ahnne?" she asked me.

"They're with me to stay. I wouldn't give them up for the world."

She shook her head disapprovingly. "You are foolish. There are many people who do not like this, a fine white girl who is teacher ruin reputation with such children."

"Frankly, I think they've finally stopped caring one way or the other."

"This is not so. Here in bush we all live together—like people in one house with many rooms. You have most important room in whole house. If people have argument with you they cannot come here. They do not wish this to happen."

"They don't come here anyway. I don't have anything to do with most of the people here."

"Ah, but you are wrong. I tell you long time ago, Ahnne, you are verree important person in settlement." She waved a hand around the room. "Here children come school—my Isabelle, Vaughn girls, Carew children, others. All these people must be friendly with you—talk with you. People come here for dance. They must talk with you or not come. You have keys Mr. Strong's store. People come store must talk with you. If they tell you truth, no more can they come. Better not to tell

262

truth, be friendly, talk. Yet inside"—she tapped her heart—"they very angry."

I'd never thought of it that way, but Mrs. Purdy was right.

"I don't think there's anything I can do about it, Mrs. Purdy."

"Indeed, Ahnne, there is something make you happy, make everybody happy." She looked over at Chuck and Ethel, picked up a handful of air and threw it towards the door.

"She pretty little girl," Chuck said after she and Isabelle left.

"She's not a little girl, Chuck. She's Isabelle's mother."

"She mudda? No fool?"

"No fooling."

At the next dance I couldn't help thinking about what she'd said. Maggie Carew was the only person who'd said anything directly to me, but when I looked around the room I realized that there were a lot of others who felt the way she did.

The schoolroom was as crowded as it had been for the Thanksgiving dance. Even though the weather outside was foul, now that it was February people wouldn't pass up the slightest opportunity to get out and go somewhere. With the wind howling outside most of the time and the days still dark, you needed to be around people more than ever, especially if you lived alone.

Elmer and Jeannette Terwilliger had come with the Carews and they brought the baby along. I didn't think I'd ever seen anything so tiny in my life as that baby. It was about two months old and just about perfect in every way, but blanket and all I bet it didn't weigh more than nine or ten pounds.

"Nine and a half," Maggie said, holding it while her daughter and Elmer were dancing. Everybody'd been standing around it oohing and ahing and carrying on and you couldn't blame them. There was something about a baby that just made you feel good, especially here. Her name was Patricia.

"Can I hold her?" I asked her.

Maggie handed her over to me. She was sleeping and I rocked her a little. "Like to have one like that?"

"I sure would."

263

"You won't as long as you got those two," she said.

The music stopped and the sets broke up. Jeannette came over with her husband. She smiled and put her hands out for the baby. I handed her over.

"How's my perfect gem?" she cooed to her. "Huh? How is she?"

"Same way she was a minute ago," Maggie said drily.

"Think she's pretty?" Jeannette asked me.

"She's beautiful."

"I wish she'd eat more," Jeannette said.

"She's doin' fine," Maggie said.

"No, she's not, Ma. She don't eat enough."

" 'Cause you hold 'er too much. Everytime she cries or makes a whimper," Maggie said to me, "there she is holdin' 'er and rockin' 'er and not givin' 'er a chance to get up an appetite."

"Oh, Ma," Jeannette sighed.

Robert Merriweather came over. "Teacher, the kids want to know if you'll get a square together with us."

"Sure."

I collected Jimmy Carew, Joan Simpson, Elvira, Lily and Chuck, which made seven with Robert and myself. Then Uncle Arthur joined our square and took Lily as his partner. Jimmy paired off with Joan, Robert Merriweather took me, and Elvira paired off with Chuck. I should have had better sense than to let Elvira and Chuck be partners, but I wasn't thinking. No sooner did the two of them join hands than Mr. Vaughn called out loud enough so everybody looked his way. "Elvira, come over here!"

I knew right away what he was mad about, but it was too late to do anything about it. Elvira went to where he was sitting alongside Angela Barrett.

"Don't you know any better?" he yelled at her. "How many times have I told you not to have anything to do with that kid? How many times?" He didn't wait for her to answer. He just slapped her. "Go on home," he said to her. She ran out, tears streaming down her cheeks. I wanted to go after her, but it would just have made things worse.

264

The whole room was quiet, everybody either looking over at our square or at Mr. Vaughn. If I'd had Angela Barrett's muscles I'd have gone over and told him exactly what I thought of him, and what I thought of him would have made what Jake Harrington said to him sound like a Sunday-school lecture. As it was though, I just stood there blushing with embarrassment and wishing one of the women still sitting down would take the empty space alongside Chuck.

Mrs. Purdy played a few notes on the accordion and that broke the silence. Ben Norvall, who was standing up on a box, pointed to our square. "One more lady over here," he called, "one more lady."

Jeannette handed her baby to Maggie, came over and took Chuck's hand, and the dance was on again.

I didn't have too good a time after that. I kept thinking of Elvira back in the cabin all by herself and blaming myself for it.

When the *Home Sweet Home* waltz was played I ended up with Joe Temple. By that time Chuck and Ethel were fast asleep so, leaving Robert Merriweather to watch them, I went over to the roadhouse with him. Maggie gave us the table by ourselves again.

I wasn't very good company. Joe tried to cheer me up, telling me not to blame myself for what happened. "I shouldn't have let you have those two in the first place," he said.

"Why not?"

"It's not doing you or anybody else any good."

"It's keeping them out of that village."

"And you in the dog house. I'm even getting the cold shoulder for giving them to you."

"You worried about it?"

"Not me. I would if I were you. Everybody's getting crankier and crankier. There's no telling what they're liable to do."

I didn't think anything more would happen, but I was wrong. The next time Mr. Strong came in he brought me a letter from Nancy's mother. Mrs. Prentiss didn't mince any words:

. . . I want you to send Nancy home with Mr. Strong right

265

now. I don't want her staying with you any more. You ought to be ashamed of yourself. First you take a halfbreed lover then you go ahead and adopt two siwash brats you got no business to. You aren't decent company for self-respecting white people. I wouldn't be surprised if you end up having a siwash of your own by that lover of yours. You do what I say and send Nancy home to me.

I didn't show Nancy the note, but I told her some of what her mother had said. When we sat down for supper that night she burst out crying right after we started to eat. I was hit pretty hard myself. She'd become almost like a sister to me.

She begged me to go over and talk to Mr. Strong, ask him if he wouldn't talk to her mother and try to convince her to let her stay for at least a while longer. "Please, Anne," she said. "If anybody can do it, he can. My mother respects him, and if he was to tell her how much I'm learning and how my being with you isn't doing me anything but good, she'd let me stay."

Finally I did. He was alone in the store when I went over and he listened to everything I had to say, then shook his head. "Her mother wants her home," he said.

"Nancy thinks if you'd talk to her she might change her mind."

"In all good conscience, madam, I cannot do that."

"She deserves the break, Mr. Strong. She's been working so hard."

"Be honest with me. Do you think she could pass the eighth-grade exam if she were to take it today?"

"She'd have a better chance if she could stay a little longer."

"Would she pass or not?"

". . . I think so."

"In that case I believe she is better off at home. She can continue studying on her own."

"You really think I'm a bad influence on her."

"I am under the impression, madam, that you do not care one way or the other what I think."

"I admire you very much, Mr. Strong. I always have and I always will."

He cleared his throat. "There is nothing I can do," he said, "and that is the plain truth."

Before I went out he said, "Generally the school board in Eagle would have made up their mind by this time whether or not to retain your services next year. We have not done so as yet, but we will do so by the end of next month, then we shall telegraph our decision to the commissioner in Juneau. I'm sure you realize what I am trying to say."

"Yes, I do." I had until the end of March to change my ways.

"I hope, madam, you will not disappoint me."

The next morning, after I told the class that Nancy was leaving, we didn't even pretend to work. None of us wanted to see her go, and until about eleven o'clock, when we heard the stable door across the way bang open, we had a little party for her.

We all went out to see her off. The sun had been up for more than a half hour, but the sky was so overcast it was almost like night. "You make sure you study everything I gave you," I said to her. I'd given her a couple of books to take along and marked the pages for her.

"I will," she said.

We'd filled a pillowcase with all her stuff. She handed it to Mr. Strong and he shoved it under the tarpaulin covering the sled.

When she said good-bye to Chuck she told him to be a good boy. "With me gone," she said, "you're gonna have to help out more—do the dishes and things like that."

He stuck out his lower lip. "I no do dishes," he said proudly. "Womans do dishes."

"Just the same, Anne's gonna need all the help you can give her, you savvy?"

"I help plenty."

She picked Ethel up. " 'Bye, sweetheart," she said, giving her a hug before she put her down. It was time to go.

"You keep studying hard," I said to her.

"I hate to go," she said.

"You'll be back to take that exam before you know it."

She swallowed hard so she wouldn't cry, then we hugged each other good-bye. "Thanks, Anne," she whispered. "Thanks for everything." She hugged me tighter. "You were right to take those two," she said. "They're good kids. I hope it works out."

It was a big thing for her to say, a real big thing, and I appreciated it. We'd both have started to cry if we said anything more, so we didn't.

Then she was clambering up on the sled and the children were all shouting good-bye to her. As soon as Ethel realized Nancy was going she started to cry.

The sled pulled out. Nancy turned around a couple of times to wave, and then she was gone. We all went back into the schoolhouse.

Right from the start the place seemed emptier without her, and came suppertime I really missed her.

Over the next couple of days, especially after school, I missed her more and more. Besides not having her company anymore, and her help with the chores, I started having trouble with Chuck and Ethel. I didn't know which one was worse. Ethel always seemed to be under my feet, clinging to me and putting her arms out to be picked up, and Chuck didn't take to it at all. He was always pushing her away from me, wanting to be close to me himself. I tried to explain to him why Ethel was doing it, but it didn't do too much good. With Nancy gone there was only me, and Chuck wanted to make sure Ethel wasn't going to take first place. So they carried on their little war, he giving her a pinch or a sock when he thought I wasn't looking, she holding on to me every chance she had.

Even with the jealousy and the rows, though, I loved having them. Ever since I could remember I'd always wanted children of my own to take care of. Once when I was a little girl there were two little kids that lived next door to me that my mother never let me play with. She said that they were dirty and had lice. One day while I was talking with them over the fence—

268

the two of them scratching and whimpering—I felt so sorry for them that I brought them into our yard and filled an old washtub full of water. I figured that if I cleaned them up my mother wouldn't mind if I played with them. They loved it and so did I—until my mother caught me. She was furious, and so was my father. He gave me a good whipping and sent me to bed without my supper, saying that would teach me not to play with trash. I didn't know what I'd done wrong, so I guessed there was just something wrong with me. If there was then the same thing was still wrong with me, because I could no more have parted with Chuck and Ethel than if they'd been my own little brother and sister. I even went to sleep when they did. It was easier than trying to get them to bed by themselves now that Nancy was gone, and it turned out to be fun. With Chuck on one side of me and Ethel on the other, I sat up in bed with a book of fairy tales and read until they dropped off. Ethel didn't have the least idea of what the story was about, but she seemed to enjoy it as much as Chuck did. In the morning I'd just get up earlier to get my work done.

A few days after Nancy left, Jeannette and her husband started for Eagle, with Jeannette and the baby tucked into the Carews' sled. They stopped by the schoolhouse before they left so Jeannette could say good-bye to Jimmy and Willard and let them have one last look at their niece. The Carews had a fairly good string of dogs, but there was an awful lot on the sled for them to pull. Since Maggie would be closing the roadhouse, she was trying to move as many things to Eagle as she could. All told there must have been about seven or eight hundred pounds there.

Ben Norvall said they oughtn't to go with so much packed on the sled. "There's a storm comin' down," Ben said, "and you're liable to run right into it."

Maggie came out of the roadhouse while they were still talking about it. She'd had second thoughts too. She came on over and looked the sled over pretty carefully. "Maybe you oughtta leave off some a them things," she said to Jeannette's husband. "You're liable to take a spill and get hurt." They argued about it for a while, then decided to take off a couple of picture frames, a whole bunch of iron pots and a small Yukon stove. Some more discussion followed, until finally they took off a couple of hundred pounds before they left.

A few hours later Ben was proved right. A really mean freeze came in so fast you could hear the nails in the walls snapping as they contracted. Even after we built up the fire till the sides of the stove were red hot the schoolroom was hardly bearable. It was the wind that did it, sweeping down from the north and bringing sleet that drove against the windows so hard I thought they'd break. It wasn't any kind of weather you wanted to be out in and for a while I thought I'd have to keep Isabelle and Joan Simpson overnight. But Mr. Purdy showed up for Isabelle about seven and Joan's father came about a half hour later.

When I was putting Chuck and Ethel to bed that night somebody knocked at the door. I yelled come in, but nobody did. After another knock I went to it. It was still sleeting out and I could hardly see beyond the edge of the porch. Right in front of the threshold was a fancy little box all done up with gleaming ribbon and cellophane. My heart gave a jump. I thought right away that it was from Fred and I poked my head out around the jamb with a smile I hadn't felt like showing in weeks. I should have known better, though, because there, hugging the wall so tight his Stetson was tipped down to his nose, was Cab Jackson. He tipped it back up and gave me that big dumb grin of his, then he picked up the fancy box and held it out to me. "Howdy, Teacher."

It was too cold to do anything but invite him in and have him get the children all awake again. Chuck was right out of bed, of course, wanting to see the present. Ethel was up too and they wouldn't go back to bed until I'd let Chuck open the box and take out the bottle of perfume that was in it. I gave them each a smell, then hustled them off to sleep, with Chuck getting the cellophane wrapping and Ethel the ribbon. Then I gave Cab a cup of coffee and made a cup of tea for myself. "I'm sorry 'bout what happened last time," he said. "I don't hardly remember any of it, but I sure wish you wouldn't be mad at me."

"I got over it."

"You wouldn't maybe want to splash a little of that perfume on and come over t'the roadhouse a spell, would ya?"

"I can't leave the kids alone, Cab."

He looked over at them and I could feel a sermon coming, so I changed the subject. "D'you come in from Eagle?"

"Nulato. Did a little business there. I'll be mushing over to Eagle when I leave here—tomorrow mornin' I reckon. Teacher," he said, "you mind if I tell you somethin'?"

"I'll have to hear it first."

"There's some mighty loose talk bein' spread about you."

"Nothing I can do about that."

"You're roonin' your whole career, people are sayin', an' they're right."

"I'll make you a deal, Cab. I won't say anything to you about whiskey running if you won't say anything to me about what I do."

"I got to," he said. "You are just too fine a person to have people talkin' the way they are. I got a good mind to let that Joe Temple have it for givin' them kids to you."

"I hope you won't," I said. "I asked him for them."

"But don't you see you're throwin' away your whole future? The only thing stoppin' that school board in Eagle from givin' you your walkin' papers right now is old Strong. He's a-tellin' 'em to wait 'n see . . . And Teacher, I don't want you to lose that job. Shucks, I was bankin' on you bein' there. I got some pretty deep feelings about ya, as you do know by now."

"I appreciate it, Cab. I appreciate everything you're trying to tell me, but I know what I'm doing and I want to do it."

"No you don't, Teacher. You got a heart big as all outdoors and you're lettin' it rule out your good sense. I'm askin' you as one who is truly interested in your welfare and your good name—you just let me mush them two kids outta here and you'll wind up the happiest female in the Forty Mile. You will."

"It's getting kinda late. I've still got some work to do."

He got up and took his mackinaw down from the drying rack. He looked at me as if he was really worried. "You sure you feelin' good, Teacher? You know—not sick or anything? Sometimes that can happen . . ."

"I'm not tetched, if that's what you mean."

He smiled. Then he said something I thought was really touching. "I guess you think I'm kinda wild and not smart. And maybe I'm *not* too smart either. But I got deep feelin's, Teacher, deep and good feelin's. About you 'specially. I wanta do somethin' for you, in the worst way. I wanna be a help to you. You know what I mean?"

"I think so . . . I appreciate it."

"Good night."

"Good night."

When I went to sleep the wind was raging, blowing so hard that if the windows hadn't been frozen in place they'd have been rattling loud enough to keep us all awake. I woke in the middle of the night. It was warmer and it wasn't sleeting. Getting up, I turned the stove damper down, then I went into the schoolroom and did the same thing. It was so quiet outside that I went to the window. Snow was falling softly. I didn't look at the clock, but I had a feeling it was about three. If it kept falling this thickly there'd be two feet on the ground before morning.

It must have stopped soon after because the next morning there were just a few more inches on the ground. It was gloomy and foggy out all that day, though, so we didn't even go outside for recess.

A little after school was over Harry Dowles knocked at the door and said he needed a couple of things from the store. Joan's mother hadn't come to pick her up yet and I didn't like the idea of leaving the children alone, so I offered to give him the key.

He said no thanks. "Wouldn't want to be accused of shoplifting. Only take a minute," he said.

I peeked into the schoolroom. The three of them were playing line cabin. Chuck had stretched a blanket over a few boxes and Joan and Ethel were inside the "cabin," while Chuck was out "trapping." They were playing so well that I didn't see any harm in leaving them for a few minutes. I told Chuck to make sure the three of them stayed in the schoolroom, then I went out.

In Mr. Strong's store, Harry said he needed some blue thread. The color he wanted wasn't on the rack with all the other thread so I had to hunt through some boxes before I found it. Then he asked for a tin of tea and five pounds of sugar. After I weighed out the sugar, he looked around, scratching his head. "Somep'n else I wanted," he said.

"Maybe you'll think of it later," I told him. I'd been gone over five minutes and wanted to get back.

"No," he said. "It's somep'n I need bad." He kept looking around making a big show of trying to think, and I should have realized then and there something was wrong, but I didn't. I reeled off a bunch of things and he kept saying no, none of them was it until I mentioned matches and he said he could use a few boxes, but that still wasn't it. Finally I told him I had to get back and that made him all kinds of nervous.

Just then from outside I heard Cab yell out "Yah-h-h-h—mush!" I didn't take particular note of it except to wonder why he was leaving so late. Last night he'd told me he'd be leaving early in the morning.

"Well," Harry Dowles said then, "I guess I can't think of it. You go ahead and tally up." He put a hand on the counter and it was shaking. I looked at him and his eyes shifted away.

And then it came to me. My first instinct was to say I was wrong, that nobody would do a thing like that. But then I knew I was right. I knew it. It was written all over Harry's face, and I felt sick.

I ran for the door, and then I was outside, running along the path to the schoolhouse and seeing Angela Barrett just ducking into the roadhouse storm entry. Cab's sled was already well out of the settlement, speeding up the trail beside Chicken Creek, and he was cursing his dogs a blue streak, yelling for them to move faster. He was running in back of it, so I couldn't really see the sled at first. But then the dogs swung to the left where the creek jogged and the sled was in full view for a few moments.

Chuck and Ethel were in it.

XX

"Cab, come back!" I yelled. "Come back!"

I started to run after him, but it was useless. The dogs were fresh and the sled was moving too fast. I'd never be able to catch him.

I kept yelling and calling, but he didn't so much as turn around. In a minute the sled veered to the left to avoid a big patch of scrub, then disappeared. I stood there dazed, hearing Cab urge the dogs on, and then I didn't even hear that anymore. I turned back.

Except for little Joan, who was standing on the porch of the schoolhouse shivering, no one was out. The whole settlement could have been deserted. Inside my quarters I asked her what happened.

She was almost too bewildered to tell me. And frightened. "They just came in here, Teacher," she stammered, "a whole bunch of 'em. They came in and took Ethel and Chuck away—just took 'em. I was scared they were gonna take me away too."

She broke into tears. It took a few minutes before she could tell me who had done it.

"Mr. Vaughn. And Mrs. Barrett. And that man whose sled it is . . . Why did they do that, Teacher?"

She looked as though she was going to cry again. "There's nothing to be scared of," I told her. "They won't be back."

I gave her a cookie to munch on and I looked around. The

275

bureau drawers were open. At least they'd taken some of the children's clothes. Ethel's dresses were gone from the wall too. Chuck's spear was still where he'd left it, though.

I couldn't think. I tried to, but everything had happened so fast that I couldn't get my thoughts together. The room looked empty, as if nobody lived in it. Dead.

I heard Joan's mother come up on the porch and knock. The sound seemed to come from another world. I must have told her to come in. When she did she saw right away that something was wrong. Joan ran over to her and told her that Chuck and Ethel had been taken away. She looked at me and asked me if it were true, but something was sticking in my throat and I couldn't answer her.

"Who took them away?" I heard her ask Joan.

"Mrs. Barrett," Joan said. "And Mr. Vaughn, and another man too."

"Oh, that's terrible," her mother said. "Anne, that's terrible." I saw her hand come over and felt it touch my shoulder. "When did it happen?" she asked me.

I said, "Just now."

She wanted to know if she could do anything for me. I said, "No. Thanks. Thanks very much. You take Joan home. I'll be all right."

After she left I sat listening to how quiet it was.

My feet began to get cold, so I got up and looked around for something to do. I started to straighten things. If I could just keep busy straightening things up, I thought, I might be able to start thinking again, figure out what to do. I shut the bureau drawers, arranged the chairs around the table neatly and then went into the schoolroom to see what I could do there. The kids had left it in pretty good order so there wasn't much to keep me occupied.

The funny thing was that I couldn't cry. I wanted to, I even tried to, but I couldn't. If I cried I wouldn't be able to think, and I had to do that. I had to think, figure out how to get Chuck and Ethel back. When I thought that, my mind started

276

working again. That's what I had to do, I realized—get them back.

Tomorrow was Friday, then the weekend. I'd get someone to take me up to the Indian village then. Maybe Joe Temple would do it. Or Fred. I'd start out right after school. I'd miss a couple of days, since I probably wouldn't be back until Tuesday or Wednesday, but I'd get them back.

Somebody came up on the porch and knocked.

It was Maggie Carew. She came in and stood in front of the closed door in her long blue coat, with her arms crossed. She made some kind of sound that could have meant anything from sympathy to "That's that."

"Did you know they were going to do this?" I asked her.

"I heard about it," she said. "It wasn't my idea, if that's what you're thinkin'."

"Whose was it?"

"What's it matter?"

"You can tell them there won't be any school on Monday. Tuesday either."

"Oh. . . ?"

"I'm going up to the Indian village. I'm bringing Chuck and Ethel back."

"The heck you will."

"The heck I won't. I'm going right after school tomorrow."

"You can save yourself the trip. Those kids are there to stay, thank God."

"Not if I have anything to say about it."

"You won't. When Cab gets through tellin' those Injuns what'll happen to 'em if they let you have those kids they'll scalp you before they let you so much as touch 'em."

"What can he tell them?"

"That if they so much as let you *look* at those kids that's the end of 'em. There's a few of 'em work on the riverboat in season. A couple of 'em get work at the Prentiss roadhouse and some more at Eagle. He'll tell 'em if they let you have those kids they won't ever work for anybody around here again.

277

He's also gonna tell 'em that Strong won't tote a blessed thing in or out of that village either. Nobody will. If that ain't enough he'll tell 'em he'll get the marshal after them. And believe me they'll listen. So like I say, save yourself the trip."

"Is that the truth?"

"You're darn tootin' it's the truth. Don't believe me if you don't want. Go on up there, but you'll be goin' on a fool's errand."

I felt weak.

"Good riddance to bad rubbish, if you ask me," she said. Then she softened a little. "They did you a favor, Annie. I know you liked them kids, but one day you'll see how much better off you are without 'em. You'll be teachin' at Eagle next year now, at least if I have anything to say about it, and I do. You'll see, Annie. You'll see it was all for the best."

"I will, will I? I'll tell you something, Mrs. Carew. You know what I feel like doing? I feel like leaving this place right now and never coming back."

"Don't talk so. You don't mean that and you know it."

"Oh I mean it all right. Do you realize what you've all done? Just because you're mad about something, because you're feeling mean about something, you're taking it out on those kids."

"I don't even know what you're talkin' about. Nobody's takin' anything out on anybody."

"You know what I'm talking about, all right. Those kids weren't hurting a soul. All they wanted was a warm place to stay and some decent food. And maybe a little kindness from people. Instead all they got was meanness."

"Not from me, they didn't. Anyway it's all water over the dam now. No use cryin' over spilt milk."

"Is that all you have to say?"

"Now looka here, I just come over to be nice. I don't know what you're blamin' *me* for. I didn't have anything to do with this."

"You could have stopped it. They're children, Mrs. Carew —just little kids. What were they doing that was so terrible?

278

Who did they hurt? Don't you realize what that Indian village is like? Don't you realize that you might as well have sent them to the electric chair?"

"I mind my own business."

"Is that what you'll tell Jimmy and Willard if they ask— that you let two kids be taken away to starve or freeze to death because it was none of your business? I'm ashamed of you."

She walked out. If she thought anything at all about what I said, she kept it to herself.

My hands were sweating and cold. I went over to the stove to warm them. I hadn't felt so bad since Fred had walked out on me. My mind was going a mile a minute. I tried to think where Cab was now. He'd probably gotten to Stonehouse Creek already. From there . . .

An idea hit me and I tried to put it out of my mind, but it kept coming back so strong that finally I knew I had to try it. There wasn't anything else I could do.

I put on a few pairs of socks under my moccasins, got my parka and went out.

There were some thin snow flurries in the air. Dry as sand, they swept in veils along the ground. I made pretty good time. It only took me twenty minutes to get to Fred's house.

Isabelle answered the door, surprised to see me.

"Is Fred home?" I asked her.

"Out in back, Miss Hobbs. Come on in, I'll go get 'im for you."

"I'll talk to him there."

I went around the back to the stable. I could hear him using the grindstone. He was sitting down, working the treadle, sparks flying from the ax he was holding. He looked up, and as soon as I saw him I could feel everything I'd kept bottled up inside me start to spill over. I was able to blurt out, "Fred, they took Chuck and Ethel away from me," and then I was in his arms blubbering and carrying on. He kept trying to get me to tell him what happened, but I couldn't. Everytime I tried I'd start crying all over again. Finally when I was able to control myself I hiccupped it all out. Mrs. Purdy came in right

279

in the middle of it and wanted me to come into the house, but Fred said maybe it'd be better if I stayed there with him.

"We'll be in in a couple of minutes. Go on back in the house, Ma," he said gently.

She left and I finished telling him the whole story, including what Maggie Carew said about my not ever getting Chuck and Ethel back once they were in the Indian village.

"They didn't have any right to do that," he said. "They didn't have any right at all."

"Fred, will you help me?"

"How?"

"Go after Cab with me."

"Now?"

"Right now. Right this minute. Please, Fred. If we can get to Cab before he reaches the Indian village I'll be able to talk to him, reason with him. I know he'll let me have them back if I can just talk to him."

He didn't say anything. "Fred, please. Please help me, otherwise I'll never get them back."

"How long ago did Cab leave?"

"About an hour."

I was asking a lot, I knew that, and I made up my mind that if he said no I wouldn't ask him again.

"You sure you want to go after him?" he said.

"I do."

"Is he toting anything else on the sled?"

"Whiskey."

He thought about it. Then he said, "Go on home. Put on your warmest clothes and pack some spares—spare parka, moccasins, socks, underclothes. I'll be by as soon as I can."

I nearly knocked him over I hugged him so tight.

"Get going," he said.

I flew getting home, and I was ready in twenty minutes. I didn't know whether he wanted me to pack food, so I put together some frozen beans, tea and some meat. Then I sat down to wait. I wondered what his father and mother would say to him. They'd try to keep him from going and I couldn't blame them. After a half hour I wondered if they'd convinced him.

A few minutes later I heard a shout and the sound of a sled approaching. I ran to the door, but it was someone else, someone carrying a passenger. The sled pulled up at the roadhouse. I shut the door.

I was ready to give up after another half hour went by. And then suddenly there he was.

I told him what food I'd packed, but he said leave it. He had everything we'd need for a week, he said.

"A week!"

"I don't know how long it'll take us to catch up with Cab or what we're liable to run into. If the trail is bad we may need everything we have."

"Somebody just mushed in to the roadhouse. Maybe you can ask him."

We went over together. The man who'd come in was a freighter, carrying a passenger to Fairbanks. The two of them were eating when we walked in. The passenger was a Dawson banker and the driver was trying to wolf down a steak and answer Maggie Carew's questions at the same time. She was worried and so was her husband. Angela Barrett was there too.

"You didn't see a sign of them at all?" Maggie was asking the freighter. She was badly upset.

"Only sled I seen was Cabaret Jackson's, 'n' that was about two hours ago," the driver said.

Her husband was trying to calm her down. "Now, Maggie, they coulda hit some bad weather and holed up in any number of places."

"You bet your boots they did," the driver said. "There was a stretch back there day before yesterday where I didn't make more'n a mile the whole day."

"How about when you passed Jamison's," Maggie asked him, "d'you see any smoke?"

"Didn't get that near," the driver said. "I stayed on the river all the way from Bonanza Bar till I hit here."

"What's the trail like through Franklin?" Fred asked him.

281

"Drifted in," the driver answered. "Unless you got somethin' won't wait I'd advise you to stay put."

"You're goin' after Cab," Maggie said to Fred.

Fred nodded and Angela Barrett said, "I hope he kills ya."

"Shut up!" Maggie snapped at her. Maybe she'd have felt the same way as Angela if she wasn't so worried about Jeannette and Elmer, but she didn't give a hoot right now about anything or anyone but them. "Be on the lookout, will you, Fred?"

"I will," he said. "But I wouldn't be worried if I were you. Elmer knows this country. He wouldn't do anything foolish."

"I know he wouldn't," Maggie said, "but they should've at least been at Steel Creek when this man went through there. He says they weren't. Last time anybody saw 'em was at O'Shaughnessy's."

"They told me at Steel Creek nobody had been through for two days," the man said.

"Maybe Elmer didn't stop there," Fred said. "Maybe he stayed on the river and then cut across to Liberty."

"You keep a sharp eye out," Maggie said.

Fred said he would, and a few minutes later we were by the sled. The runners had frozen in.

"Gee!" Fred yelled.

The dogs dug in, then swung to the right, and with a crack the sled was free.

He told me to get in, but I suggested that I run along with him for as long as I could hold out to save the dogs work.

"You'll be doing plenty of that," he said. "We better save you as much as possible."

"Mush!" he yelled once I was in. And we were off.

For the first few miles we moved along fast. The dogs were eager and the hills were gentle. Then the trail toughened, and I got out to trot alongside or help push and shove the sled through scrubby spruce, down and up sharp banks and across hummock-littered tundra. I kept watch for anything that might make the sled tip or get caught, and for a while I congratulated myself. I was pulling my own weight on a tough trail. Then I became careless and didn't see a rock slick with ice. One of the runners ran over it, the sled tipped and before I could stop it it nosed off the trail and into a drift. The two of us struggled to get it out, but a runner was caught on something. We couldn't budge it.

"We'll have to unpack some of the load," Fred said.

"But we'll waste so much time!"

"Nothing else we can do," he said.

We worked at unpacking slowly—too slowly, I felt. Mad at myself for being so careless, I tried to work fast. Fred kept stopping me. "Slow down," he said.

"He'll get away."

"You're not in the schoolroom now. You're on the trail. Slow down and keep that scarf over your face."

I knew he was right. You had to pace yourself, not move fast enough so that you started breathing through your mouth, taking freezing air into your lungs. It was the first rule of the trail —don't exhaust yourself. We had to take off half the load before we could free the runner, then reload, again working at the same maddening slow pace.

"Couldn't we have gone around all this?" I grumbled, tossing a package of raw meat into the sled.

Fred pulled his scarf down. "Take a look over there." He pointed to the distance. "See that saddle between those two hills?"

I could see it through the grayness—a dip stretching between two crags that rose up above the timber line.

"We're heading for that," Fred said. "It'll be a long trip. You won't make it if you don't take it easy. We'll go as fast as we can."

I felt small. "I'm sorry," I said.

"Forget it. We'll catch up with him, don't worry."

Once we left the tundra behind it was like moving along in a slow-motion dream, following a trail that wound ahead without any end, dipping across a creek, narrowing around a hill, then around still another hill when that was left behind. The dogs never let up, trotting along at a fast willing pace when we hit the flats, digging in almost as if they enjoyed it

283

when the going was rough. Night came on fast and black and the Northern lights billowed like curtains across the starlit sky. We didn't talk. There was no need to, even if we weren't using all our strength to keep up a steady pace. We were on the trail, stumbling along, snowshoeing across snow ten feet deep, plodding through drifts and sometimes sailing when the trail was smooth enough.

We reached the base of the saddle three hours later, a long slope of white with nothing to mark it but the twin lines of Cab's sled running up as far as we could see. And alongside of it were the small footprints of Chuck and Ethel. I wondered how they were making out, whether Cab was pushing them too hard or being impatient with them. Halfway up, Ethel's footprints stopped and I could see where she'd sat down. She'd been too tired to go any further. Cab had gone on a short distance beyond, then come back, picked her up and brought her to the sled.

I thought that when we got to the top of the pass, maybe by some miracle we'd be able to spot Cab's sled, but we didn't. It was too dark to see anything but endless stretches of black forest and the dark winding outline of the Forty Mile River.

The ride down was worth the climb. For two miles straight Fred rode the runners, the only sound the squeaking of the sled and the *plop plop plop* of the white clods the dogs threw up behind them. I wondered how they could do it, go on like that for hours taking that burning cold air into their lungs. But they did. They even gave each other a playful nip once in a while when they didn't have to pull too hard.

We rode down a long slough to the river, then once we were on it we went like an express train, swinging around big drifts and patches of rough ice. Again Fred was able to ride the runners for long stretches and I hardly had to get out. If we hadn't been chasing Cab I'd have been in heaven. The moon came out after a while. The river widened, and we began to pass little islands. We were sailing along so smoothly that even Fred must have let his guard down, because without

284

any warning Pancake suddenly veered off to the right and Fred lost his balance. He fell off the runners, fought to stay on his feet, then jumped back on. Pancake was still moving to the right, making a wide sweep. "Haw!" Fred yelled at him, but he kept moving until Fred had to stop the team.

Fred went up to him and he was really mad. "What the heck is the matter with you?" he yelled. "Don't you have any better sense than that? You nearly killed me, you blasted fool!" He said a couple of other things that weren't very complimentary. Pancake hung his head and took it all. "Now you darn well better go where you're supposed to," Fred warned him. Once in back of the sled he yelled haw, but sure enough Pancake veered off to the right again.

Fred stopped the sled again and this time I thought he was really going to give it to Pancake, but he didn't. Instead he looked over the area that Pancake had been so stubborn about avoiding, scanning it carefully. He'd told me long ago how many times a man had to depend on his dogs to stay alive and at it turned out this was one of them. "Well I'll be darned," he finally muttered.

He went to Pancake then, got down on his knees and put his arms around his neck, then he rubbed his cheek against Pancake's head, telling him what a good dog he was. I didn't realize what it was all about until Fred showed me. "See that over there—where the snow's a little darker, almost a little yellow?" I saw it finally. It was like a shadow. "It's a warm spot," Fred said. "Water. At the least we'd have wound up with wet gear. Probably worse. Pancake smelled it."

It was three weary hours later that we pulled up by a small cabin buried up to the eaves. The owner had dug a path from the door and uncovered the window, but otherwise you'd have hardly known there was a cabin there at all. "You stay here," Fred said. "I hear this man isn't too friendly."

There was smoke coming from the stovepipe and a faint yellow light coming through the window. Inside, a dog growled threateningly when Fred knocked.

"Who's there?" a gruff voice asked.

"Fred Purdy."

"I heard of you. You live up to Chicken."

"That's right," Fred said.

"Keep on a-goin'," the voice said. "Don' know you and don' wanna know you."

"I have a lady with me. We've been on the trail over six hours and we'd like to stop a few minutes."

"This ain't a roadhouse."

"We don't want any of your grub. All we want is to get warm."

"Build yourself a fire. Keep a-goin', bud."

Fred muttered something I couldn't hear and I said, "Fred, let's go. We don't have to stop here."

"Listen to the lady, bud," the voice said. "She's makin' sense. I got a thirty-aught-six pointed at that door and it'll blow your head clear to White Horse you try to come in here."

Fred jumped away from the door fast. "Did another sled mush by here in the last few hours?" There was no answer. "Did you hear me?"

"I heard you."

"Well, did it?"

"I ain't sayin' it did and I ain't sayin' it didn't."

Fred was mad. He walked back to the sled, took out his rifle and unsheathed it. Then he went over to the cabin door and threw the bolt. "Did you hear that?" he said.

"I heard it," the voice answered with a little less gruffness.

"Now, you inhospitable beast," Fred said. "I'm gonna ask you the same question again. If I don't get an answer I'm gonna knock out every darn pane in the window. Did another sled mush by here recently?"

". . . Yeah."

"How long ago?"

"Maybe three hours. Cab Jackson it was. He wanted to come in and I told'm the same as I told you."

"You sure it was that long?"

286

There was a pause. "Three hours and fourteen minutes. I got a book here I wrote it down in. I always write it down when anybody mushes by."

"Thanks." He came over to the sled. "He'd go on to the O'Shaughnessy roadhouse. Probably stay there overnight. It's eight miles. We can build a fire and rest a while or we can push on. I'm for pushing on if you can make it."

"I can make it," I said meekly. He looked so mad I'd have said I could do double cartwheels on the sled if he wanted me to. I'd never seen him like that before. In a way I kind of admired him for how tough and hard he could be, but it upset me too. Up to then I hadn't thought about what might happen when we caught up with Cab, figuring that somehow I'd be able to reason with him and talk him into letting me have Chuck and Ethel back. But suppose I couldn't? Cab could be pretty unpredictable. He could get mean about it and start saying some nasty things. Fred just wouldn't stand by and let him. I began to conjure up all kinds of things happening, maybe even shooting.

"Fred, will you promise me something?"

"What?"

"When we reach O'Shaughnessy's, you'll let me handle Cab."

"Promise."

"Cross your heart? I don't want you getting into a fight with him."

He smiled. "That makes two of us."

Those eight miles to the roadhouse must have taken us almost four hours. Even though Cab was following the trail the freighter had broken for him coming in, and he was breaking it even more for us, it was still hard going. And I was holding us up. You needed stamina for the trail—the kind of stamina you don't have unless you're used to it. All I had to do was trot alongside the sled most of the time, but I was still a drag. Fred never said a word about it, never told me to move faster. He just kept going.

The wind didn't help any. It started coming at us right after

287

we left the cabin and beat at us so hard for a while that we were pinching ice off our eyelashes every few minutes. Then one of the lead lines broke and we had to spell each other mending it, each of us working till our fingers were too cold, then the other taking over.

When the O'Shaughnessy roadhouse came into view I felt I'd never seen anything so warm and inviting as the yellow lights in its windows. We pulled up to the welcome yips of dogs tied up in the barn and no sooner did we stop than a bundled up figure came out of the roadhouse door. It was Mr. O'Shaughnessy.

"Inside with ye," he yelled over the wind when he saw I was a girl. "Oi'll help yer man put up the dogs."

I didn't need any urging. I went to the door so sure Cab would be on the other side of it that my stomach started doing flip-flops. When I opened it the wind shoved me in and nearly tore the door out of my hand. A man who'd been sitting down jumped up and closed it behind me. The heat of the place hit me with a lovely warm sting and the quiet almost made me reel. Mr. O'Shaughnessy's Indian wife had already pushed the table close to the oil-drum heater. She took me by the arm and led me over to it. "You sit down quick, Teacher. Get warm," she said comfortingly, then bustled over to the stove to pour a cup of hot tea. I was surprised she remembered me. I hadn't seen her in over five months, when I'd stopped with Chuck and Mr. Strong.

I plopped down and looked around. There was no sign of Cab. Some blankets were strung across part of the room to shield the bunk beds and I wondered if he and the kids were behind them. Mrs. O'Shaughnessy put the cup of steaming tea down on the table and helped me off with my parka. The man cleared his throat.

"Some night to be out on the trail," he said to Mrs. O'Shaughnessy. He was really talking to me, but he was being courteous. When people came in off the trail they were cold and tired and you didn't talk to them until they talked to you first. A snore came from behind the blanket.

288

I kept my voice low. "Is Cab Jackson here?"

Mrs. O'Shaughnessy shook her head. "No."

"You looking for him?" the man asked me. From the way he asked it I had the feeling he already knew the answer. He was tall and pale, and he wore glasses. One of the lenses was cracked and ringed with adhesive tape.

"Yes."

"That's too bad," he said. "He's been here and gone. Left about a half hour ago."

XXI

"No, ye'll not catch oop with *that* bludy rascal bafore he's ta the Indian village," Mr. O'Shaughnessy said in his thick accent. A friendly pixie of a man with sauerkraut eyebrows and a veined nose, he was trying to convince Fred and me it wouldn't be any use for us to try and catch Cab. "Stay an' have yersilves a good noight's sleep. It's too foine a sthring of dogs the man has. *Too* foine fa the loikes uv him. Not that yer own sthring ain't a dandy," he said quickly to Fred, "but thim a his are greased loightnin'. An' gracious, man," he exclaimed, "he's an hour'n a half hid start on ye already!"

Cab had stayed only long enough to warm up and eat, he'd told us after we'd changed clothes. He'd made up his mind not to stop for sleep until he reached the Indian village.

"You're sure that maybe he won't stop anywhere else?" I asked him.

"An' where would he be stoppin'?" He seemed surprised I'd even ask such a thing. "There ain't nahthin' 'twixt here 'n the Injin village but one lone cabin."

The steak his wife had pan fried for us was thick and delicious, but I could hardly finish half of it. Once I found out that Cab had pushed on I didn't have much of an appetite.

"What made him go on?" I asked. "What's his hurry?"

Mr. O'Shaughnessy looked over at the man with the broken glasses as if asking him, then answered the question himself.

"Because he's daft! Oi told'm he wuz daft, too. 'It's an outra-a-a-geous hardship for the little tykes,' I sez to 'im. Wud he listen? He wud not. 'Oi've made up me moind,' sez he. 'Oi has a mission Oi'm on, 'n' Oi shall not sleep until Oi've finished with it. Oi makes no stop till Oi've done whut Oi've set out ta do.' Did he say that or shall Oi be kicked inta a ditch seven toimes for loyin'?" he asked the man.

The man nodded. He was a neighbor named Joshua Potter and he'd just dropped by for a visit. "That's just about what he said," he agreed.

"Oi'm sorry, lass," Mr. O'Shaughnessy said to me.

Mrs. O'Shaughnessy came over to the table. "You not eat," she said.

"I'm not hungry," I said.

The man sleeping in the bunk started snoring again and kept it up until Mr. O' Shaughnessy went behind the blanket and poked him. He hadn't waked up the whole time we were there.

I looked over at Fred. There were dark circles under his eyes. He'd hardly spoken a word since we'd come in. "Suppose we went over The Drop," he asked Mr. O'Shaughnessy. "You think we'd have a chance of catching him then?"

"The Dhrop?" He crooked his head and made a grudging sound. "It's a bad toime for takin' that trail. Bad indeed."

"It would save us two hours."

Mr. O'Shaughnessy looked at the other man. "Phwat do you think, Josh?"

"You might catch him," he said to Fred, "if your sled holds together."

"You have some chain I can borrow?" Fred asked.

"All ye need," Mr. O'Shaughnessy said.

Fred glanced at me. He was tired. We both were. He looked away quickly. "If you'll tell me where it is I'll go get it," he said, standing.

"I'll go with ye."

Fred collected his clothes. As he was about to go out, I said, "Hey, you're forgetting something."

"What's that?" he said.

"My duds," I said, getting up. I'd used the term to make him smile and he did.

"Oh. Yeah . . ."

I collected my own clothes and gave them to him.

"What's The Drop?" I asked Josh after they went out.

"Ptarmigan Drop. A pass. Bad one." He raised one hand and held it flat. Then he tilted it steeply. "Drops like this," he said. "This time of year it's half ice."

I thought about Chuck and Ethel. "Is there any chance Cab would take it?"

"Probably would if he weren't carrying whiskey."

"How about children?"

"Be glad he's got the whiskey," he said.

I heard the dogs yipping as Fred and Mr. O'Shaughnessy led them out of the barn. I sat back and closed my eyes, enjoying the last few moments of warmth and thinking how nice it would be to sleep before going out again. It was almost two in the morning and we'd been on trail for over eight hours. Suddenly I thought of something that made my eyes pop right open—the way Fred had almost walked out without my clothes. I was up like a shot.

I slipped and almost fell before my moccasins held onto the caked-down snow. The dogs were all harnessed and Fred was bending down in front of the sled. He was checking the spring fastening that held the main towline to be sure it was holding. It had given us trouble. As soon as I reached the sled I knew I had been right in coming out when I did. The tarp was lashed down over the load and Mr. O'Shaughnessy had my clothes bundled under his arm.

"You were going without me," I said to Fred.

"Cab's got a big head start," he said. "I'll have a better chance of catching him if I'm alone."

"I'm going."

"Anne—"

"You're not going alone. I mean that."

"It's going to be tougher from here on, and you're tired . . ."

"You're not going to catch up with him all by yourself."

I stood my ground and he gave in. We had to re-pack the load to make room for me to ride when it was possible, then we went back in and said good-bye to everyone.

I was able to ride for about a mile, and every time I thought about what he'd intended to do I'd get a lump in my throat. When we came to the bank of a slough we had to cross I got out. I put a hand on his arm.

"Fred." I pulled my scarf down. "I'm so proud of you."

He put his arms around me and held me for a few moments. "I feel the same way about you," he said. Then he let me go and we went on. I felt as if I could take on anything after that.

For as long as I lived I'd never forget those next six hours. Old-timers like Ben and Uncle Arthur had told me dozens of stories of forced mushes they'd made, and of how more often than they wanted to remember they'd almost frozen to death, but on that trip I found out I hadn't had the least idea of what they meant.

Compared to the trail we now took, traveling on the river had been a breeze. We sidled up hills that grudged us the narrow paths that bordered them and kept trying to edge the sled off. Twice, for stretches of a quarter of a mile, Fred had to put on snowshoes and break trail across snow that would have swallowed us up to the waist, while I stayed at the handle bars inching the sled forward. Time and again we both had to push from behind as the dogs labored to pull the sled up a steep bluff or the sharp bank of a creek. Half-buried bushes caught in the runners and tore at our moccasins.

Aggravated from lack of sleep, exhausted from pushing and falling and being whipped by the wind, I sat down once and cried, telling Fred to go on and leave me, that I couldn't go any farther.

It wasn't all bad, though. Rounding a sharp turn in the trail once while I was on the runners and Fred trotted alongside, the

293

dogs decided to speed up suddenly and I lost my grip on the handles. I went flying off down an embankment, and braced myself for a sickening jolt. Instead I did a flip, landed on my back and sank down in a soft fleecy bed, with my legs straight up in the air. I stared up at the sky, while Fred ran after the sled. I was still in the same position when he slipped down the embankment and his face loomed over me. "Anne, are you hurt?"

I knew how ridiculous I had to look, like a bug on its back. "Hurt my eye." I wiggled my legs for him. It was just what we needed. The two of us started to laugh hysterically. Even after we were on the way again all we had to do was glance at each other to make us giggle.

It was almost as if it was a turning point, because in a little while the trail eased and we pushed ahead up a winding creek. Even the wind started to help us, blowing at our back and giving us an extra nudge to speed us up.

"There it is!" Fred yelled finally, "Ptarmigan Drop!"

I looked for it, but I didn't see anything that resembled a drop. "Where?"

"The other side of that hill."

It looked pretty steep from where we were, but not half as steep as it did when we reached the base of it. The top was half a mile away, and it seemed impossible that the dogs would be able to pull the sled up. It was an obstacle course of ledges and clefts, boulders and stunted spruce. Even with the wind in back of us, it would be a tough climb.

"Isn't there another way up?"

"There is, but we'd lose too much time," Fred yelled. "We'll make it. Let's go!"

I got behind the sled with him and we both started pushing to help the dogs. After a few minutes I had to stop and rest. It was like trying to roll a boulder uphill, shoulders behind the handlebars, struggling upward a few hundred feet, then rest. I could feel every stab of willow, every rock, through my moccasins. It was as hard on the dogs as on us. They panted and

294

clawed for purchase where there wasn't any, panted and strained where there was.

And finally we were at the top, all of us flopping down limply as if we were parts of one big body. My feet were bruised and I knew a couple of my toes were bleeding. I lay on my side, taking in huge gulps of air. Fred lay beside me.

"If you feel like crying," he said between deep breaths, "go ahead. I'll join in."

A couple of minutes later I sat up and looked out over the country that lay beyond us. We were at the top of the world, and even as played out as I was my spirits lifted. The gray wide line of the river wound northeast through mountains whose sides were shrouded in mist. Above the mist loomed white pinnacles that stood out sharp against a midnight blue sky spangled with stars. Stretching directly below us was a long sweep of slope that was as inviting as a magic carpet, a carpet that led into a wonderland of dark green distant forests. It was dizzying.

I wondered how far down the slope went. After the climb we'd just had it looked like a dog musher's dream. The dogs would be able to ake it at an effortless trot while Fred and I rode in style.

"That couldn't be The Drop," I said.

"No. It's down below."

"How far?"

"Couple of miles."

We took them as easily as I thought we would, leaving the wind on the other side of the hill. It was like traveling through a stage setting, the air clear and tingling, the moonlight sparkling off bushes laced with frost. The slope ended in a plateau and we veered to the right, skirting a sheer drop until the ground dipped and we rode down a wide trough for a short distance. The left side of the trough gradually lowered, the curved bottom flattened out and we came out onto a narrow ledge. There below was The Drop. I thought of how scared I'd been to ski down the hill at Joe Temple's cabin. This one made Joe's seem level. I didn't have to ask how it had gotten its name. It

295

was obvious: you needed wings to climb it and wings to go down. It was just one long cascade of snow and ice-covered rock that ended half a mile below at Ptarmigan Creek. Even on foot you'd have to slide down most of it.

"Fred, we can't go down that in the sled—it's suicide!"

He was already untying the dogs.

"We're not. I am."

Now I saw what Mr. O'Shaughnessy's friend had meant when he said it could be done if the sled held together. If it got out of control and went too fast it would be smashed to pieces. The driver could be badly hurt, even killed.

I kept trying to talk Fred out of it, but he wouldn't listen to me. He'd done it before, he said, although not this late in the year when there was crusty snow and ice. "I'll make it," he insisted. He kept unharnessing the dogs, so I couldn't get him to look me in the eye to see if he was as sure as he sounded. Then he swung the sled around to face The Drop.

We were almost finished rough-locking the runners with chain when Fred pointed to something way off. "Look."

All I saw was the long flat sweep of the river.

"It's Cab," he said. My heart skipped a beat. "There on the river, all the way to our right. See?"

Then I saw it—a faint long speck darker than the gray around it. From this distance it looked as if it was barely moving.

"You sure it's him?" I began to feel excited.

"It's him," Fred said. "He may be a little ahead of us when we hit the river, but not much."

We finished chaining the runners quickly, then Fred told me to start down with the dogs. "I'll catch up with you."

"Fred . . ." I was torn between the excitement of catching up with Cab and the fear that Fred might be hurt.

"Go on," he said, "I'll make it, don't worry."

I started down with all the dogs except Pancake. Fred needed him to keep the sled pointed. I didn't have to walk. All I had to do was keep my balance and practically slide down, the dogs nipping at each other and frisking around. I was halfway down when Fred let out a yell. I made the dogs whoa and sat down fast, bracing one moccasin against a rock.

By the time I looked up the sled was moving. Pancake was on a long lead, and the line was taut. Whether he'd be able to keep it taut once the sled picked up speed was another thing. Chains jingling, Fred on the runners, the sled nosed down in a straight line. Underneath the soft surface snow was hard crust, so Pancake had no trouble running, but the same crust was greasing the way for the sled. It picked up speed fast, even rough-locked as it was. A shower of sparks flew out from under the right runner as the chains scraped across a slab of rock. It didn't slow the sled down, though. Once over the rock the sled jumped forward and a spray of white flew out from behind as Fred rode the brake. Pancake had to run like sixty to keep the line from going slack. It was either that or get out of the way.

"Mush Pancake!" Fred yelled. "Yah-h-h—mush!"

By the time it was close to passing me the sled was rocking from side to side and Fred had to lean hard to keep it from tipping. Once abreast of me it hit a bump that sent the front of it two feet in the air. It came down with a punishing whump that I felt in the soles of my feet and Fred was bounced off the runners. I screamed, sure he wouldn't be able to get back on, that he'd end up tumbling like a rag doll, neck broken. But somehow he got one foot back on. In a kneeling position, he grabbed at the lashings and pulled himself up. Then he was standing, foot on the brake again, yelling to Pancake.

Once he was past the sled disappeared in its own boiling mist. In the next moment I thought my arm was going to be pulled from its socket. I was jerked forward by the dogs and went tumbling down the hill after them. Too excited to stand still, they were running after the sled, dragging me with them. It happened so fast I didn't have time to think or try to free the line from around my mitten. All I saw was a violent white world flying around me. Then my mitten was pulled off and I slid to a stop.

By the time the world stopped spinning and I got my wits

back the dogs were a snarling, yipping mass of confusion. Tangled up in the lines, they rolled and fought their way down towards the bottom of the hill. I didn't give one hoot about them, though, because there, all the way at the bottom was Fred. He'd made it and was already scrambling up towards the dogs.

Twenty minutes later we were on our way again, mushing down Ptarmigan Creek. I had a sore right arm and a couple of the dogs sported a red slash or two from the fight they'd had, but we were all in one piece. When we spilled down a cleft and onto the river I was disappointed. Cab was nowhere in sight.

"How far ahead is he, Fred?"

"Maybe half a mile."

"How far is it to the Indian village?"

"Another ten maybe."

"Fred, we've got to catch him!"

"We will—don't you worry. Pancake!" he yelled, "Domino! Samson—mush!"

"Mush!" I yelled right along with him. "C'mon, the whole bunch of you—mush!"

They mushed, too. They must have picked up the scent of the dogs ahead because they dug into their collars and surged as though they knew they were in a race and they had to win. We sped down the river like the wind.

We caught our first glimpse of Cab's sled when it was going around a bend in the river. That was all it was—just a glimpse before it disappeared around what must have been a gravel bar. A few minutes later when we rounded it ourselves there he was no more than a quarter of a mile away. We kept narrowing his lead until Fred called out to him. "Cab!" The hills picked it up and echoed it: *Cab. Cab. Cab.*

He stopped his team and waited. I couldn't see Chuck or Ethel behind him. I saw him take off a mitten and rub his eyes, trying to see who we were. As soon as he recognized us back went the mitten and he was off again.

"Cab—wait up!" I yelled. *'Ait up. 'Ait up. 'Ait up* . . .

But he wasn't trying to get away. He was letting us catch up to him gradually.

"Howdy there!" he called when we pulled alongside of him. His scarf muffled his voice. Between that and his furred hood I could only see his eyes, but I knew he was grinning. Chuck and Ethel were all bundled up. Chuck looked at us as if we were ghosts. "Tisha!" he called out. Ethel waved. The two of them were all right.

"Cab," Fred called over, "hold up a minute, will you?"

For answer Cab speeded his dogs up. "Cab, please stop," I called.

"You got a hundred dollars, Fred?" he called back. "A hundred spondulicks says I make it to Cross Creek before ya!"

"No!"

"No race, no stop."

"Take the kids off."

"No race, no stop," he repeated. "C'mon, boy, it's an easy mile, nary a bump nor a bang. How about it?"

I waited, wondering what Fred would decide. Ahead, the river looked fairly safe. Here and there were a few humps and some gnarled jags of ice, but they could be avoided.

"You're on!" Fred called back.

Cab let out a blood-curdling screech. "Mush, you buzzards," he roared. "Yah-h-h!" At almost the same time Fred let out a yell of his own and our sled jumped forward. We'd gone fast a few times on trail, but it was nothing like the way we went then. We flew across that snow with the wind behind us and the sled rocking like a cradle.

"Down!" Fred yelled at me.

He didn't have to tell me. That sled was a bare two feet wide and with someone sitting up it was no trouble at all to tip it over from the slightest bump. I slid down until I could just barely see ahead.

I looked over to Cab. We were running almost neck and neck, with him a few feet ahead. "Yah, Pepper!" Cab called to his lead dog. "Move that butt! Pull, you darn crow-bait, or I'll skin your hide! Yah!"

The teams knew they were in a race and they were pulling their hearts out. A few seconds later both sleds separated to avoid a jag of rough ice. Cab came around his side too wide and he lost a few feet. Once we were straightened out we were a little ahead of him. The dogs were going so fast they were peppering me all over. One gob got me in the eye and I couldn't see for a couple of minutes.

Before I came to Alaska I'd always thought river ice froze the way it did on Christmas cards, smooth and even. But it didn't, at least not as far as a sled was concerned. If this was what Cab thought was without a bump or a bang I wondered what he'd consider rough. A couple of times I thought we'd turn over, but Fred held the sled steady. I looked over at Cab to see how Chuck and Ethel were making out. They'd both scrunched down as far as they could and were probably enjoying the ride.

A half-mile later Cab was a little ahead, but then his dogs had to veer off from some branches that had been blown onto the river and we were two team-lengths ahead of him. He and Fred were yelling up a storm, the echoes bouncing off the hills and yelling it all back to us.

Neither of us was going in a straight line. We veered all over the river, trying to keep to the smooth. One minute Fred and I would be in the lead, the next it would be Cab. When we both hit a stretch of soft snow at the same time and slowed down, Fred and Cab were off the runners and pushing. Cab moved ahead of us.

Once we were through it, both men on the runners again, Cab was still ahead. We were off to his left by this time, closer to shore and gaining on him when all of a sudden a rabbit appeared out of nowhere dead ahead. Pancake saw it, broke stride for just a moment as if he was going for it, and stumbled. It could have been a disaster. As it was it lost us the race. The dogs piled into each other and we ran into the wheel dog. He went down with a yowl and we plowed into three more of them before we could stop. None of them was hurt, but by the time Fred got all the harness straightened out Cab was too far ahead to catch.

He was waiting for us a quarter of a mile away. He let us come pretty close before he mushed on, but we never caught up with him again. We'd gain a little every now and then, but Cab reached Cross Creek a full two minutes before us.

Fred stopped the sled far enough away from him so the dogs couldn't get to each other, then he just stood for a couple of minutes trying to get his breath back. Cab was out of breath too. I got out of the sled and went over to Chuck and Ethel. They weren't any the worse for wear, but they were scared. Ethel put her arms out to me and I started to lift her out.

"Leave 'er be, Teacher," Cab said. "Sorry you came all this way, but I can't let you have 'em."

"Why are you doing this?"

"I ain't gonna let you roon your life."

I tried to convince him that he was wrong. No matter what I said he shook his head. He was doing it for my good.

"Let her have them, Cab," Fred said.

"I wouldn't butt in if I was you," Cab said.

"If Anne wants those kids it's her right to keep them."

"I'm takin' them where they belong," Cab said. He took off his mittens. "That's the way it's gonna be." He spoke so softly that if you didn't see his eyes you'd have thought he was being friendly.

"Fred . . ." I tried to take his arm, but he shook me off. He went to the sled and made as if to lift Ethel out. He never got to touch her. Cab charged right into him and gave him a hefty shove that almost made him lose his balance. "That's the way you want it, that's the way you got it," Cab said.

I wanted to stop it there and then. It wasn't fair. Fred wasn't a fighter like Cab. You could see just by the way he stood that he'd probably never had a fight in his life. He just stood there with his mittens bunched up in front of him as if he wasn't sure how you went about the whole thing. But not Cab. He knew what to do. He circled around Fred, his fists bobbing, while he moved in a little closer with each turn. Then all of sudden his left fist streaked out. Fred tilted his head back, but it didn't do him any good. Cab hit him on the side of the jaw

301

with his other fist and it made such an awful sound I thought I was going to be sick. Fred fell right down, stunned. He didn't even know what had happened for a few seconds. He just sat there shaking his head, his legs spread open. He spat a chunk of blood out and there was a tooth in it. I started to go over to him, but Cab said, "Leave 'im be, Teacher."

I thanked God he wasn't drunk, because if he had been he'd have been all over Fred, trying to tear him to pieces. Instead he just stood over him, his fists holding invisible ski poles. "You get up, boy, and you're crazy," he warned. "You just say uncle now and we'll call it quits. Hey?"

Fred looked terrible. He wiped his mouth and smeared blood all over his chin, then he looked down at his tooth. When he looked up again I hardly recognized him. It wasn't only the blood, it was something else, that same expression he'd had when he'd almost fought Cab back in Chicken. I'd seen him get it on the trail when we had tough going. There wasn't any fear in it. It was calculating and deadly. His face was as gray as death and as cruel as numbing cold. All of a sudden I knew that the last thing he was going to do was call it quits.

"What do you say?" Cab asked him again.

Chuck and Ethel were on each side of me, Ethel holding on to me for protection. Scared, they'd clambered out of the sled and come right over to me.

Fred didn't get up fast, but when he did it wasn't like a man getting up, it was like an animal that was using every muscle in its body even before it was on its feet. As he did it a sound came from deep inside him that I didn't know a human being could make. When I heard it I felt that something terrible was about to happen, felt it even before Cab got hit the first time. Cab didn't have a chance. One second he was standing there with his fists weaving in front of him and the next there was blood spurting out of his nose and he was backing off with Fred wanting to kill him. I don't know how many times Fred hit him before he just toppled over backwards and his head hit the ice with an awful sound. Then Fred pounced on him, his knee landing on the side of Cab's neck. He wanted to get

302

at him so bad that he sprawled past him only to scramble right back and start pounding him as if he'd gone insane and Cab wasn't a man, but something to be beaten down into the ground. Cab kept trying to protect himself, but it didn't do him any good. Fred didn't care where he hit him, just as long as he could hit him. He pounded him in the ribs and there was a snap, then he pounded his face.

I kept trying to grab him and pull him off, but he didn't stop until Cab's head was lolling like a dead chicken's, his face smeared so heavy with blood it looked like a messed-up jelly apple.

We sat him up against his sled and put his mittens on him, then Fred set about trying to wake him up. We bathed his face with snow. Even after we got most of the blood off, he still looked terrible. His nose was broken and one eye was almost closed. Even after he healed, he wouldn't be looking the way he had before the fight.

He didn't come to for almost ten minutes, and at first he couldn't remember what had happened. One thing you had to say for him, though, was that once it all came back to him he didn't hold any grudge. In fact he acted just the opposite. As soon as he could stand up he told Fred he truly admired him, that he hadn't any idea Fred could handle himself that way. Fred said that Cab was pretty good himself and that he hoped he hadn't hurt him too much. Cab said No, he'd gotten beat up worse than that one time in Redman's Hall at Eagle.

He had to stuff some cotton in one of his nostrils and he didn't make a whimper. I was really worried about his being able to make it as far as the Indian village and so was Fred, but Cab said he'd be all right. In a way it was almost funny, Fred worrying over him and asking him if he was sure he was fit to travel and Cab telling him not to worry at all, he'd make it. A little while before they'd been trying to bash each other's brains out. Now they were carrying on like buddies.

Cab even got out a bottle of whiskey and offered Fred some. "Half-breed or not," he said, "you're a white man."

Fred turned the drink down and Cab took a few swallows

while Fred and I started putting Chuck and Ethel into our sled.

"I could go back with you as far as O'Shaughnessy's if you want," he said. "Looks like you might run into some bad weather." He pointed way far off to the southwest where the mountains were disappearing in a darkening sky. Fred told him we'd make out all right, so Cab just leaned back and watched us. We had Chuck and Ethel all bedded down and were about ready to go when Cab's dogs started sniffing the air and getting to their feet, a couple of them growling and baring their teeth. Ours started to do the same thing and I thought that maybe they were going to start something between them, but they weren't. They were all looking back up the river.

Something was coming our way. All there was at first was a tiny patch of white fog moving toward us, then a dotted black line that turned into a string of maybe a dozen dogs. There was a man riding the sled behind them, another one trotting alongside. They were still too far away to make out who they were, but Cab's dogs turned so mean that they wouldn't settle down until Cab got a length of chain out and waded into them with it.

"Indians," he said, after he'd calmed them down. "My dogs don't take to 'em."

They were Indians, and one was Titus Paul. They must have been on their way back from their trapline because their sled was loaded. They stopped some distance away, their dogs as ready for a fight as Cab's. The other man stayed with them while Titus walked over.

It's funny how things strike you all of a sudden. I'd never thought about why Indians and Eskimos always ornamented their parkas with bright beadwork and plenty of color. I'd just figured that was their way. Until I watched Titus walking toward us. His caribou parka was a real beauty, white fur speckled with brown, topped by a wolf-fur hood, but as he came nearer I suddenly realized that after being on trail all this time I'd become tired and bored of seeing green and white. Looking at Titus was like seeing the whole world suddenly take on color, the slash of it at the hem of his parka, even the braided leather mitten-string that was attached to his collar. He looked like a Northern prince. Even the way he walked was kind of prince-like, long-legged and slow, chest out, and that small head of his above it all, making him seem taller than he was.

"Howdy, Titus," Cab called, "you make good catch? Take plenty fur?"

Titus nodded so you'd hardly notice, taking in Cab's condition without changing expression, then his eyes went flick-flick-flick, taking in me and Chuck and Ethel and dismissing us. Then they flicked to Fred and the dogs, and finally settled on Fred. Fred took off a mitten and offered his hand. "Fred Purdy," he said.

Titus took off his own lynx paw mitten. "Titus Paul," he said. Like his partner, he was all dressed in skins. His moose-hide breeches were tucked into knee-high "husky" boots—moccasins made from the leg skin of the wolf above the ankle and moose leather below.

Cab took another swallow from the bottle and offered it to him. He took a couple of swallows, then handed it back. "You go Indian village?" he asked.

"Sure am," Cab said.

"You come see Cathy?" he asked me.

"No, Fred and I are going back to Chicken."

"We just had a little difference of opinion before you showed up, Titus," Cab said. The whiskey had already gotten to him, you could see. He was getting a mulish look to him that said he was thinking about something hard and coming to a conclusion about it. I smelled trouble and I wished Fred and I were gone. No doubt Titus had seen Cab's sled trail farther up the river and then seen where ours joined it. He looked at Chuck and Ethel, then asked them something in Indian.

Chuck pointed to Cab, explaining, then to me.

"You take kids from *skooltrai?*" Titus asked Cab.

305

"Yeah, I take 'em," Cab said, glancing at Fred and me. "I bring 'em back to Indian village where they belong," Cab answered. "People in Chicken no like they live there."

Titus looked at Fred. "Why *you* take from *him?*"

"Anne wants them."

I said, "Titus, they belong to me, their father gave them to me."

"They Indian kids. Indian kids belong Indian village."

"Glad you say that, Titus," Cab said. "Them two kids make this little lady lotsa trouble. Lotsa trouble. White people in Chicken no like *skooltrai* keep them. Make too much very angry with her she keep them. Make angry with whole Indian village too!"

"Cab, you're a louse," I said.

Cab didn't pay me any mind. "You take these kids, Titus. Take to Indian village an' white people be lotsa happy."

Fred spoke up. "Titus, those two kids belong with Anne. She's been taking care of them. She wants them and they want her."

"Why you want?" Titus asked me.

"Because I love them."

The minute I said it I felt tears coming up and I was furious with myself. The last thing I needed right then was tears. I needed to be tough. Titus, he didn't know anything about tears, so I screwed my face up, and I gave him the meanest look I could manage. "What's wrong with that?" I said. "Is that a crime?" Somehow it didn't come out tough.

"Teacher," Cab said, grinning that dumb fool grin again, "you are the cat's whiskers."

"Cab, if you don't shut up—"

"Hold on a minute, Teacher. Titus, I ask you question. You have law in village—no brave go 'way from village without Council say yes. You savvy me?" Titus didn't say anything. "This little boy belong in village until Council say he can go. Am I right?"

Titus nodded.

306

"Well then I think you better take him and the little girl too."

He came over to where I was standing beside the sled and started to undo the ties. I don't know what happened to me then. As soon as Cab put his hands on Ethel I saw red. "No!" I yelled, and it was the strongest no I'd ever given to anyone. I didn't think and I didn't care. I just gave him the hardest push I could and he went sprawling. He looked as surprised as he had when Fred had hit him.

"These children are mine!" I yelled at him. "They're mine and nobody is going to take them away from me."

Cab stayed lying where he fell. One leg up in the air, he played the clown, looking up at me as if he were seeing me for the first time. Then Fred came over and stood beside me. "Calm down, Anne," he said.

"I'm *not* going to calm down. Ever since I came here everybody's been telling me what I'm supposed to do and what I'm not supposed to do. Now I'm going to do what *I* want to do!"

Titus' dogs weren't any friendlier than Cab's, so the Indian who'd stayed by the sled found a jag of ice he could chain them to. Then he came over and joined Titus. It was Arthur Jack. He looked over at Chuck, then said something and Titus nodded. I got in front of Chuck.

"Better let 'em have 'em, Teacher," Cab said. "They can get pretty mean."

I stayed put. "Titus, please, let me keep them," I pleaded. "Don't take them away from me. What chance are they going to have there in that place? What chance will Chuck have—the chance to grow up speaking broken English and maybe get a job sweeping up at a roadhouse? Or going to work on the riverboats? What chance will Ethel have except maybe to wind up living with some white miner the way her mother did?"

"They belong Indian village," Titus said grimly.

"They belong with me! Their father gave them to me."

He thought a moment. "You take girl," he said. "We take Chuck."

307

"Take him to what? What are you taking him to? Lame Sarah, who can't even feed herself?"

"You come talk Council. Not my business. Chuck Indian boy. You take him you make him white boy."

"I'll make you a promise. Let me keep him and Ethel and I swear I won't let them forget their own people. I'll never let them forget where they came from."

He was softening. I could feel it. "Titus," I said, "don't take them. I can make them strong, I can help them to be proud and stay proud. Let me do it."

He stared at me for the longest time, then his eyes flicked to Chuck and Ethel. Before he could say anything, Cab spoke up.

"Titus," he warned, "you no take these kids, them people in Chicken are gonna be mighty *sahnik* with ya. You gonna have Mr. Strong to deal with an' everybody else here in the Forty Mile. Now you be smart an' do the right thing, you hear? I'm warnin' you."

A wind came up, sending swirls of snow across the frozen surface of the river while Titus mulled the warning over. Then he asked Chuck a question in Indian.

"*Aha*," Chuck answered. Yes.

Then, just like that, Titus turned on his heel and headed back for his sled, Arthur Jack following. It happened so fast I didn't realize for a few seconds that Chuck and Ethel were mine. Cab did, though. "You know what the heck you're doin'?" he called after Titus.

Titus didn't pay him any mind and Cab took a few steps after him. "Titus! Darn it, are you deef?"

Titus finally turned around when he reached his sled. Cab stood with his back to me and Fred. I thought Cab was going to start more trouble, but he was as unpredictable as he was stubborn. "You wanna race to the village?" he called to Titus.

"You give me start," Titus called back.

"No, I ain't gonna give you no start," Cab said. "I got half a load of whiskey."

"I got full load fur."

"Give you a quarter mile 'n' betcha fifty dollars."

308

"Bet," Titus answered. "I fire two shot."

Titus' sled drove off and Cab came back. "Teacher," Cab said, "don't be mad at me. I was doin' what I thought was right."

I didn't pay any attention to him because I'd made up my mind I'd never say another word to him again.

"If it means anything," he went on, "I ain't gonna say anything to anybody about Titus lettin' you have those two kids."

"You really mean that?"

"I truly do. Shoot, I'm no snitch. I did my best an' that ugly weasel called my bluff. So how about lettin' bygones be bygones."

"All right."

He still looked in bad shape. I didn't see how he could have the energy left over to run another race. He did, though. He smiled at me. "Teacher, I'll tell you somethin' and I mean it from the bottom of my heart. You're an Alaskan."

"Thanks, Cab."

Fred released the brake on the sled and I got on the runners.

"See ya soon," Cab called.

"See you soon," I called back.

And that's the way we parted.

XXII

Fred found a place off the river that was out of the wind, then after we fed the dogs and built a fire we had some beans and jerky washed down with tea. Dead tired, Ethel fell asleep practically in the middle of eating, but Chuck was wide awake.

I'd asked him if Cab had treated him and Ethel all right and he said he had. He was confused, though. Too many things had happened too fast. "Where we go now?" he asked me.

"Back to Chicken."

"I not like that," he said.

"Why not?"

"Want go Indian village."

"You *want* to go to the Indian village?"

"Yiss. You come too there."

"I could take you there, Chuck, if that's what you want, but I couldn't stay." I was disappointed. It was the last thing I'd expected him to say.

"We go other place maybe. You know other place?"

Then I realized what was on his mind. He wanted to be with me, but he was scared to go back to Chicken, scared of being grabbed again by Mr. Vaughn and the others.

I pulled him close to me. "Nobody'll take you away like that again," I said. "Don't you worry. I promise you, they'll be too scared to do anything like that. Isn't that right, Fred?"

"It sure is," Fred answered. His jaw was swollen, and it was

310

all black and blue. "They try anything like that we'll beat 'em all up."

"You do that?"

"Sure will," Fred said.

Chuck smiled. He liked that. His head pressed into my shoulder, the fur around his hood tickling my nose.

Starting out, we piled Chuck and Ethel into the sled and Fred and I took turns riding the runners and trotting alongside. We'd take the route Mr. Strong followed, Fred said, along the river. If the weather held we could make the O'Shaughnessy roadhouse in seven hours, stop there to sleep, then push on for Chicken. He didn't say what we'd do if the weather didn't hold and I didn't ask. It never occurred to me it might not.

It would have been an easy trip if it hadn't been for the wind and the fact that we'd been up for almost twenty-four hours. The longer we kept going the more I couldn't help but wonder at the courage of men like Uncle Arthur and Ben. They'd come into this frozen land as newcomers, before it had hardly even been mapped, and they'd built cabins and made a go of it without any help from anyone. Uncle Arthur had told me he'd never even used a thermometer for the first ten years he'd been here. In the winter he'd just leave a vial of quicksilver out on the windowsill. "And if the quick froze, you knew it was too cold to go out," he'd told me.

Even now, thirty years after they'd settled here, the land was just as raw as it had ever been. Maybe it was settled a little more and had more people, but it was still a long lonely distance from one bleak outpost to another.

We'd been traveling for almost an hour. It must have been around nine o'clock and the sun should have been coming up. Instead it was growing darker and the wind was getting worse, lifting drifted snow and hurling it at us like balls of smoke. I was trotting alongside the sled when all of a sudden a blast came along that banged at us so hard I was nearly bowled over. Even the sled rocked. Fred stopped it and the dogs immediately dropped on all fours and started curling up.

"We're in for it!" he yelled.

The snow drove at us like a wall. We couldn't even talk. The two of us got down behind the sled and sat, waiting the blast out.

"Is it over?" I said after it died down.

"It hasn't started," Fred said, getting up. "This is just a lull."

"What'll we do?"

"Keep our fingers crossed. There's a cabin we can head for. A couple of miles farther up. We can hole up there."

A few minutes later the wind was at us again. It wasn't strong enough to keep us from going on, but it was meaner and colder than ever. I began to feel thirsty, and I had to stop myself from eating some snow. In this kind of cold it would be the worst thing to do, sucking precious body heat and giving nothing in return. The temperature was dropping fast and evaporating every bit of moisture. Even when we hit smooth ice the sled was balky and Fred had to trot behind it. The wind kept snapping at us like an icy whip, teasing us, then whacking at us hard. My mouth felt dry as dust.

We swung around a small delta, and Fred headed the sled for a big cleft in the bank, a slough. "Cabin's about a quarter mile up!" he yelled.

It was a long quarter mile. No sooner had we started up the slough than the lead dogs almost disappeared. Too deep and soft, the snow swallowed them up. Fred had to get out his and Chuck's snowshoes and the two of them moved ahead of us breaking trail while I drove the sled after them at a snail's pace. We moved up the side of the slough after a while and traveled along its bank, but even there the snow was piled too deep for the dogs.

The land leveled off a little, and finally Fred stopped. He and Chuck went off to look around. There was wood around us and it helped against the wind. I leaned an elbow on the handlebar and tapped the back of Ethel's hood. She turned around, brown expectant eyes staring at me over the mask of her scarf.

I smiled, then I remembered she couldn't see my mouth.

I pulled my scarf down. "Where's the monkey?" I asked her. She thrust it out from the fur robe around her. It was her favorite toy, a fuzzy red monkey with brown button eyes. She'd held onto it even when they'd dragged her out.

"Monkey," she said.

"A happy monkey?"

"Monkey," she repeated, offering it to me. I made as if to grab for it, and she pulled it back under the robe. When it appeared again I made another grab and it went right back under.

Fred and Chuck came back.

"I can't find that cabin," he said.

"You sure it's here?" For a second I had the awful feeling we might be lost, but Fred nodded.

"Somewhere. It's probably drifted in." He put a hand on Chuck's shoulder, pointed. "Take a look over towards that rise," he told him.

Chuck went off in one direction, Fred in another, and I had to marvel at how fast they could move on snowshoes. Using them exhausted me, but Fred and Chuck swept around on them without the slightest effort. Fred kept moving farther and farther away, looking for landmarks, anything that would give him a bearing on where we were.

The dogs had been lying down quietly, muzzles flocked white. Now, one after the other, they got to their feet, sniffing the air. Either the wind had shifted and they smelled something they hadn't smelled before, or something was around that hadn't been up to now.

Pancake uttered a low growl, the ruff around his neck bristling. The other dogs were doing the same thing, and some of them began to whine. I called to Fred and he snowshoed over.

"What is it, boy?" he asked Pancake.

Pancake hung his head and kept growling. He was scared.

"Whatever it is, we can't worry about it," Fred said as Chuck joined us. "We'll head over that way." He pointed to where a double line of straggling willow and birch marked the path of a creek. "It's got to be around here somewhere."

He and Chuck started off, and I mushed the sled after them. A few minutes later we came to a clearing where the snow wasn't that deep and Fred and Chuck were able to take off their snowshoes. Fred took the sled from me. We mushed across the clearing, then down a sidling trail. We ended up beside the slough again, a little above where we'd left it. Below us were our own trail marks.

"It must be above us. We didn't come up far enough," Fred said. "Mush!" he yelled at the dogs. They started to move up the slough, then stopped dead, and no matter how much Fred yelled at them they wouldn't move. Pancake's hair was really up now. Fred moved up to him, grabbed his collar and jerked him forward with a curse, but Pancake braced his forelegs and wouldn't budge. When Fred tried to pull him forward again he snarled and bared his fangs. He meant business. I could feel the hair on my own neck start to rise.

"Fred, maybe there's a good reason why he won't go."

"He has to. We can't stay here. We've got to find that cabin!" His face above his scarf was dotted with pinpoints of blood from the driving wind.

He dragged Pancake forward a few feet and then that was the end of it. Pancake simply lay down and whimpered. *Do what you want to me,* he was saying, *I'm not going.* The other dogs did the same. It was eerie. Whatever was a little farther on had them too frightened to move.

"Stay here," Fred said to me and Chuck. He moved along the edge of the slough, then when he was almost out of sight I saw him stoop down and pick something up. He came back with it—a length of dog harness. It had been chewed. "There's what's left of a dog over there, just the skull, a few bones and some hair."

"Bear?" I asked him.

"Wolf," Chuck said.

Whatever Fred was thinking he kept to himself. He chained the dogs to a tree, then took his rifle out of the sled. "You

314

stay here with the kids," he said to me. "I'm going to take a look around."

"Oh no. We're going with you." Nothing in the world was going to keep me there with him gone. I took Ethel out of the sled.

We slogged after him. I knew that wolves didn't attack people—at least not people who were alive—but I still felt nervous. Any minute I expected something to come running out at us from behind a bush or a tree. I held Ethel's hand tightly. Instead of going straight up the edge of the slough, Fred made a wide circle, then started working back towards it. Before we reached it we found the remains of another dog. Again it was only a skull, the wind had swept the rest away. There was something else too. Chuck found it snagged in a bush—a small length of polished hardwood with some webbing attached. It was part of a sled.

We went on a little farther until we all stopped at almost the same time. There a little above us was some kind of a ledge where there shouldn't have been one. It was right smack in the path of the slough, almost as though someone had built a curved platform across its banks. But it wasn't seeing the ledge that made us stop. It was what was on it: a pack of wolves circled around something. We were downwind from them, so they hadn't caught our scent, and with the wind blowing they hadn't heard us approach.

I counted seven of them. The smallest wasn't under a hundred and fifty pounds. They looked like ghosts through the flying drift, all of them staring at something, milling around as if they didn't know how to get to it. And that was the weird part. There was nothing there, at least nothing I could see.

Two of them were more restless than the others. Long-legged, with a gait like a cat's, they kept loping around the perimeter of something, stopping every so often to peer down. I didn't know what it was about wolves that made people think of them as enemies, but people did. Maybe it was because they were so smart, working together to bring down what they were after. Or maybe there was just something in the human

315

mind that couldn't help itself, like the way fishermen hate sharks. But after I'd just seen what was left of the two sled dogs they'd taken, I didn't feel too friendly to them myself.

They saw us a few seconds later. Whatever it was that interested them, they didn't want to leave it, so they waited to see what we were going to do. The way they sized us up made my skin crawl. I'd always thought of wolves as smart dogs. This close they didn't resemble dogs at all. No dog had the huge head and powerful jaws these animals had, and no dog had their cold, shrewd gaze either. They were almost human. Or inhuman.

Fred went down on one knee, took aim, and his rifle cracked. The biggest of them, which must have weighed close to two hundred pounds, went right down. He rolled down to the end of the ledge, then just disappeared into a bed of soft snow below it. The rest of them took right off.

Fred told us to stay where we were and made his way up along the border of the slough. He glanced over to where the wolf had disappeared below, then moved out onto the ledge. I still couldn't figure out what it was, an ice bridge across the banks or what.

Fred went down on his hands and knees and inched forward. He stopped at right about the place where one of the wolves had been peering down and I thought I heard him call out, say something to somebody. I couldn't stand the waiting any longer.

"Fred, what is it?" I called to him.

He turned and waved me over. "Leave the kids there," he said.

I followed the same path he took, stepping in his tracks. I didn't know what I expected to see when I got there, but something told me it wasn't going to be pleasant. The ledge was bigger than I'd thought, bulging up a little towards the center. It wasn't solid either. There was a jagged hole almost in the middle of it. It was big, maybe four feet wide and three times as long. The whine of a dog was coming from it.

Fred pushed himself back from the hole before I reached

316

him. He stood up, the front of him painted with snow. He pulled his scarf down, and his expression was awful. "Take a look," he said, "but be careful . . . It's Jeannette and Elmer."

I crawled up to the edge of the hole and peered in. My first thought was that whatever I was seeing couldn't be real. It was like a scene from another world. Underneath me was a huge domed ice cavern, and there in the darkness a dozen feet below, her face partially covered with a fur robe, her eyes boring into mine, lay Jeannette Terwilliger. I thought she was dead until her eyes blinked, and I saw the glint of tears in them. I heard myself say, "Oh dear God."

She was lying on her side among the rocks of the slough bed, a fur robe wrapped around her. Beside her was the smashed sled. She pulled the robe down a little, but her face was still hidden by her scarf. Elmer was a short distance away from her. All I could see were his legs. He'd crawled up the side of the slough, where he lay now, not moving. I couldn't tell if he was alive or dead.

In a split second I saw it all as it must have happened: the loaded sled moving across the innocent-looking snow, the domed roof of ice under it giving, shattering like an egg and the sled falling, crashing to the ravine below. It must have happened so fast that they were falling before they heard the hollow sound of the shell ice breaking under them.

Two dogs had been pulled down with them. One of them had already clambered onto the over-turned sled and was making motions as if to jump up at me, whining in eagerness. But the distance was too great. The other dog lay among the rocks, its neck broken. Jeannette hadn't taken her eyes from me.

"Jennie?" I managed to croak out her name.

She made some sounds. That was all.

"We'll get you out," I said. Then, knowing I'd burst into tears if I stayed a moment longer, I inched back and the scene disappeared.

"You're not going to cry," Fred said harshly. "We don't have time for crying. We've got to get her out of there."

I bit my lip. "What'll we do?"

Chuck and Ethel had come up on the ledge and Chuck started to edge forward. "Stay away from there," Fred said.

"Want see," Chuck said.

"You'll see later. I need you with me."

We followed him to a big fallen spruce where he started scooping snow out on the side of the trunk that was out of the wind.

"You'll stay here with Ethel," Fred said when there was a hole big enough for Ethel and me to huddle in. "I'll take Chuck with me." He gave me his rifle. "Hold onto this. You probably won't need it, but keep it anyway."

"Where are you going?"

"To find that cabin. I know where it is now."

He and Chuck went off to get the sled. From where Ethel and I were we could see the whole ledge. Ethel pointed to it and asked me something in Indian.

"It's a hole," I said. "There was an accident there. A bad accident."

"Hole?"

I thought about the baby. I hadn't seen her. I'd been afraid to ask Jennie about her, afraid she was dead. Now a whole bunch of terrible images crept into my mind. She could be under the sled, crushed, or she could have been thrown out. I kept seeing her flying out of Jennie's arms as dogs and sled crashed through the ice, kept seeing her lying in the snow and the wolves moving toward her. . . . Finally I couldn't stand it anymore.

"Stay here, Ethel," I said. I crawled back to the edge of the hole and looked down. Elmer was in exactly the same position as before. He must have been dead.

"Jennie . . . Jennie?"

She turned her head a little, but her hood still hid her face.

"Can you answer me?"

She groaned.

"Patricia—where is she?"

Her arm moved under the robe that covered her, then her

318

mittened hand pulled down her scarf and I saw why she couldn't talk. Half of her face was white as snow, dead-looking. It was frozen.

"Ee-e-e-uh-h-h," she groaned.

"Here? Is that what you're saying? She's with you? Nod your head if you can and I'll know it's yes."

Her head moved slightly and I thought, thank God. Then I wondered if she was alive, but I couldn't ask Jennie that. "Hang on, Jennie," I said, knowing how stupid it sounded, but not knowing what else to say.

I went back to Ethel and while the two of us huddled together, I kept thinking about the accident and how it had happened. Jennie and Elmer had probably done exactly what Fred and I had—hit bad weather and come up here looking for the same cabin. Like us, they'd had trouble finding it, so they'd searched around blindly. Maybe they'd been caught in ice fog, or blizzard, but for some reason they hadn't seen that the ledge was false, a covering for a huge hollow blister. It had probably formed when water came rushing down the slough in a flash flood. The water must have gotten dammed up in some way and been held fast. By the time it drained out the surface of it had frozen, leaving just a shell. And Elmer hadn't seen it until it was too late. The same thing could have happened to anybody—to me and Fred. I'd heard of it before. I wondered how long Jennie had been down there. It could have been as much as three days, three days of lying in a frozen dungeon with hardly the barest chance of being found, and the wolves circling around above. If it hadn't been for the wolves we'd never have gone to the spot at all. She and Elmer probably wouldn't have been found until spring, maybe not even then, for then water would have come rushing down the slough, tons of it, washing everything before it into the river.

Over an hour must have passed before Fred came back with the sled. "We've found it!" he said. It was drifted in, just as he'd thought. He'd left Chuck to finish the job of clearing the door. He'd brought a strong slender birch trunk with him that he'd chopped down. Tying a rope around the center of it he went

319

over to the ledge and placed it across the narrowest width of the hole. After he made sure the ice on each side would hold, he let himself down the rope. I watched from above.

The dog that was uninjured was overjoyed. Fred had to cuff it a few times before it would stop jumping all over him. Then he lifted the sled off of Jennie. Half of the load was still in it, the rest of it—picture frames, a gold scale, mining tools, traps— was scattered all over the ravine bed.

He made Jennie as comfortable as possible and put another robe over her before he looked around. The slough was flat at the bottom, the banks sloping up gently to where the ice met them. He picked up a mattock that had spilled from the sled and chopped a good-sized rock loose from the frozen ground. "Anne, move over that way about ten feet." He pointed to where the ceiling arched down to meet the top of the bank. "Tell me if you can hear this rock hitting." His voice sounded hollow, as if it came from a tomb.

I did as he told me, listening. *Thump. Thump. Thump.* I scrambled back to the hole.

"I heard it."

"I'm going to try to dig out of here."

"You want us to come down?"

"No. Somebody's got to stay up there just in case."

"Fred, what about the baby?"

"I think it's all right. It's under her parka."

"Can you hand it up to me?"

"Jennie's arm is broken. I don't want to touch her until we can get her out. . . You're going to have to make out as best you can. I don't know how long it's gonna take to chop through this ice."

He moved out of sight and I heard him start chopping.

I went back to Ethel and we waited. She fell asleep again before Chuck came back. When he did I told him what Fred was doing and he went over to the hole to see if Fred needed him. He must have, because Chuck swung himself over the birch trunk and disappeared.

It began to snow.

I got up once or twice to stamp around and keep the circulation going in my legs. The dogs had all curled up, still in harness. Nothing bothered them, not the wind or the driving snow. Noses tucked into tails, they lay as contentedly as if they were in a warm living room, letting the white pile up around them.

I kept looking towards the spot where I thought Chuck and Fred would come out for so long my eyes started doing tricks on me. Then finally I saw a small hole appear. After that the snow began caving in like quicksand, and I roused Ethel. Chuck's head popped up and he levered himself out of the hole as Ethel and I headed over towards him. "We digged out!" he yelled excitedly. The uninjured dog scrambled out right after him, yelping and frisking around Ethel and me, almost knocking us over.

I lowered myself into the hole slowly. My feet touched the solid bank and I felt Fred grab me. Then I was below the ice and Fred helped me down the bank.

It was like a gloomy world where time had stood still. Overhead was a dome of ice that stretched across from one bank to the other and maybe thirty feet up and down the slough. Outside the wind was howling, but it was quiet in here, snow flakes drifting down through the opening above. Elmer was stretched out on the bank opposite, his head almost touching the ice above him. He was frozen, one hand still upraised. There was a hunting knife in it, and above him you could see where he'd tried to chop away at the ice. One of his legs was horribly twisted, bent at a sharp angle where there was no joint. He'd managed to crawl up the bank, and he'd died there.

I went over to Jennie.

"Jennie . . ."

She opened her eyes.

"Jennie, do you want me to take the baby?" My voice bounced off the ice above.

She nodded. I pulled away the furs that Fred had covered her with, and lifted up her parka. The baby was lying against her stomach. Somehow, even with a broken arm, she'd managed to protect her. She was still wrapped in her blanket. When I lifted the blanket from her face my heart sank. At first I thought she was dead. Her face was a sickly blue, her little body still. She wasn't dead, though. The barest wisp of vapor curled from her mouth. I put her inside my own parka and she felt cold next to me, a cold little thing that didn't move.

"S-s-s-e-e-e." Jennie said. "S-s-e-e-e." Her eyes pleaded.

"Let her get warm first, Jennie," I said. "She's cold." I didn't want her to see the baby the way she was. She had enough misery already. Her eyes closed.

Ethel and Chuck had come down through the hole. Fred set Chuck to work making the hole wider, then he knelt beside Jennie. "She's out," he said. "Thank God." He picked up a man's shirt that lay in a pile of other clothes. "Rip that up," he said. "I'm going to set her arm."

He went after the sled with an ax until he had two lengths of wood for splints. After that he rolled Jennie on her back and eased the broken arm out of her parka. Even under the sleeve of her long underwear, the break was clear. He sat down and braced one foot against her armpit, then pulled on her wrist slowly. I turned away until I heard the bone snap into place. While he set her arm in the splint I walked up and down the slough bed, hoping I could jostle the baby into making even the smallest move. It didn't do any good, though. She lay still.

Fred kept working methodically and I marveled at how he could act so coolly. If everything had been on my shoulders I'd have broken down long ago. When he was finished he climbed up the bank alongside Chuck, took the mattock from him and chopped some more ice away. When he was done he tossed the mattock down and looked over at me wearily.

"How's the baby?" he asked.

"She's not moving." *She's going to die* was what I thought, but I didn't want to say it.

"You'd better give her to Chuck," he said. "I'll need your help with Jennie."

I handed the baby over. "Hold her tight," I said. I could have saved my breath. He was eight years old, but if ever I'd seen a boy act twice his age it had been him.

Fred lifted Jennie's shoulders and I took her legs. Halfway up the bank one of them slipped out of my grasp. Her foot dropped onto a rock, making a horrible sound—as if it was a rock itself. I glanced up at Fred, cringing inside. His mouth set itself in a tight line. Only one thing could have made a sound like that—a foot that was frozen solid.

XXIII

Somehow we managed to get Jennie up through the hole and into the sled.

We made a few trips back in to bring out food and things for the baby. Then Fred dragged out the dead dog and left it some distance away. There'd been some traps on the sled, and before we left, he brought five of them out and set them around the hole. We hoped they'd keep the wolves away from Elmer's body.

When we reached the cabin I wondered how Fred had found it at all. It squatted so low against a hill that I didn't even see it until we were practically on top of it.

Inside, the sloping ceiling was too low for Fred or me to stand up straight except by one wall, and there wasn't too much room to move around. It was shelter, though, and it was all we needed. There was oil in a dusty lamp. After Fred lit it we brought Jennie in and laid her on a rickety canvas cot, then Fred started a fire in the small Yukon stove.

I took Patricia out from under my parka. When I looked at her I almost groaned. Her face and hands were a sickly violet in the light of the oil lamp, and there wasn't anything I could do for her except sit by the stove and hold her close to me.

After we stored our gear and filled some pots with snow, I started some stew thawing while Fred and Chuck went to work on Jennie. Fred filled a small washtub with snow, then took the moccasin and socks off her frozen leg. It was hard as marble, white up to the knee. He put it into the washtub and began to bathe the leg with snow while Chuck bathed her face. She hadn't regained consciousness and I hoped for her sake that she'd sleep for as long as possible. Once feeling came back to her she'd be in terrible pain.

It took a long time to boil water for tea. The stove had to be coddled, since the sheet-metal sides were too rusted and flaky to chance a big fire. Someone had laid a piece of sheet metal across the top to reinforce it, otherwise we wouldn't have been able to cook on it at all. Even so, it didn't throw out much heat.

I handed some tea over to Fred and Chuck, then poured some for Ethel and me. None of us had said a word since we'd come in. We were all played out, just going on nervous energy. Jennie moaned softly and moved her head. Some snow fell away from her face.

"How bad is she, Fred?"

He didn't have to say anything. His look was enough. He shook his head. "How about the baby?" he asked me.

"She hasn't moved."

"We have to decide what to do," Fred said. "Jennie's foot's frozen to the bone. The leg may be too, I can't tell."

"What can we do?"

"Get her to a doctor."

Outside the wind was blowing hard as ever, making the stovepipe hum. "How can we?"

"We have to. *I'll* have to . . . Even if she does get to a doctor she's going to lose her foot, maybe the whole leg."

"Where's the nearest one?"

"Dawson."

That was over a hundred and fifty miles.

"I could take her as far as Forty Mile," he said. "There's bound to be someone who could take her to Dawson from there."

Forty Mile was the first town across the Canadian border,

but it was still ninety miles. I didn't see how he could make it, not as tired as he was. The weather outside was as mean as ever. "That's a long trip, Fred."

"I know," he said. "I'd have to get some sleep first, a few hours anyway, but I could do it. There are places I could stop at on the way. I've traveled in worse weather."

"When would you start out?" I asked him.

"After we eat and I get a few hours sleep. You'd have to manage here alone."

It was a grim meal. I hardly tasted the food. When Chuck and Ethel finished they sat stupefied. They couldn't stay awake anymore. They used a pail to relieve themselves, then they bundled up together in a sleeping bag we'd taken from the Terwilligers' sled. They were asleep before we buttoned the bag up.

Fred and I had another cup of tea.

"I hate to leave you all alone here," he said.

"How long do you think it might be?"

"Mr. Strong's due up the river in a day or two. I'll leave word at Steel Creek that you're here. With the weather like this, well, you'll be here a couple of days. Maybe more."

"You better get to sleep," I said.

"You think you can stay awake?"

"I'll have to." Somebody had to wake him up.

I took Patricia out of my parka to look at her again. She was losing the blue color. Her little hands were pink. If she woke up she'd have to be fed, so I had another reason for staying awake.

Fred laid out another sleeping bag and told me to wake him in three hours. He fell asleep almost as fast as the kids had. My watch had stopped, so I set it at twelve, then sat down on the edge of the cot. Jennie's face had begun to blister. Her foot was still in the washtub, the skin on her leg beginning to wrinkle. I leaned over, picked up some snow and bathed her leg with it. When my hand touched the flesh it made me shudder.

After a few minutes I felt sleepy and got up. The dog that

326

had been in the slough was lying between the stove and the wall. He lifted his head. We'd chained him up outside with the other dogs, but they'd attacked him, so we'd brought him in. I stood by the high wall for a few minutes, then I sat down on a stool by the stove. I took the baby out and rocked her. I brushed her cheek with my lips. It was warm, soft as a flower petal. She looked like Elmer around the cheeks and eyes, but she had Jennie's mouth, kind of pouty and nice. "Patricia?"

I'd changed her diapers and gone over her carefully to see if there was anything wrong with her. She had a black and blue mark on her thigh and it had swelled a little, but she didn't have any broken bones. Outside of some chafing from wet diapers she seemed all right. I rocked her some more and talked to her. She squirmed a little and there was a flash of pink tongue before she sucked it back in her mouth. Then she yawned. Excited, I walked back and forth with her. I had a bottle filled with diluted condensed milk, all set to be plunked in a saucepan if she woke. "Come on, Patricia. That's it," I said. "Just wake up and start yelling. You can do it . . ."

She stopped and was still.

There was a small fruit crate lying by the stove with some kindling in it. I emptied it out, laid some newspapers on the bottom, then wrapped a blanket around Patricia and placed her in the crate. After that I put some more wood in the stove. The sides of it were so thin that the fire gleamed through in places.

I sat down on the edge of the cot again and bathed Jennie's leg. I fell asleep right in the middle of it. I caught myself falling forward and my knees almost touched the floor before I woke with a start. For the next couple of hours I kept putting snow on my face and neck to stay awake.

A half hour before I was supposed to wake Fred, Jennie began to scream.

She kicked away the washtub and I had to grab her to keep her from falling off the cot. It happened so suddenly that I was terrified. One moment everything was still and the next I was wrestling with Jennie and sobbing hysterically for Fred. She thrashed around, screaming in pain. And finally Fred was on the other side of the cot, holding her in a firm grip, talking to her while she stared at us wild-eyed. She kept trying to talk, but her mouth was twisted in an ugly sneer and her words were just a babble of sound.

"Jennie, you're here with Anne and me," Fred kept repeating. "You're safe. You're safe, Jennie. Try to understand."

The wild look went out of her eyes. She stopped struggling and fell back in exhaustion. She realized where she was. Her eyes closed and tears of pain welled up from them. "Eeshuh," she said quietly. "Ee-shuh."

"Patricia's here, Jennie," I said. ". . . She's sleeping. Do you want to hold her?"

She nodded.

I brought the baby and laid her in the crook of Jennie's arm. She raised her head to look at the baby a moment, then slumped back and closed her eyes. The pain she was suffering must have been excruciating, but she lay still. She had her baby.

"Jennie," Fred said, "I have to get you to a doctor . . . you understand?" She nodded without opening her eyes. "Anne'll stay here with the baby and take care of her." She only made the barest movement. She understood.

Chuck and Ethel hadn't waked up. They'd lived in close quarters all their life. They were used to all the noise that went with it.

While Fred made preparations to leave I warmed up a chunk of vegetable soup and fed the broth to Jennie. She was able to drink only a little of it. Once in a while she moaned softly, but from the moment I'd given her the baby she'd hardly made a sound. The only way I knew what she was going through was when I looked into her eyes. The pain was there, the pain of losing her husband and leaving her baby, and the pain in her tortured body. I could hardly imagine the suffering she was going through.

When Fred was ready we carried her out. The cabin and the

hill in back of it gave us little protection from the wind as we lashed her into the sled. Gray sleet drove at us, the cold pressing like water. When the lashings were secure I leaned over Jennie to say a hurried good-bye "I'll take care of the baby, Jennie. I'll take good care of her."

She moved one mittened hand feebly and pulled the scarf from her mouth. One side of her mouth twisted up before her hand dropped. She had tried to smile.

Fred was ready to go.

There were so many things I wanted to say to him—how much I admired him, how much I needed him and wanted him, how deeply I loved him. But there was no time. Instead I said, "Please be careful, Fred."

"I will. Just don't you get scared."

"I've got the easy part."

I didn't wait for him to kiss me. If I did, I'd have waited till Kingdom come. I kissed him hard enough so that maybe it would keep him warm and safe and alive all the way he had to go.

Then he was gone, the sled disappearing in a gray swirl. I turned back into the cabin.

After a while I knew I couldn't stay awake any longer. I'd kept walking back and forth with Patricia as long as I could, coaxing her to wake up. It wasn't doing any good. She'd move a little, open and close a tiny fist, and that was all. She was a perfect little thing and inside of her there was a struggle for life going on, but there was no way I could help her. I felt myself caving in. I put some more wood in the stove, then crawled into Fred's sleeping bag with her. Even if the stove went out we'd all be warm enough.

I didn't know how much later it was that I started to wake up, thinking there was an alarm ringing somewhere. Groggy, at first I thought it was my father's alarm clock and I wondered why he didn't turn it off. It seemed to keep ringing for hours and it made me angry until I realized it wasn't an alarm at all. It was a baby crying.

Then I was awake. Beside me, Patricia was spluttering in

rage—the most wonderful sound I'd ever heard.

I was out of the sleeping bag in a moment. I stood up too fast and bumped my head on the ceiling. The fire in the stove was just embers. Shaking the ashes down, I heaped up some paper and kindling, then wood on top of that. It caught right away and I plunked the bottle I'd prepared into the saucepan. Then I turned up the oil lamp.

Chuck and Ethel were still asleep, the top of Chuck's head poking out of the bag. I rocked Patricia in my arms, talking to her, telling her she'd be eating soon, filling up on all she needed. I looked at my watch. It said 8:30. That meant I'd slept almost five hours since Fred had gone. I wondered what the real time was, whether it was day or night. I'd lost track and there was no way to tell. Sleet was needling at the window. It was iced over and it looked to be night outside. I couldn't be sure, though. I kept going over to the stove to check the bottle, but it always seemed as cold as ever and Patricia kept yelling. Her fingers found her mouth and she shoved them into it, gums clamping down on them. They satisfied her for a couple of minutes before she realized nothing was happening, then she bawled again for the real thing.

The bottle was tepid when I gave it to her. I just couldn't wait for it to get any warmer. She grabbed at the nipple, struggled with it, then pushed it out. I tried again and the same thing happened. I checked the nipple and it was all right, but when I gave it to her again the milk dribbled down her chin. She wasn't getting it.

I started to feel helpless panic, afraid I was doing something wrong, but I didn't know what. Patricia screamed louder than ever. Chuck's head popped out from the sleeping bag. He looked over at me, not really awake, then his head disappeared.

I put the bottle back in the saucepan, thinking that maybe it wasn't warm enough. Every few minutes I tested it on my wrist. When it felt warm I gave it to her again. She still wouldn't take it. I tasted it to see if there was anything wrong with it, but there wasn't.

Ten minutes later she was asleep again. I sat looking at her, wondering what could possibly be wrong, if maybe she'd been injured internally in some way. If she had been then there was nothing I could do but sit here and watch her die. I crawled back into the sleeping bag with her and lay there in a half stupor.

The next time she woke I was up before she began to cry. I'd refilled the bottle with fresh milk, and this time I waited for it to heat to the right temperature before I gave it to her. She still wouldn't take it. She twisted and turned, avoiding the nipple, screaming as though she were in pain.

Sick with fear, I sat and stared into space. I couldn't help her. Whatever she needed, I couldn't give it to her.

Chuck's head popped out of the sleeping blanket. He eased himself out of it, shivered, then slipped on his parka. He watched while I tried to get Patricia to take the bottle again.

"Baby no hungry," he said.

"She is hungry, Chuck. That's why she's crying. She hasn't eaten in a couple of days. I don't know what to do."

Chuck wiggled his fingers in front of her. She stopped crying to look at them, then he put a finger in her hand. She grabbed onto it and held it for a few moments before she let it go.

"Tiny liddle baby," he said.

"Did you ever see anything like this happen?" I asked him. "I mean where a baby wouldn't eat?" I was so desperate I was asking an eight year old for help. He shook his head.

I tried the nipple again, but it was the same. She took it, then spat it out and started crying. I handed the bottle to Chuck and put her over my shoulder. The bottle seemed bigger in his hands, awfully big. Maybe that was the trouble. She hadn't eaten in two or three days and she was weak. Maybe she was too weak to hold onto the nipple. "Chuck, get me the first-aid kit. It's over there on the shelf."

He brought it over. There was a medicine dropper in it. Unscrewing the cap on the bottle, I asked Chuck to hold it, pulled some milk up into the dropper and put it in her mouth.

She wouldn't take it, but I kept at it. For I don't know how long the milk kept dripping out of her mouth. Then when I was almost ready to give up she began holding on to some of it. First just a few drops, then more.

"She's taking it, Chuck."

He leaned over her, interested. She fussed and fumed, frustrated every time I pulled the dropper out to fill it up again, but she was taking it, all right. When she dropped off to sleep there was about an inch and a half of milk gone from the bottle. She hadn't taken much, hardly more than a couple of mouthfuls, but at least she'd taken something.

I put her back in the fruit crate, then set about getting a meal ready. The dog came over to the stove while I was cooking. I sent him out to do his business and he was at the door again almost right away, scratching and whining to get in.

Ethel woke up just before the meal was ready and the three of us sat down and ate—biscuits and stew. When we were done Chuck and I did the dishes and Ethel sat beside Patricia, talking to her. I couldn't seem to get my mind going. What I needed to clear it was about twelve straight hours of sleep. I felt as if I was going to burst out crying any minute. I wondered where Fred was, how he was making out. If the weather kept up like this it could take him four or five days to reach Forty Mile, with stopovers for sleep. If it eased up he might make it in two.

With the dishes done the three of us sat on the cot while I fed Patricia again with the medicine dropper. Chuck was thumbing through a yellowed magazine. He pushed it over to me and pointed to a page. It was a drawing of a trim, neatly dressed housewife standing alongside of an electric washing machine. She was barely touching the clothes as they went through the wringer and dropped into the laundry basket.

"You like?" Chuck asked me.

"I sure would," I said.

"One day," he said, "I have lotsa money. I buy for you."

"That's nice of you."

"You no more wash and wash and wash." He imitated me scrubbing at the washboard. "How much cost it that?"

I looked at the price. "A hundred and two dollars."

He thought about it, but didn't say anything.

The Terwilligers' dog woke up and sniffed the air. Then it began to whine. A few seconds later a wolf howled somewhere. It wasn't the long lonely cry, but the excited hunting call and it was answered right away by the other wolves. I wondered if they had somehow found their way into the slough bed.

Chuck said something to Ethel in Indian. She answered, "*Aha*"—yes. I thought it was something about the wolves. I asked him what he'd said.

"I tell Et'el this good place, ask she like stay here. She say yiss."

He was still worried about going back to Chicken. I wondered what *would* happen when we got back, what Mr. Vaughn and Angela Barrett would say. But I didn't really care one way or the other. They didn't seem important anymore, not after all this. The only one I was concerned about was Maggie—what she'd be going through when she found out about Jennie.

Time passed. We couldn't go outside, so we made the best of staying inside. To pass the time we played games—Hot and Cold, Hide the Thimble. Their favorite game was one they made up themselves. They'd run across the room and I'd try to give them a light whack on the bottom as they went by. If I missed they won.

Each time Patricia woke up, every hour or so, she took a little more milk. I kept trying her with the nipple, until finally—it must have been almost a day later—she took it. She finished a whole bottle, then threw half of it back up, but she was getting stronger. In the next few hours she took two more half-filled bottles.

The only thing I'd have wished for was some uninterrupted sleep. Patricia wouldn't sleep for more than a few hours at a time even after she started taking the bottle. Sometimes she'd cry for what seemed hours, and I'd walk up and down with her in a daze until she settled into an uneasy sleep and I'd do the same. I started to get cabin fever, snapping at Chuck and Ethel for no reason at all, then hating myself for it. They were helping out as much as they could, bringing in wood and snow, helping with the dishes and keeping things in order. Chuck even warmed the bottle and helped me feed the baby once.

After two days of it the time came when I just couldn't bring myself to wake up. Patricia began to cry when we were all asleep. I nudged Chuck and asked him to put the bottle in the saucepan, then I gave Patricia to him and told him to wake me when the bottle was ready. I ducked down into the sleeping bag and that was all I remembered until I woke up some time later to hear her crying again. I didn't know how long I'd slept but Ethel and Chuck were awake. She was sitting on their sleeping bag holding Patricia. Chuck was at the stove, warming a bottle.

"Chuck, how long have I been asleep?"

He shrugged. "Long time, I think."

I got up, feeling pretty good. "Don't you have any idea how long?"

He shook his head. "You give me baby. I give milk for him. He go sleep, I go sleep. He wake up, I wake up, Et'el wake up. You not wake up. You have one good sleep."

I took Patricia from Ethel. "You and Ethel fed her?"

"Yiss. I do good?"

I hugged him. "You did marvelous. I needed that sleep bad."

He beamed. "You happy me, I glad."

"Happy? I adore you. And that goes for you too," I added to Ethel.

Only then did I notice how quiet it was. The wind had stopped blowing. I went to the door. Outside the sky was bright with stars, the air still. It was so bitterly cold that my breath snapped into crystals. I came right back in.

From then on I wasn't worried about a thing. I knew we'd

make out and that someone would come for us eventually. All we had to do was wait.

The next day the weather was lovely. The sun shone bright in a cloudless sky and it was warm enough to walk around with parka hoods down. Chuck and Ethel went out early and busied themselves building a "roadhouse," then played hunter for a while. In the afternoon, I brought one of the sleeping bags outside, laid it against a stump and just sat taking in the sun with Patricia on my lap. The sun felt so good that I started to drowse, listening to Chuck make the sounds of a rifle as he tried to "shoot" Ethel the Moose or Ethel the Caribou for the nth time. I heard her squeal with delight as he missed her, then silence as she fell and he started to carry her back to the roadhouse for skinning and eating. Then I heard another sound, a sound I'd become so familiar with the past few months that I knew I wasn't hearing things. It was coming from the direction of the river. I opened my eyes to see Chuck and Ethel standing stock still, listening. They'd heard it too.

It was Mr. Strong's sled. Chuck let out a yell and ran down towards the river and disappeared. A few minutes later I heard him yelling and calling to Mr. Strong, the sound of the bells on the sled getting louder and louder.

I ran into the cabin and put Patricia on the cot, then went out to wait until the two of them appeared, making their way up towards me, Chuck hopping and jumping like a sparrow, Mr. Strong clumping along after him. I was so happy to see him that I threw myself into his arms and almost knocked him over.

"Now, madam," he cajoled, "don't take on so. The situation is well in hand. We'll be out of here in no time."

He hadn't seen Fred, he said, but Fred had left word where I was at Steel Creek.

He stayed long enough to bring Elmer's body into the cabin, and there he left it covered with a blanket, the knife still clutched in Elmer's frozen hand. Then we started out.

We stopped only once on the way, at O'Shaughnessy's, and

335

then only long enough to take a hot meal and a short rest before we went on again.

Later on, a few days after we were back and school was open again, the one thing that stuck in my mind was the moment when the settlement came into view. Ethel and I and Patricia were tucked away on one side of the sled towards the back, where Mr. Strong had made room for us among a whole load of parcel-post packages and dry goods. We were wrapped up pretty warm, the tarpaulin top over our heads like a tent. Chuck was sitting up in front with Mr. Strong. I didn't know we were almost there until the sled stopped and Chuck came crawling back along the side of the sled and pulled up the tarpaulin. He didn't want to be all alone up there with Mr. Strong when we came in.

When he lifted the tarp, there was the settlement in the distance. Chimney smoke had darkened the snow all around it, making it look like a gray little island. Sure enough, everybody was waiting, a bunch of black dots speckled in front of the post office. When we came nearer the whole place looked strange to me, as if I'd been away much longer than five or six days. I felt as if I'd left it a long time ago, almost as a little girl, and now I was coming back all grown up.

The horses started slowing down automatically as we neared the post office, and I lifted the tarp up to let everybody see we were in the back. But we didn't stop there. Mr. Strong let out a shout and I heard his whip crack. The sled jerked forward and I caught a flash of the surprised look on everybody's face as we went by—Mr. Vaughn's all displeased at seeing Chuck and Ethel, Angela Barrett's screwed up in anger. Mr. Strong halted the sled in front of the roadhouse and he'd already jumped down and was pulling the tarp back from us when everybody came running up.

I was too stiff to move, and there everybody was, staring at me and the children, Mrs. Purdy startled, wondering where Fred was, nobody saying a word. I had Patricia beside me, all swaddled in a wolf robe with just an opening for her to breathe, so nobody saw her until I picked her up. Like every-

336

one else, Maggie Carew and her husband had come running. As soon as Maggie saw what I was holding she knew right away it was Patricia and the life seemed to drain right out of her. Everybody else realized it too and they made way for her. I handed the baby down to her and she took her from me, her eyes asking the questions she couldn't bring herself to ask out loud.

Mr. Strong lifted me down from the sled and after that I hardly knew what was going on. Everybody was pressing forward, Mr. Carew asking me in a croaking voice where Jennie and Elmer were, Mrs. Purdy wanting to know about Fred, all the faces around me stunned, none of them angry anymore. Then Chuck and Ethel were beside me and Mr. Strong was herding the three of us into the roadhouse and trying to keep people back, telling them to give me a chance to get inside and warm up before they made me answer all their questions.

XXIV

For the whole first week I was back Maggie Carew made me and the children come over to the roadhouse for supper. She said that I'd been through an ordeal and that she wanted to make sure I had plenty of good hot food and didn't wear myself out. I didn't want her to go to any trouble for me, but she insisted. Her husband had left with Mr. Strong the next day, headed for Dawson, and she was all alone except for Patricia and the children. Having me there helped her feel better, she said, helped her feel closer to Jennie.

She blamed herself for what had happened. God was punishing her, she said, for something she'd done. He must have been, she insisted, because Jennie was the dearest and sweetest girl in the world, and had never harmed a soul. So she, Maggie, must have done something wrong. She tried not to keep asking me whether I thought Jennie would be all right or not, but she couldn't stop herself. "What do you honestly think, Annie," she'd ask me over and over. "You think she'll pull through?"

No matter how many times I told her I thought she would, she kept torturing herself by asking me more questions: how badly frozen had Jennie's leg been? Her face? If she did pull through, did I think she'd lose her leg or part of her face? All I could tell her was that I didn't know. When I told her how Jennie had tried to smile she broke down and wept.

Even when Fred came back we didn't know much more. He

pulled into the settlement in the early afternoon eight days later, completely bushed, and a few minutes later we were all in the roadhouse listening as he told us what had happened. He'd mushed Jennie as far as Forty Mile, just as he'd set out to. There he ran into Percy de Wolfe, which was a stroke of luck. Known as the Iron Man of the North, de Wolfe carried the mail up and down the Yukon between White Horse and Eagle, and he had the fastest team in that part of the country. Almost minutes after Fred arrived, they transferred Jennie to his sled and he'd mushed off with her to Dawson. There was a telegraph station at Forty Mile and they'd wired the authorities at Dawson that Percy was carrying an injured woman who was going to need treatment. "Before I left," Fred said, "Dawson wired back that there'd be a doctor at the hospital ready to work on her right away."

It wasn't until the end of March, three weeks later, that Maggie received a telegram from her husband. By then the days were sunny and long. Gentle chinook winds were melting the snow so fast that traveling by sled was almost impossible except at night when the slush froze up. Mr. Strong brought the telegram in on his last sled trip of the season. It didn't go into any details. It just said that Jennie had been in very serious condition for a while, but that she was going to pull through. Mr. Strong would tell her the details, the telegram ended. Mr. Strong broke it to Maggie as gently as he could. Jennie's face wasn't going to be scarred, he said, but they'd had to amputate her foot to well above the ankle.

Maggie took it pretty hard, as might be expected, and it worked a big change in her. Not that she became soft, just a little more tolerant. I knew that deep down she still felt that I had no business having Chuck and Ethel with me, that I was making a mistake, but she didn't look at them anymore as if they carried the plague or something worse. She even had them come over to the roadhouse every so often to play with Jimmy and Willard. Everybody else who'd been mad at me kind of eased up a little too. Maggie had a lot to do with it, I was sure. She swung weight in the settlement, and when

339

people saw her having me and the children come over to the roadhouse they started acting a little more sociable. Then one night when I went over to the roadhouse to pick up Chuck and Ethel, Maggie asked me a question that surprised me.

Mr. Vaughn and Angela were there playing cribbage, and Uncle Arthur was helping Chuck clean the new .22 rifle I'd bought for him. I'd been so proud of him for how he'd acted during our "ordeal," as Maggie called it, that I'd taken him into Mr. Strong's store and told him to pick out anything he wanted. I'd had some misgivings when he chose the .22, but he knew how to handle it. He'd had one ever since he'd been five.

Ethel and Willard were playing back in the bunkroom, having a pillow fight and Chuck's rifle was all apart, so I had a cup of tea while Uncle Arthur helped him reassemble it. Right out of the blue Maggie popped the question.

"You done anything about buying yourself a cabin in Eagle?" she asked me.

"No," I said.

"How come?" she asked me. "They don't have any teacher-age there for ya. You gotta provide your own quarters."

"I know," I said, "but I still don't know whether I'll be teaching at Eagle."

"What makes you think you won't?" she said.

She knew the answer to that as well as I and everybody else in that room did. Angela and Mr. Vaughn didn't look up from their game, but they were listening to every word. They weren't any crazier about me than they'd been before, but at least they said hello now whenever they met me.

"Well, nobody told me I *wouldn't*," I said, "but I didn't think the chances were too good."

Maggie's lip curled into that disgruntled sneer of hers. "I know everybody on that schoolboard," she said, "and if they got any objections I wanna hear about it . . . How much you want to pay for a cabin if they take ya?"

"I haven't even thought about it," I said.

"How big a one might you want?"

"Well . . . big enough so maybe Chuck and Ethel could have their own room."

She didn't bat an eye. "What do you think, Arnold?" she asked Mr. Vaughn deliberately. "Think it'll be easy to find one?"

He mumbled something and Maggie said, "I didn't hear ya."

"I said probably," he said.

"We'll find you one," Maggie said. "Far as I'm concerned a bird in the hand's worth two in the bush. We know what we got with you. Lord only knows what they're liable to send out from Juneau if we let'm . . . From what I hear about that Rooney, she's a real darb. Pinches the kids till they're black and blue and goes ga-ga over everything that wears pants."

Having Maggie on my side went a long way. Nobody came up to me and told me they thought any better of me than they had before. That wasn't people's way. It was just something I could feel, something in their manner. Like at the next dance we had. We didn't hold one until the Friday after Maggie got the telegram from her husband. Up to then it just hadn't seemed right to have one, to be dancing and laughing and having a good time when almost right next door Maggie would be sitting and wondering if Jennie was going to live or die.

When everybody came in they gave me a big hello or a howdy instead of just a grudging nod as they usually did, and a couple of them even talked about the weather with me. Now that spring was getting close everybody had their own idea about when the river was going to break up or when the creeks would be running so that sluice boxes could be set up. Nobody ever ran out of things to say about it and they didn't generally talk about it with cheechakos or somebody they didn't want to talk with in the first place. One or two even made a point of admiring the map of Chicken on the wall. As big as it was, they'd never seemed to notice it before. Now

341

they said they'd never seen anything like it, and how clever all the kids were to have made it.

Chuck was making out better too. His standing among the kids was upped practically from the first day of school. They stopped snickering at him and making fun of his accent. In fact for the first few days the boys all chummed up to him, wanting to hear all the gory details of how he'd found Jennie and Elmer and how Elmer had looked when he was dead and frozen. Chuck didn't have too much to say about it and didn't do any bragging, which impressed the kids more than if he'd gone on and on about it.

The only thing that didn't change at all was the way things were between Fred and me.

"If you wanna teach in Eagle," Maggie had told me in private, "you better behave. You got away with takin' those kids. Start chasin' after that half-breed again and you won't get away with anything. Now don't go givin' me any Bolshevik speeches. I'm givin' you the straight goods."

I didn't see him again for almost three weeks after he got back, and then only when he came in to pick up some hardware he'd ordered from Mr. Strong. He'd made up his mind he was going to stay away from me for my sake and that was that. No stain on my reputation was going to come from *him*, no sir. He showed up for the dance and when we danced together you'd have thought we were doing a minuet he held me so far away. I had the hope in the back of my mind that maybe Uncle Arthur would put on the *Home Sweet Home* waltz for us, but I wasn't surprised when he didn't. It didn't matter that Fred had saved Jennie's life and even risked his own: he was still a half-breed and I was still pure Northern womanhood.

Sure enough, came mid-April Mr. Strong brought me the news that I'd been accepted to teach at Eagle. I was happy about it. Yet at the same time I wasn't. Chuck and Ethel were worrying me. Ever since I'd brought them back to Chicken we hadn't been getting along.

More than ever, I wished that Nancy was still with me.

Between the two of us we'd have been able to figure out what was wrong and do something about it. For the life of me, I couldn't figure it out by myself. I had to keep after them all the time—to dress neatly, to be clean, to help me keep my quarters in order and to mind their manners around people. I wasn't doing it just to be bossy. It was for their own good. Even though the uproar over them had died down, most people still looked at them differently than they looked at other children. If they did something wrong or got into mischief it wasn't because they were kids and didn't know any better. It was because they were Indian kids. Almost everybody felt that way, even people who liked them.

One day when Uncle Arthur gave Chuck some candy, he waved his hand tolerantly when I told Chuck to say thank you. "Don't pay it any mind, missis," he said, "they just don't know any better." He didn't say "he." He said "they"—those Indians. It was the same way with other people. Every time Chuck or Ethel made a mistake it wasn't because things were new to them and they didn't know the ropes. "They" just didn't know any better.

It put me on the defensive. It shouldn't have. I shouldn't have paid it any mind and seen it for what it was, ignorance, but I couldn't. Stupidly, I felt that any criticism of them was criticism of me and I decided I wasn't going to give people a chance to criticize. I made Chuck and Ethel toe the mark. Once we were in Eagle they'd have to take their place alongside of other children and I wanted them to be able to do it as fast as possible. Nobody was going to laugh at them or point out how different they were if *I* had anything to do with it.

I really kept after them. At the same time I nearly worked myself to death ironing dresses for Ethel, scrubbing, washing, and keeping my quarters neat so that people would have a good impression when they came. I was especially tough with Chuck, always reminding him to hang up his clothes, not to throw things on the floor, to mind his manners, speak correctly, be good.

The two of them kept fighting me on everything, or at least

343

that's the way it seemed. Ethel started soiling her dresses, eating half the time with her hands and getting food all over her. She stopped picking up English too, and pretended she didn't know what shoes or socks were. One time she got up on a chair, pulled down some of her newly-ironed dresses from the wall and stomped all over them. Chuck changed too. I had to force him to wash up all the time and getting him to take a bath was a major battle. He became lazy in his schoolwork and surly around the house. I even had to remind him to bring in wood where before he was always one step ahead of me. I began to feel that he and Ethel were in league against me, whispering together in Indian, laughing between themselves. If I asked Chuck what they were laughing at he said it was nothing. Sometimes I even thought of sending them back to the Indian village I was so disgusted.

Something had to give, and it did.

They both ran away. It wasn't the first time for Chuck. The week before, he'd left the house and not come back until almost nightfall. Fit to be tied, I told him that if he ever did it again I'd give him a spanking.

This time he didn't come back. When dusk settled in at about eight they were still gone. Uncle Arthur and a few others helped me look for them. We tramped through the wet woods, yelling and calling, but there was no sign of them. Around midnight everybody went home, telling me not to worry. "They'll turn up, missis," Uncle Arthur assured me. He and everybody else promised to help me look again in the morning if they didn't. It was the beginning of May, the nights short and kind of dusky–daylight. I stayed out until past two before I gave up and went home to change out of wet footgear and go looking again.

I couldn't think about sleep. Just the thought that something had happened to the two of them kept me on the verge of panic. Over and over I imagined them lying at the bottom of a cliff, or swept away by a swollen creek, or attacked by a bear. And over and over I asked myself why they'd done it.

344

I'd been tough on them, I knew that, but I didn't think I'd been bad enough to make Chuck do something like this. I had a cup of tea and I forced myself to sit down and try to think calmly where they might have gone. The first thought that occurred to me was that they might have headed for the Indian village. A couple of times when I'd bawled Chuck out he'd threatened to. If they were headed there it might take all day to catch up with them.

The sun was nudging in the window, tinging everything with gold. I looked around the room, something I hadn't done before. I didn't see Ethel's little red monkey around anywhere. It wasn't in the schoolroom either when I looked, so she must have taken it with her. I noticed that Chuck's rifle was gone too. And his parka. The last time I'd seen him he'd been wearing his mackinaw, which meant he must have taken the parka out some time before he left. The more I looked around the more I noticed things missing: a few of Ethel's dresses, a dress suit I'd bought for Chuck, a couple of blankets, two pillow cases. There was only a little bread left in the breadbox, and I knew there should have been two loaves. Chuck must have been removing things bit by bit over the last few days and caching them somewhere. My heart started to pound: they'd taken too many things with them to carry them all at once, especially if they were going to the Indian village. If they were anywhere it was someplace in the vicinity. And if I was right there was only one place where they could have gone. I ran out.

The spicy odor of willow buds was in the air when I reached the trail that led down to Mary Angus' shack. The place was in worse shape than ever. Someone had taken out the window frame, and the stovepipe was gone too. As soon as I saw the place, though, I knew they were in there: the wolf robe was draped in the opening where the window used to be.

I pushed the door open and there they were, the two of them lying on a bed of spruce boughs, huddled together under a couple of blankets. Chuck's .22 was on the wall, along with

345

their clothes. The food they'd brought with them was piled in a box.

I bent over them and stared at them a long time before I woke Chuck up. They were beautiful. I'd never realized how beautiful. I remembered them living here with their mother. They'd been cold and hungry more often than not, but that hadn't mattered to them because they'd had *her,* the one person in the world they'd loved and trusted, the one person who knew them and understood them. Here in this shack she'd touched them and held them. Not me. Her. They hadn't asked for me. Even though I was the only one in the world who cared anything about them, they hadn't asked me to take them. I was a stranger to them. I fed them and gave them clothes, but I was still a stranger. So they'd run away from me and come back to where there was nothing but a memory—the memory of someone who'd held them close, spoke to them softly and loved them the way Granny Hobbs had loved me.

"Chuck . . ."

He woke up slowly. I watched his eyes, wanting to see what would be in them when he was aware of me, whether he'd be looking at a stranger or at someone who cared for him. What I saw hurt. He just stared at me the way I used to stare at my father when I wondered if he felt mean, telling myself that I didn't care what he said.

"Morning, Chuck," I said.

"What you want, Tisha?" It was a simple question, no more than that.

"I came to take you home," I said.

He shook his head. "No."

"You can't stay here."

"I stay for a while. Hunt. Get meat. Then I go Indian village."

"The Indian village is pretty far away."

"You think I not find?"

"I guess you could. You're a pretty smart boy. I just wonder why you want to go there."

"I go live with Indian mudda."

346

He meant Lame Sarah, the old woman he'd lived with in the Indian village. "I see. I guess that means you don't want to live with me anymore."

"No more."

"Why?"

"I hate you, Tisha," he said simply. "You not nice me. Alla time you *sahnik* me."

Ethel woke up, innocent and beautiful as the morning. She stared at me the way he had.

"Am I angry at you all the time?"

"Alla time. Alla time angry me, angry Et'el too."

"Does Ethel hate me as much as you do?"

"More. Say you white devil-woman. Make scare her. She no more live with you too. We live with Indian mudda. She like us."

"Chuck, will you believe me if I tell you something? I love you. I love you very much. You and Ethel."

"Tisha, you tell one very big lie."

"I'm not lying at all. I mean it."

"Oh, no. You hate me, say I bad boy. All time bad boy." He was getting aggravated.

"Is that what I do?"

"Foreva! All day long you say, 'Chuck, you bad boy, you make floor dirty. Oh, Chuck, you bad boy, you make mud all over clothes. Chuck, you not have good manners, dirty, make table dirty, make big mess, make everything dirty.' Tisha," he spluttered, "soon you tell me I make whole world dirty!"

I didn't want to cry, but what he said next cut the ground from under me.

"Once upon a time, Tisha, you be nice me. You be so nice I love you truly." He shook his head. "No now. Now you shame me. Shame way I talk. Shame everything me. You no love me, Tisha. You hate me."

He said it so simply and honestly that I burst into tears, ashamed of myself. Before I was able to stop, I was sitting on the dirt floor, he and Ethel worriedly patting me. Then we talked. He told me how much I'd picked on him and tried to get him to do things in the past month that were too tough, and the longer we talked the more I realized he was right. I'd been ashamed of him, and of Ethel too. In class I gave everybody extra help but him. At lunchtime I asked nobody else to mind their manners but him. It didn't matter why I'd done it. I'd been wrong. Instead of hugs and pats for the things he'd accomplished I'd given him criticism for the things he hadn't.

In the end he and Ethel came home with me, and I promised him things would be different.

That night when I put him to bed he told me that once when he was in the Indian village he'd chopped twenty cords of wood. I'd lectured him more than once about telling the truth, but this time I kept my mouth shut. I must have shown my doubt, though.

"You no believe," he said.

"Oh, yes I do," I assured him.

He wasn't convinced. "You think I tell lie."

"Let me feel your muscle." He flexed his arm, and gritted his teeth. "That's some muscle, all right. If you say you cut twenty cords I believe you."

He smiled and hunched down, pulling the covers up to his chin. "I fool you," he said. "I not cut twenny cords. Too much for me myself."

"No?"

"No," he said. "Maybe cut ten."

348

XXV

After that I stopped trying to make Chuck and Ethel into model children. All I had to do was remember how Granny Hobbs used to be with me and I knew exactly what to do. The last thing she'd ever cared about was my etiquette or my cleanliness. The first thing she'd cared about was making sure I was happy. And that's what I did with Chuck and Ethel. If they weren't the cleanest kids and didn't have the best manners, they weren't the dirtiest either and their manners were better than most, so I stopped worrying about it. I stopped worrying about their messing up my quarters, too. Granny would never have given a hoot about something like that, and when it came right down to it I didn't either. As for what other people might think about it, there was nobody I cared that much about impressing anyway, except maybe Fred, so I let them go ahead and mess.

They tested me a few times. They spilled things, splashed water from the barrel and insisted on wearing the same clothes for too long, wanting to see what I'd do. When I didn't pay any attention to it they stopped by themselves. In fact, about a week after they ran away, when I was dumping some of my own clothes in the wash boiler, Ethel came up to me with a little blue dress that was her favorite.

"What do you want me to do with it?" I asked her.

"Do."

"Do what?" I knew full well what she wanted, but I loved to hear her talk.

She pointed to the wash boiler. "Do?"

"Wash? You want me to wash it?"

"Yiss," she said. "Watch."

She followed Chuck's lead and literally worshiped him. If he was happy she was happy. And he seemed to be. It hadn't taken much to please him in the first place, and once he felt I was on his side he settled right down. He had a good sense of humor, too. One time when Jimmy Carew stayed to have lunch with us, Chuck asked for a slice of "brode," as he called it.

"Brode," Jimmy mimicked sarcastically. "It's not brode, it's *bread*!" He chuckled. "Brode . . ."

Isabelle and Joan were having lunch. They started to laugh, and Chuck shot me a quick glance.

"What's wrong with saying brode?" I asked Jimmy.

"It's just wrong."

"Well, where my grandmother used to live in Missouri, the people used to say brayd. Mr. O'Shaughnessy pronounces it brid. What's the difference as long as people know what you're talking about?"

Jimmy shrugged uncomfortably. I hadn't been too fair to him, but Chuck needed the points more than he did. I put a slice of bread on the plate. "Here's your brode," I said.

"Brode not correct," Chuck said archly, imitating me, "we say bread."

After they'd been back another week, he and Ethel no more wanted to live with anybody else than I'd have wanted to marry Mr. Vaughn. They were with me for good.

It was just around then, in mid-May, that spring came. Up to then the weather had been so changeable you couldn't tell what to expect. March had really been freakish. One day the sun would be out hot and strong—bouncing off the snow, dazzling your eyes and setting eaves to dripping—and you'd be convinced spring was on the way. The next day, and for days after that, gray monster winter would settle back in and you'd be just as convinced that spring would never arrive at all.

April had been a darling. With the class wanting to get in all the last-minute sledding they could, I'd had trouble getting them back in school after lunch. Water had been drip-dripping everywhere, and wet shoes and socks were always drying around the stove. Soon the first crocuses, purple faces splashed with yellow, had pushed up through the snow, and blossoming crow-foot cascaded down hillsides. After that the creek broke up and everybody became restless. Spring still hadn't been close enough so that we'd been able to shed our winter underwear, and sleds had still creaked by in the half-dusk that was night, but it was closer. It was there in the brown spots that appeared on the hills, and the islands that eddied out around trees. People had scattered ashes in their backyards to melt the snow faster so they could start planting vegetable gardens, and pale green buds sprouted on birches.

Then spring exploded. The sun came and stayed, and soon we were able to open the schoolroom windows to the tangy smell of running sap and the spicy odor of willow. Sometimes we'd run out just to see the great flocks of Canadian honkers passing overhead, the loud beating of their wings making the air seem thick as water. The schoolroom felt so musty and confining that I was as glad as the class when Friday came and we could toss our books away. Each long sunny day blended into warm mild dusk, dusk into gentle morning.

And suddenly the snow was gone. Tender shoots of grass sprinkled the hills and wild canaries flashed through trees haloed in green. I started taking the class on field trips again and we'd see rabbits all over the place, their white winter coats already turned ash brown. On one trip we saw a moose, gaunt and needing a haircut badly. It was a bull, his racks still fuzzed with winter white. We even started our own garden. I wouldn't be around when it came up, but it was fun just the same.

At the end of May Nancy came back to take the territorial exam. She took it in my quarters on the last morning school

351

was held, while I rehearsed the class in the schoolroom for the pageant we were going to put on after lunch. For the whole time she sat behind the closed door I was on pins and needles. Even though I knew she'd pass I couldn't help worrying. She'd made all kinds of plans for going to high school in Fairbanks. If she failed I didn't know what it would do to her.

When she was finished she came in and handed the test to me, then went outside while I looked it over. I couldn't grade it for her. That would have to be done in Juneau, which meant waiting six weeks before the official word came back, but I could tell her whether she'd passed or not. She passed, all right, and when I let out a yell for her to come on back in and hear the good news the class let out a cheer.

Before the pageant started we had an exhibit of all the best work the class had done over the school year. Compositions, drawings, book reports, graphs and booklets decorated the walls. Set out on the shelves were fossils and birds' nests, pot holders and samplers, papier mâché masks and everything else the class had made and collected. A couple of Rebekah's papers were on the wall too. She'd already mastered a first-grade reader and her penmanship was so beautiful I'd put up some samples of it.

Seeing it there and watching the kids showing it all off to the parents, I felt proud. Without any fancy equipment, without even all the books they should have had, they'd worked hard and sopped up everything I could teach them. They'd helped each other, taught each other at times, competed and cooperated. And they'd learned. It was a grand day for everyone, including me. The pageant was all about the Gold Rush days and it went off without a hitch. The old-timers enjoyed it more than anybody. After that we served ice cream and cake, and when it was all over everybody helped clean up for the dance we were going to have that night. Maggie Carew was the last to leave.

"Well, that's the end of 'er," she said, looking around the room. " 'No more pencils, no more books,' like the kids say. She's gone now."

She meant the school. There just wasn't enough enrollment to keep it open. There'd never be another school here again.

"What'll happen to it?" I asked Maggie.

"Angela's claimin' it," she said. "Gonna turn it into a roadhouse after I'm gone. You did a good job."

"Thanks." Coming from her it was a high compliment.

"Only thing I don't understand is how come you didn't give the kids marks."

"I didn't see any reason to. They all knew how well they did."

"How'd they know?"

"They just did. I told them where they did well and where they needed improvement, but they already knew."

"Suppose you did give'm marks—what would mine've got?"

"Offhand I couldn't say."

"Suppose you *hadda* mark 'em?" she insisted.

"Well . . . I'd say maybe an A for Jimmy, B for Willard."

"How about the others?"

"Maybe an A for Elvira, C for her two sisters, A for Lily, B for—"

"How come you give Lily an A and my Willard a B?"

"Lily's a very bright little girl."

"That don't mean she's smarter'n my Willard. No half-breed's smarter'n a white," she said without thinking. I didn't answer her and she colored. "See y'at the dance," she said as she went out.

It was still light out about 8:30 when everybody started showing up. It would stay light until about eleven when dusk would set in for a couple of hours until the sun came up again in the middle of the night. I still wasn't used to it, going to bed in almost broad daylight and then trying to sleep with the sun nudging at me at two o'clock in the morning. It gave me a kind of a guilty feeling, as if I ought to be awake and doing things. Sometimes I'd only be able to sleep for a few hours and so I'd just get up and start the day at three in the morning, then take a nap later. It was kind of fun in a way because it was the thing you'd always wanted when you were a kid—never to have it get dark. But it was unsettling too, like living in an Alice-in-Wonderland world.

Everybody kept crazy hours. Miners would be out working their claims right through the night, setting up sluice boxes, digging ditches or excavating ground. They only had three good months to get their work done and they didn't want to waste any time. A few of them didn't even bother with dress-up clothes when they came to that last dance. Sprouting beards for protection against mosquitoes, they showed up in clean workclothes, all ready to go back to their diggings when the dance was over. Fred and his mother came too, and that made the evening for me.

Everybody kept asking me if there was anything wrong with me, wanting to know if I was having a good time. I was, but I couldn't help feeling sad. In a few days I'd be leaving, yet when I looked around the room it seemed to me as if it was only yesterday that I'd arrived. In less than a year I'd lived a whole lifetime here. There were still a few papers on the walls and one of the green shades had a message written on it, left over from the class party: "Farewell, Miss Hobbs." Underneath it, Jimmy Carew had scrawled a P.S.: "See you in Eagle."

With Fred playing the banjo during most of the square dances, I only got to dance with him once. If it was up to me we wouldn't have left each other's side. On this night of all nights especially I wanted to be with him as much as possible. Even after Uncle Arthur wound up his gramophone and the round dancing started we didn't get to dance together that much. Since I was going away, Uncle Arthur and Joe and some of the other men insisted I had to dance with them at least once. I didn't mind it early on, but as it started to get late and there was more and more chance that Uncle Arthur would play *Home Sweet Home*, I began to get nervous.

I'd just danced with Jake Harrington when Fred ambled over to me. He looked grand. He had on a starched blue and white striped shirt, and the sun had tanned him really dark. He had a big smile on his face.

"You look like the cat that ate the canary," I told him.

"Funny you should say that. I was just licking my chops."

"Over what?"

"Over the supper you and I are going to have."

Uncle Arthur had already put the next record on and was lowering the needle. The *Home Sweet Home* waltz began to play. Then I saw that there were a whole bunch of people staring at the two of us—Jake Harrington and Rebekah, Ben Norvall and Nancy. They were all smiling. Uncle Arthur gave me a little wink. "We had it all arranged," Fred said.

His arm slipped around my waist, and like the first time we danced that waltz together the walls of the schoolroom moved right back and everybody disappeared. Even the music didn't sound the same. To me it wasn't an old scratchy record playing an old-fashioned waltz, but Paul Whiteman's full orchestra. I was so far away in my mind that not until the record was over and everybody began to clap did I realize that no one else had danced. All of them had stopped to watch Fred and me.

Chuck and Ethel were asleep on the bed along with Joan Simpson, so Robert Merriweather stayed with the three of them while we all went over to the roadhouse.

It was almost two in the morning and everybody was just about done eating when a couple of chords sounded on the piano. We all turned around in time to see Joe Temple point a finger at the kitchen area, and while he played a march Maggie Carew came out carrying a huge chocolate cake with a candle in the center. She set it down in front of me. "Good Luck" was written on it in icing. I was too surprised to say a word, even more so when Uncle Arthur walked over with a beautifully wrapped box and handed it to me. "We passed the hat around and got this for ya," he said. "A little token of our appreciation."

Inside the box was about the most expensive camera you could buy, all black leather and nickel plate. Everybody clapped and yelled for me to make a speech.

"I wish I could," I said, "but I'm not very good at making speeches. All I can say is, thanks—I appreciate it."

355

"No more than we appreciate you, Teacher," Ben Norvall said. "There isn't a soul in this room that doesn't think you're a fine honest girl and a true-blue Alaskan to boot."

Jake Harrington said, "Ben, that's the first time in all the years I know you that I heard you tell the unvarnished truth."

Joe started to play *Auld Lang Syne* on the piano, and then Fred and everybody were singing. I never could hear that song without getting a lump in my throat to begin with. By the time they got to the end I was on the point of crying. I wasn't the only one either. Maggie's and Nancy's eyes were wet, and Uncle Arthur burst into tears.

It was almost three in the morning when Fred and I left the roadhouse. We went over to my quarters to see if everything was all right. Robert was asleep on the couch, Chuck and Ethel on the bed, just as I'd left them, so I tiptoed out and Fred and I went for a walk.

As soon as we were out of sight of the settlement Fred took my hand. The woods were as quiet as if the sun in the sky was just pretending to be there and it was really night.

We talked a little about Eagle and what it would be like living there with Chuck and Ethel. I asked him how he thought the kids there would treat them and he said he didn't know. A family with three half-Indian children were already living there, he said, but he didn't know how they got along with the white kids. He said he wanted to come and see me after the freeze-up.

We went on until we came to Fourth of July Pup. Swollen to creek size with runoff, it was too wide to jump across. Before we sat down on the grassy bank we scooped up a drink. The water was cold and sweet, dyed clear amber from roots and dried hillside moss.

"I guess you're relieved," I said, lying back. The ground was warm.

"About what?"

"That I'm going."

"Why should I be?" He lay down on his stomach and leaned on his elbows.

356

"You won't have me chasing after you anymore."

"You didn't do that," he said.

"Yes, I did. I'm doing it right now. I'll be leaving in a few days, so what does it matter? It's the truth." He didn't like hearing that, but I didn't care. I didn't have a bit of shame left in me and I was glad of it. He could be a gentleman if he wanted. I was sick of being a lady. "I've been chasing after you almost from the time we met."

That made him squirm. "Anne, if I could give you a home, if I had money enough to take care of you, I'd ask you to marry me right now."

I felt like growling, or shaking him, doing anything to wake him up, anything to make him realize I didn't care how much he had or how little, that all I wanted was him. There was no point to it, though. We'd been through all this before, so I just stared at him long enough until he couldn't do anything else but kiss me. I ran my fingers along the back of his neck and played with his hair. He murmured my name and for the first time in my life it didn't sound plain to me. It sounded lovely, all mixed in with the rush of water running below us and the sweet smell of the earth.

I didn't want to open my eyes. I wanted to keep them closed and have him hold me. I realized ever so faintly that I wasn't too sure of what I was doing, but I knew I was in love, and I knew that he loved and cared for me. When I finally did open my eyes and looked into his I loved what I saw. I thought to myself that I sure wished I'd known about this kind of feeling a few months before. At the same time I was glad I hadn't. I'd have been a goner. He said, "Anne," his voice husky and deep, and I could smell that wonderful odor of wood smoke coming from him. My fingers went to his lips. "I want to say something to you," I told him.

He waited while I got it all straight in my mind, and I said, "I don't know what it is you think you have to have before you want to keep company with me, but you just remember this. I love you. I won't be chasing after you anymore because we're going to be far away from each other, but some day, when you get ready, you better come and marry me. Because I'm never going to marry anybody else. I mean that, Fred Purdy. If you don't marry me some day I'm going to be an old maid."

"No you won't," he said.

"Is that a promise?"

"That's a promise."

"You better not break it."

"You better not break your promise either," he said.

A little while later we started to walk back arm in arm, stopping every so often to linger and embrace. We went on that way until we came in sight of the settlement, then we let each other go.

September 16, 1975

THAT'S HOW Fred and I parted those many years ago, with the promise that one day we'd be married. Thinking about that promise now, I almost have to smile. Trying to keep it was like making a trip by dog sled in a snowstorm: you know where you want to go, but you can't be sure how long it's going to take or where you'll wind up along the way.

Fred and I didn't get married until over ten years later, on September 4, 1938. By that time Chuck had graduated from high school, Ethel had entered it, and I'd adopted three more children.

It was worth all the waiting, though. We had a grand life together. Fred mined in the summer, and in the winter sometimes we stayed home, sometimes we packed up the family and went Outside. We did whatever we liked. One winter, maybe the finest we ever spent, we took on the job as teacher and custodian in an Indian village. As for children, Fred loved them as much as I did, so we went ahead and adopted four more.

I'm 67 years old now. Fred passed away ten years ago, and although I've since gotten over the sharp pain of losing him, I still miss him badly at times, mostly when there's a gentle rain falling. I think of it falling so quietly all over the hills, soaking into the ground to bring out new life, and it's hard for me to accept that I'm never going to see him again or hear that wonderful laugh of his. It's as hard as trying to imagine springtime without the sound of birds.

Occasionally I look back on those early years we spent without each other and I feel a little cheated. Then I think about the 28 wonderful years we had together. Everytime I do I realize how fortunate I've been, because as much as I love children and sunlight, I know that the sun would never have shone as brightly for me, nor children's smiles seemed so lovely, had I spent those years without Fred.　　　—Anne Hobbs Purdy
　　　　　　　　　　　　　　　　　　　　Chicken, Alaska

AUTHOR'S NOTE AND ACKNOWLEDGMENTS

Throughout this work I've tried to keep as close to actual oc-
currences and facts as I could, adding to them or altering them
only when I deemed it dramatically necessary.

Many Alaskans, particularly those who live in the Forty Mile
country, will note that I've taken some license with geography.
For instance, the Indian village in these pages is described as
being located on the Forty Mile River. The actual Indian
village from which Chuck and Ethel came was, and still is,
located on the Yukon. Today there is a modern, well-equipped
school there. In 1927, however, it was pretty much as I described it.

There are many who helped in the creation of this book,
both in Alaska and in the Lower 48:

To Charles Bloch go my deepest thanks both professionally
and personally. More than an advisor and supporter, he has
been a friend and a guide. Without him this book would not
have been completed.

To Linda Price, my editor at Bantam Books, I owe a special
debt of appreciation. Her patience and judgment were indis-
pensable.

Nor could I fail to mention Julie Garriott of St. Martin's
Press for her incisive criticism and enthusiastic support. She is
a gifted editor.

Among others who helped in different and important ways are: Grace Bechtold, Orrin Borsten, Leonard Brean, Jackie Carr, Everett Chambers, Van Dempsey, Julia Fenderson, John and Dora Funk, "Dean" Galloway, Jack Guss, Borgil Hansen, Lynne Specht Klein, Martin Lowenheim, Charles Mayse, Sanford and Patricia Mock, Isabelle Purdy, Michael and Georgina Ritchie, Marjori Rogers, Zelma Rose, Walter Schmidt, Dee Sclar, Beulah Thornburg, Norman and Erna Toback, Vernon and Beth Weaver, Marguerite Wilson, Jack Young.

I am grateful to them all.

—R.S.